NUCLEAR ENERGY POLICY

A Reference Handbook

NUCLEAR ENERGY POLICY

A Reference Handbook

Earl R. Kruschke
Byron M. Jackson
California State University, Chico

CONTEMPORARY WORLD ISSUES

ABC-CLIO

Santa Barbara, California
Oxford, England

© 1990 by ABC-CLIO, Inc.

Library of Congress Cataloging-in-Publication Data

Kruschke, Earl R. (Earl Roger), 1934–
    Nuclear energy policy : a reference handbook / Earl R. Kruschke and Byron M. Jackson.
       p.   cm.—(Contemporary world issues)
    Includes bibliographical references.
    ISBN 0-87436-238-5 (alk. paper)
    1. Nuclear energy—Government policy—United States. 2. Nuclear industry—Government policy—United States. 3. Nuclear energy. 4. Nuclear industry.   I. Jackson, Byron M.   II. Title. III. Series.
    HD9698.U52K78   1990   333.792′4′0973—dc20   89-18132

ISBN 0-87436-238-5 (alk. paper)

97 96 95 94 93 92 91 90   10 9 8 7 6 5 4 3 2 1

ABC-CLIO, Inc.
130 Cremona Drive, P.O. Box 1911
Santa Barbara, California 93116-1911

Clio Press Ltd.
55 St. Thomas' Street
Oxford, OX1 1JG, England

This book is Smyth-sewn and printed on acid-free paper ∞.
Manufactured in the United States of America

To my brother, Dennis Bernard Kruschke,
and to my sister, Sidonia Mae Kruschke,
both of whom witnessed the dawn of the nuclear age,
but neither of whom survived
to experience its triumphs or
to be challenged by its potential terrors

To my sister, Gail Jackson Quarles,
for her years of encouragement

Contents

Preface

THE LITERATURE ON NUCLEAR ENERGY is nothing short of overwhelming. The senior author of this book personally examined hundreds of books, journal articles, popular magazine articles, book reviews, pamphlets, newsletters, government documents, laws, legal cases, treaties, and other pieces of related literature and audiovisual material—and he failed to make what he considers a significant dent in what is available worldwide. To attempt to exhaust the literature in this field would clearly take more than one lifetime.

Yet we offer the reader still another source. This might seem ironic, but this brief book is intended as an introduction to some of the literature and other materials available in this field. The book has been specifically prepared for the layperson—more precisely, for the high school student, the college undergraduate, and the curious general reader.

In Chapter 1 we discuss the major issues involved in nuclear energy policy in the United States. We attempt to lay out some of the arguments involved in the controversy over nuclear energy and to present the major dimensions of the issue. Chapter 2 contains a chronology of significant events in the unfolding drama of nuclear energy developments. In Chapter 3 we present brief biographies of some of the figures who were prominent in the development of nuclear physics and nuclear energy policy as these evolved in the United States.

Chapter 4 covers several primary facets of the nuclear policy field—well-known speeches and communications, laws that helped shape policy, major government documents and reports, important court cases, treaties that illustrate some aspects of nuclear energy policy, a list of nuclear reactors, and several more detailed documents of interest to the reader concerned with the finer aspects of nuclear energy policy.

Chapter 5 presents a brief list of some of the organizations involved in nuclear energy policy making, and Chapter 6 is an introduction to some of the major references—bibliographies, handbooks, encyclopedias, books, journal articles, etc.—available to the serious reader. Chapter 7 lists some of the nonprint materials available to the researcher and the more casual reviewer, and is followed by a brief glossary of frequently used terms in the nuclear energy and nuclear energy policy fields.

It is the hope of the authors that all of this material will serve to introduce the reader to the subject and to stimulate the more serious observer to engage the subject—a subject that carries with it endless fascination and, indeed, frustration. Although it is certainly not an exhaustive overview of the subject, it is the authors' hope that this book is a clear introduction that will whet people's appetites to pursue the subject further. The subject of nuclear energy often invites and, indeed, incites controversy; this brief book is intended to serve as a simple foundation so that people might be able to approach the subject from a more objective, less hostile, vantage point.

For any errors of commission or omission, the authors alone assume responsibility. The goal of the authors is to provide the underpinnings for further inquiry and, in particular, greater understanding of this fascinating and controversial subject.

1

Introduction

Nuclear Energy Policy in the United States

So that we may effectively discuss nuclear energy policy, we need first to define several important terms. Public policy may be understood as "a course or pattern of activity and not simply a decision to do something" (Anderson, *Public Policy-Making*, 1979, p. 2). As a course of action, public policy is directed toward certain goals and accomplishments. In this sense, public policy deliberately sets out to solve a problem by means of concerted action. The public policy process involves largely bureaucratic procedures and governmental decision makers or groups who are authorized to seek solutions to problems that fall within governmental responsibility.

The question of how and which problems receive government attention is also important in understanding the policy process. A major means of stimulating government attention is through the making of policy demands or claims to get public officials to act on a perceived problem. For example, in a community located adjacent to a factory whose chimneys emit excessive amounts of smoke, residents who are troubled by this problem can appeal to their local governing body for action to alleviate the smoke. In other words, the citizens of the community may attempt to place the issue on the public agenda. If the group succeeds in getting their local government, the local office of the Air Quality Control Board, or the

Environmental Protection Agency to act on their behalf, they have effectively placed the problem of excessive smoke emission on the public agenda. The public agenda should thus be perceived as the list of problems acknowledged by government officials and the forum in which these officials begin to seek resolutions for the problems identified.

The consequences of specific problem-solving activities by public officials are called policy outputs. Policy outputs are the actual accomplishments of government, rather than what the government promises to do. Policy outputs are preceded by policy statements, which have been defined as "formal expressions or articulations of public policy" (Anderson, *Public Policy-Making*, 1979, p. 5). These policy statements contain references to the activities and goals the government hopes to accomplish. Frequently, policy statements are ambiguous and vague and do not clearly explain the purpose of a policy. By looking closely we may notice many times that actual policy outputs may differ from policy statements. In other words, rules or regulations may go unenforced or ignored; not all policy statements are realized in terms of policy outputs.

The public policy process involves essentially five stages: (1) establishment of the policy agenda, (2) policy formulation, (3) policy adoption, (4) policy implementation, and (5) policy evaluation (Kruschke and Jackson, *The Public Policy Dictionary*, 1987, *passim*). As stated above, the policy agenda involves official governmental recognition that a problem seriously affects a group or groups and that it therefore requires government action. Establishing the agenda constitutes the major initial step in the policy process because it signifies that some official body realizes that a solution to a problem is important to an affected population. A policy is then formulated or designed, and specific courses of action are chosen. Once the proposals for action are reviewed, evaluated, and approved, the policy proposals are accepted by those legitimately authorized to fund and pursue the course of action. This stage of the process is referred to as the policy adoption stage. The policy is implemented by designated officials who apply specific proposals to deal with the problem. The final stage of the policy process is evaluation of the policy application. Questions of evaluation focus on such matters as the effectiveness and impact of the policy on the problem itself and on the clientele it affects.

If we apply these stages to the previous example of the excessive smoke problem, the first effort would be to get the problem on the public agenda. The most difficult aspect of this stage of the policy process is assuring that government officials acknowledge the serious nature of the problem as it has been brought to them by the affected population. Frequently, government agencies, legislative bodies, or official representatives are slow to react or reluctant to pursue controversial actions. But if the smoke emissions from the factory are obvious and appear to present a hazard to the general community, then the local government would be obligated to act.

Let us assume that the community's city council and the local Air Quality Control Board recognize a responsibility to correct the problem. They might meet to formulate a joint solution that would require the factory owners to reduce the level of smoke emissions or "clean" the smokestacks by placing "scrubbers" in the stacks to eliminate some of the smoke before it reaches the atmosphere. These would be two possible policy solutions or examples of the policy formulation process. If these possible solutions seem workable and if they provide effective measures for reducing the amount of smoke emitted, then the city council and Air Quality Control Board would agree to adopt these policy solutions and the factory owners would be notified of the decision.

Given the nature of the policy process (involving, as it does, a large element of political competition), as well as the nature and process of the legal system in the United States (based, as it is, on due process), the factory owners would be given an opportunity to contest or appeal the joint decision. If no changes are made during this stage of the process, then the policy would be implemented and the factory owners would be granted a specified time period during which to comply with the new policy. After the specified compliance date, an evaluation or reassessment of the smoke abatement policy would take place to see if it should be continued, changed, or discontinued.

As stated above, policy making, whether it be in the area of smoke abatement or nuclear energy, is political activity. Politics involves the activities of individuals and groups who, in competition with others, attempt to maximize their values by use of whatever resources they can muster (Kruschke, "Toward a Brief Formulation of a Definition of Politics," 1973). Thus, it involves their efforts to influence the policy process to satisfy their own needs and objectives. Those groups possessing the greatest resources are most likely to see their influence maximized. The policy process related to the creation of a nuclear energy policy has been particularly notable for the role played by a wide variety of political actors using a wide variety of resources. Let us move, then, from our introductory example of general policy making to the issue of nuclear energy policy and observe how the policy process has evolved in that area.

Although there is considerable debate over whether the United States has an energy policy, it is nevertheless obvious that nuclear energy—whether fission or fusion—is one of the most important elements of the nation's efforts to create an overall energy policy. Up to the early 1970s, the energy posture of the United States appeared rather strong and healthy. Gasoline was inexpensive, natural gas was plentiful, nuclear plants were being built to deal with the country's increasing need for electricity, and energy conservation was not yet a major item on the nation's public policy agenda. The private sector had the responsibility of providing the nation's energy. The involvement of the U.S. government in the development of nuclear energy had consisted, up to that point, of a series of regulations designed to maintain a stable price for energy producers (Cochran et al., *American Public Policy,* 1982, p. 60).

Energy policy in the United States prior to 1973 was thus based on an optimistic assessment of the energy future. Policy did not appear to be concerned with the prospect of diminishing energy supplies. Cochran et al. observed that the regulations adopted by both state and federal governments tended to encourage consumption with minimal concern for waste (Cochran et al., *American Public Policy,* 1982, p. 60). The Arab oil embargo in 1973 caused energy experts to reconsider the previously optimistic projections for U.S. energy security. The embargo marked an end to the period of U.S. self-sufficiency in energy resources. And, while oil supplies have declined since 1973, there has been an increasing demand for energy combined with a drop in domestic energy reserves.

When the Atomic Energy Act was passed in 1946, the prospect of diminishing fossil fuels did not appear to be an immediate national problem. The onset of the atomic age, which began with the Manhattan Project, and the ultimate destruction of Hiroshima and Nagasaki by the newly invented atomic bombs provided, perhaps ironically, the opportunity for U.S. and foreign scientists to explore the peaceful uses of atomic energy. The Atomic Energy Act of 1946 created the Atomic Energy Commission, which was responsible for promoting and regulating the development of the U.S. atomic energy program. The early development of U.S. nuclear energy policy was in part a response to fears that the Soviet Union would acquire atomic secrets and perhaps even use atomic weapons against the United States. As a result, the Atomic Energy Act of 1954 and the Price-Anderson Acts were passed, which offered support for the development of the commercial nuclear energy industry. This legislation encouraged participation of private industry in the development of nuclear energy and provided financial protection to the public and to the Atomic Energy Commission licensees and contractors in case of nuclear accidents.

The Energy Reorganization Act of 1977; the Nuclear Safety Research, Development, and Demonstration Act of 1980; and the Nuclear Waste Policy Act of 1982 are all important public laws that have a direct impact on the future of nuclear energy in the United States. The Energy Reorganization Act of 1977 created the Department of Energy and combined the Energy Research and Development Administration with the Federal Energy Administration. The Department of Energy is the parent agency of the Nuclear Regulatory Commission, which was created under the earlier Energy Reorganization Act of 1974. The Nuclear Safety Research, Development, and Demonstration Act of 1980 was designed to provide rules and safeguards to improve the safety of nuclear power plants. This act dealt with the investigation of and setting of standards for the manufacture of components and materials used in the construction of nuclear power plants. The Nuclear Waste Policy Act of 1982 was designed to initiate a process of environmental assessment that would lead to the choice of a site for the nation's first nuclear waste repository. The choice of a site to permanently store high-level nuclear waste is of critical national importance, from both political and scientific perspectives. The unpredictable nature of nuclear wastes and the immensely long half-life of nuclear-contaminated material suggest that rational and accurate analyses of the nuclear waste storage problem are required from both policy makers and scientists.

In the United States, there are currently over 100 nuclear energy plants in operation and at least a dozen more are under construction. In 1987, 35 states had nuclear power plants, which provided 12.6 percent of net U.S. energy generation (Pearman and Starr, *The American Nuclear Power Industry,* 1985, p. 3). The first plants to become operational were those at Shippingport, Pennsylvania; Dresden, Illinois; and Yankee Rowe, Massachusetts. The greatest growth and expansion of nuclear power facilities took place during the 1970s. Since then, however, there has been a marked decrease in construction of proposed nuclear facility units. In addition, the licenses of some units have been revoked, mainly because of safety concerns, construction problems, and the obsolescence of older facilities.

In the 1950s and 1960s, a major advantage of nuclear power appeared to be its relatively low cost. Nuclear power was seen as a cheap energy source when looked at over the long term. But nuclear fission energy is no longer regarded as an inexpensive alternative to more traditional energy sources. In the late 1970s, heightened financial problems, construction delays, safety concerns, and operating difficulties increasingly affected the development of nuclear power in the United States.

Increased regulatory action has also had an impact on the cost of proposed or existing nuclear facilities. The Nuclear Regulatory Commission, created under the Energy Reorganization Act of 1974, is responsible for regulating all nuclear power facilities as well as for regulating nuclear materials in the states. The Nuclear Regulatory Commission regulates the licensing of nuclear reactors, a process that involves standardization of the licensing procedures, inspection of reactors, approval of technical specifications of reactor and facility components, quality assurance inspection, emergency preparedness of nuclear generating facilities, management and organization of facility employees, safety reviews and inspection, and indemnity and financial protection of facility operators. The Nuclear Regulatory Commission is also required to regulate activities related to the nuclear fuel cycle, which include: (1) materials safety, (2) incinerator licensing, (3) interim spent fuel storage, (4) licensing of uranium enrichment facilities, and (5) the decommissioning and decontamination of facilities. Another aspect of the fuel cycle subject to regulation is the transportation of radioactive materials. The Nuclear Regulatory Commission regulates the transportation of defense-related, high-level waste and spent nuclear fuel shipments as well as the security and safety of transportation of nuclear fuels (U.S. Nuclear Regulatory Commission, *Annual Report,* 1987, p. 184).

An increasingly controversial aspect of Nuclear Regulatory Commission regulation is nuclear waste management. The areas of concern here are the mining and waste of uranium and the location and storage of spent fuels in the form of high-level and low-level nuclear waste. Standards and regulations for disposal of mill tailings and nuclear wastes are established by the Office of Nuclear Material Safety and Safeguards, which was created by the Nuclear Waste Policy Act of 1982. Another law related to waste regulation was the Low Level Waste Policy Act of 1980. This act made each state responsible for the disposal of its own nuclear wastes. Low-level wastes include materials other than spent fuel that have become contaminated or exposed to radioactivity during use. For example, low-level waste is generated by hospitals, research facilities, industries, and universities. The difficulty in the implementation of this act is that all states do not need disposal sites; they are therefore encouraged to develop joint disposal plans with neighboring states. The specific point of controversy emerges in what has been referred to as the NIMBY (not in my backyard) syndrome, which implies that no states want a low-level radiation site placed within their borders or that they do not wish to be responsible for any other state's waste. The three low-level waste disposal sites presently in the United States are at Barnwell, South Carolina; Beatty, Nevada; and Richland, Washington.

Why is nuclear energy such a controversial issue in the United States? A colleague once suggested that people fear nuclear energy because they cannot hear it, see it, or smell it, and thus it remains a mysterious unknown. Perhaps this is an oversimplification of the real reasons people have for being suspicious of nuclear power. Real or potential nuclear accidents—the malfunction of nuclear reactors, which may release radiation into the atmosphere—seem to be the most significant underlying factors accounting for people's reluctance to wholeheartedly support the nuclear energy alternative in the United States.

At the end of World War II, the introduction of the nuclear era gave rise to the belief that atomic power could be used for broad-scale peaceful and generally beneficial purposes. This was true then, and it remains true today. Admiral Hyman G. Rickover, who was influential in the development of nuclear propulsion programs for the U.S. Navy, was a major force in the early development of and support for nuclear energy as a source of commercial power for public use. The prevailing view held by many representatives of the U.S. Congress and by the various presidential administrations during this early era was that nuclear power could be the solution to many of the nation's critical energy needs. The partnership of government and industry would forge a strong alliance for the development of nuclear power as an inexpensive energy source.

In 1965, U.S. utilities placed their first orders for nuclear plants for which the manufacturers no longer provided price guarantees (Stobaugh and Yergin, *Energy Future*, 1980, p. 136). This created a buyer's market for utilities wanting to build nuclear plants, because they could approach the separate manufacturers for secret bids and then negotiate and bargain for the lowest bidder. Low cost projections were proclaimed to those utilities considering joining the nuclear power fraternity. However, analysts who made these early cost projections for nuclear power development were soon to be proven incorrect. By the end of the 1960s, more accurate and less emotional assessments of the cost of nuclear power indicated that the real costs were much higher than had originally been perceived. Although breeder-reactor technology was improving and there were continuing problems in the development of the light-water reactor system, government research groups and the Atomic Energy Commission had become committed to the light-water reactor system, without fully understanding that the costs of these facilities would multiply significantly by the time the nuclear reactors became operational.

Frequently in the public policy process, experts and specialists tend to dominate debate and to steer the course of discussion on an issue. In the development of nuclear power in the United States, nuclear scientists, engineers, and members of the Atomic Energy Commission and its affiliated agencies were particularly influential in controlling the debate and the flow of information regarding nuclear energy and its potential uses in the production of electricity. These experts were largely optimistic about the health and safety aspects of nuclear energy and they were often impatient with "outsiders" who were critical of their assertions and projections. The Brookhaven Report of 1957, for example, was intended to assuage public fears about the safety of nuclear energy.

The focus of criticism and opposition to nuclear power, in the 1970s and today, has been largely on the technical capabilities of the nuclear power industry to assure the safety of nuclear reactors; to demonstrate that temporary storage of spent fuel rods at nuclear generating facilities can be safe; to assure that the environment in which nuclear generating stations are located can be kept free from long-term radiation contamination; to de. strate that the transportation of nuclear materials can be secur. from terrorist attack and can withstand accidents during transport; and to assure that long-term storage of spent nuclear fuel rods and other nuclear wastes will not be harmful to the surrounding environment and especially to people in the region. A 1984 survey done by the U.S. Office of Technology Assessment showed a significant decline in support for nuclear power after the Three Mile Island accident in 1979 (U.S. Congress, Office of Technology Assessment, *Nuclear Power in an Age of Uncertainty,* 1984, p. 211).

A more recent development in the nuclear power debate has to do with the economics of nuclear power. Can nuclear energy be realistically considered an inexpensive source of power when we are forced to confront the increasing costs of technology? The discussion of the economics of nuclear power focuses on the investment costs of nuclear generating stations; the most effective way of managing inflation in allocating the investment cost to each kilowatt-hour of electricity produced by the plants during their assumed lifetime; fuel and fuel-related costs; and the appropriate way to estimate cash flows and fixed and variable costs (Stobaugh and Yergin, *Energy Future,* 1980, p. 145). General Electric Corporation estimated that between 1975 and 1984 the costs for nuclear power plants would increase 41 percent (Myers, *The Nuclear Power Debate,* 1977, p. 23). Each side of the nuclear power debate in the United States has a set of valid claims, but the economic factors associated with development of nuclear generating stations have slowed construction and caused delays in planning new nuclear power facilities.

The nuclear power industry is a highly centralized, technically complex, capital-intensive industry that is perceived by many to have the potential for long-term environmental danger. Some scientists have therefore suggested that coal-fired plants should be considered as potential alternative energy sources. But a major economic factor related to coal plants is the cost of stack-gas scrubbing equipment that removes sulfur dioxide from plant emissions (Myers, *The Nuclear Power Debate,* 1977, p. 23). The environmental hazards caused by emissions from coal-fired plants are also sources of controversy and concern. Clean coal combustion is still in the testing and development stage and has not yet reached commercial application, although in 1985 the United States received 57 percent of its electricity kilowatt-hours from coal and only 15 percent from nuclear plants (Electric Power Research Institute, *Electricity: Today's Technologies, Tomorrow's Alternatives*, 1987, p. 29). At this juncture, therefore, the use of coal as a clean source of power to replace nuclear energy remains controversial.

Between 1957 and 1977, the nuclear power industry experienced a period of significant growth. President Dwight D. Eisenhower's Atoms for Peace plan served as the U.S. government's statement of official support for research and development of peaceful uses of the atom. Since nuclear energy had therefore become a priority of the national government, a massive infusion of money stimulated investigation into, and production of, nuclear power capability. As indicated earlier, the establishment of the Atomic Energy Commission placed nuclear power on the national public agenda, and that agency was charged with promoting the development of nuclear power in the United States.

With the passage of the Energy Reorganization Act in 1974 and the creation of the Nuclear Regulatory Commission, a stronger regulatory emphasis became part of national policy. Implementation of the national nuclear energy policy has been attempted largely through support and encouragement for the building of nuclear power plants by private sector utilities. But with accidents at such locations as Browns Ferry in Alabama, Three Mile Island in Pennsylvania, and the most disastrous accident at Chernobyl in the Soviet Union, serious questions have been raised about nuclear energy as a safe and viable element in future energy planning. This, coupled with the increased costs involved in establishing nuclear energy plants, has significantly slowed the pace of the construction of additional nuclear facilities.

Thus, an evaluation of nuclear energy policy in the United States is still underway. The hopes for developing inexpensive nuclear power have not been abandoned, but the incentives for utilities to enter the nuclear power business have been diminished.

Other nations are facing a similar dilemma in deciding whether to invest in or to continue the development of nuclear power as a source of energy. A significant element of this discussion is the proliferation of nuclear power and, beyond that, whether some nations that might develop nuclear power will—or already do—use the power to create weapons. What, then, is the nuclear power situation in other countries? What have been the routes for the inclusion of these nations in the international nuclear community? And what are the prospects for the future? We will now briefly examine some of the issues affecting nuclear policy in other nations.

The Proliferation of Nuclear Power

The United States, England, France, the Federal Republic of Germany, Italy, Japan, Sweden, Canada, Switzerland, and the Soviet Union are all industrially developed nations that have the capacity to generate electricity by means of nuclear power. The Netherlands, Ireland, Belgium, Spain, Australia, Austria, and Denmark have research reactors that may lead to their capacity to use nuclear power as a source of energy. Other nations that either have or are developing nuclear power capability include South Korea, the Philippines, India, Brazil, Iraq, Argentina, South Africa, Israel, Libya, Taiwan, and Pakistan.

Many complex issues face nations in their attempts to decide whether to commit precious resources to the development of nuclear power capability. Katz and Marwah (*Nuclear Power in Developing Countries*, 1982, p. 21) offer a set of factors that have an impact on a nation's decision concerning whether to invest in nuclear energy technology. One of the first considerations is the sheer scale of the energy project. Can a nuclear reactor of necessary size be built, and can it be operated efficiently? The United States, the Soviet Union, Britain, France, and Canada sell reactors and nuclear technology to nations in the process of developing nuclear energy capability. But the preparatory and infrastructural costs in creating a nuclear power program are immense for any nation, let alone for a less-developed country. The country must also face the problems associated with the range of activities involved in the nuclear fuel cycle—including such factors as access to natural uranium, its conversion and enrichment, and the actual fabrication of reactor fuel elements. Still other important considerations include the creation of structures and institutions to establish and sustain a nuclear power program, the regulation and safety of operations, and the development of a supply of qualified personnel (Katz and Marwah, *Nuclear Power in Developing Countries*, 1982, p. 27).

Katz and Marwah also point out that the issue of the actual location of a nuclear power plant looms as a major consideration.

Finding suitable sites for nuclear reactors presents a special set of difficulties. For both economic and technical reasons, it is important to place a reactor close to a large body of water that would provide cooling and the environmentally acceptable diffusion of waste heat (Katz and Marwah, *Nuclear Power in Developing Countries,* 1982, p. 28). Seismic activity must also be taken into account. The reactor should be placed in an area where earthquake activity is low or nonexistent. Finally, the safety of nearby populations must be considered. A nuclear facility should be located as far away as possible from population centers.

In 1981 prices, a rough estimation of capital costs for a 600-megawatt reactor unit installed by an international contractor would be in the range of $1.5 to $2 billion (Katz and Marwah, *Nuclear Power in Developing Countries,* 1982, p. 28). A 600-megawatt reactor is considered to be the most economical to build and operate (Katz and Marwah, p. 26). However, such a reactor would obviously constitute a major capital investment—and it should be recognized that these are only essential startup costs. Nations seeking to enter the nuclear power community thus face a significant hurdle in the scale of an economical plant and the financing of the undertaking.

Yet another consideration for nations seeking nuclear power status is the question of security: Can a nation maintain a secure supply of uranium to fuel the nuclear power program? Can it provide the security necessary to keep the machinery functioning throughout the entire course of activities, from the extraction of uranium to the transformation of uranium and finally to the storage of nuclear wastes? Can a nation protect its nuclear installations against sabotage and terrorist attacks? These are fundamental questions that must be carefully addressed by any nation seeking or utilizing nuclear facilities.

Finally, a nation must determine the compatibility of entering into a nuclear program within the context of its social, economic, and technological fabric. Variables to consider in this context would include the nation's long-range energy plans, its international policies, its level of scientific and technical education, and its aspirations and capacity for future development. These problems may sometimes be daunting (Katz and Marwah, *Nuclear Power in Developing Countries,* 1982, p. 39).

Listed below are the nations possessing nuclear reactors as of 1987 and the number of reactors operating in each (Martocci and Wilson, *A Basic Guide to Nuclear Power,* 1987, p. 19).

Nuclear Reactors Operating, 1987

AFRICA, 2
South Africa, 2

NORTH AND SOUTH
AMERICA, 130
Argentina, 2
Canada, 19
United States, 109

ASIA, 58
India, 7
Japan, 37
Korea, 7
Pakistan, 1
Taiwan, 6

EUROPE, 227
Belgium, 8
Bulgaria, 4
Czechoslovakia, 7
Finland, 4
France, 49
East Germany, 5
West Germany, 21
Hungary, 3
Italy, 3
The Netherlands, 2
Spain, 8
Sweden, 12
Switzerland, 5
United Kingdom, 38
USSR, 57
Yugoslavia, 1

Nuclear Power and Energy Production

How does nuclear energy provide a source of power? The nucleus of an atom is made up of particles referred to as protons and neutrons, which are held together by very strong forces. Nuclear fission occurs when the nuclei of certain atoms are split; this splitting releases energy that can be harnessed to produce electrical power. Commercial production of electricity from nuclear fission relies on uranium as the fuel to begin the nuclear process. The uranium-235 isotope splits or "fissions" if it absorbs a neutron. This fission process takes place when the uranium produces two new atoms of lower atomic weight, which are called fission products (Nader and Abbotts, *The Menace of Atomic Energy,* 1979, p. 39). The fission process is designed to produce many neutrons, which are then absorbed by uranium atoms. This process enables the nuclear reactor to be self-sustaining and to generate heat at a steady, constant rate. The heat generated is kinetic energy, which is then transformed into heat energy. Water is heated to produce steam that passes through a turbine to generate electricity. Thus, nuclear energy is derived from the continuous chain reaction that creates heat, which raises the temperature of the water, which creates steam, which in turn generates electrical power by use of the turbine. The only major difference between a coal-fired plant and a nuclear power plant is the method used to heat the water. It should be emphasized, however, that there are a multitude of potential problems associated with constructing and housing the facilities to harness and process the fission and the nuclear chain reaction. The materials that make up the reactor walls and cooling pipes must be able to withstand extraordinary heat, pressure, and the effects of corrosion in order to prevent potentially disastrous releases of radiation in the event of a plant failure.

Nuclear reactors in commercial use in the United States are called light-water reactors—reactors that use ordinary water as a coolant. These reactors have four major components (Martocci and Wilson, *A Basic Guide to Nuclear Power,* 1987, pp. 4–6):

1. Fuel rods, which contain pellets of uranium fuel that has been enriched
2. A moderator, which slows down the neutrons given off during fission so they are more easily absorbed by other nuclei
3. Control rods, which contain substances that absorb neutrons and slow down the chain reaction
4. A coolant, which acts to cool the fuel rods and carries their heat to another part of the power plant, where it is used to produce power

Light-water reactors are to be distinguished from heavy-water reactors. Heavy-water reactors use deuterium—also known as heavy hydrogen, the isotope that is twice the mass of ordinary hydrogen and occurs in water—which acts as a moderator and offers greater efficiency of production (Nader and Abbotts, *The Menace of Atomic Energy,* 1979, p. 43). The water circulates around the assembled clusters of the fuel rods. The fuel-rod assemblies make up what is known as the core or fuel pile of the reactor, which is covered by the water contained in the reactor vessel. Approximately 100 fuel rods are required to fuel a reactor; a typical fuel rod is about 12 feet long. A moderate-sized reactor may require 40,000 fuel rods weighing 100 tons or more (U.S. Atomic Energy Commission, *The Safety of Nuclear Power Reactors and Related Facilities,* 1973, pp. 1–6).

The energy content of nuclear fuel is very high. This means that it takes very little nuclear fuel to create power. For example, the fissioning of one pound of nuclear fuel releases as much energy as the combustion of about three million pounds of coal. Compared to fossil fuels, nuclear fuel has a very high potential for energy production and is, to that extent, a highly desirable source of energy. Although not all of the fissionable material in the fuel rods is available for use, the rods can be reprocessed to recover unused uranium-235 and newly formed plutonium-239 for future use.

This reprocessing of the fuel is an important stage in the entire nuclear fuel cycle. The nuclear fuel cycle consists of the following stages: (1) mining and milling of natural uranium, (2) enriching the uranium, (3) processing the uranium for use in fuel rods, (4) fissioning the fuel in the reactor, (5) recovering the remaining fissionable material, (6) refrabricating the material for reuse, and (7) disposing of the nuclear waste.

Representatives of the nuclear power industry state that, on average, nuclear power offers lower-cost electricity than any of the fossil fuels. The capital costs of building nuclear plants are high, but operation, maintenance, and fuel costs are comparatively low. Industry proponents also assert that nuclear plants have an advantage over nonnuclear facilities in that they do not emit the atmospheric pollutants for which fossil fuel plants have often become notorious. Thus, it is argued, there is no smog problem with nuclear power generation and expensive cleanup of the air is unnecessary. These assertions, however, do not go unchallenged. Critics of this argument state that "thermal pollution" occurs from the waste heat that is emitted into the atmosphere by the billowing clouds of water vapor discharged from the cooling towers. Spokesmen for the nuclear energy industry respond by saying that thermal pollution cannot occur from vapor clouds because the clouds dissipate so quickly that they cannot heat the atmosphere.

Claims of pollution may be more accurate when nuclear plants are located adjacent to large bodies of water such as rivers or bays; superheated water discharged into these water systems may have an adverse effect. But operators at nuclear plants take great pains to cool the water that will be discharged into surrounding systems, to prevent negative impacts upon the wildlife. The Diablo Canyon Nuclear Power Facility in California, for example, heavily monitors the water temperatures in the bay adjacent to its nuclear facility to assure that the facility does not disrupt the marine environment and tidelands in the vicinity.

Costs and Benefits of Nuclear Energy Policy

Relatively precise measurements of the pros and cons of nuclear energy policy may be made with a simple cost-benefit analysis of the factors affecting development of nuclear power in the United States and elsewhere.

Katz and Marwah, for example (*Nuclear Power in Developing Countries,* 1982, p. 21), offer a useful cost-benefit device for discussing the broad categories requiring attention in the nuclear power controversy. These authors suggest the benefits that may be expected from a national nuclear power program can be classified under three broad headings:

1. *Energy Economics.* What are the advantages of centrally generated electricity, and does nuclear fission offer a means of generating electricity at a lower cost?
2. *Energy Security.* Does the introduction of nuclear power help diversify energy and electrical supplies? Does it thus diminish dependence on any one source of supply? Does it reduce dependence on imported energy sources?
3. *Economic and Technical Modernization.* Does access to advanced technology and industrial skills necessary in a nuclear power program raise the level of scientific and technical development as well as serve as an optional path to economic development?

Katz and Marwah also consider the apparent costs of nuclear power development, two of which are pertinent to our discussion:

1. *Investment Capital.* Can the nation soundly and reasonably invest in nuclear electricity production? Does it have the necessary industrial and regulatory infrastructure?
2. *External Dependence.* If a nation adopts a nuclear energy program, can it realistically reduce its dependence on

other nations for imported fuels or for equipment, services, and technology?

The present authors might add a third consideration that has to do with the multitude of potential health and safety concerns related to nuclear power development:

3. *Health and Safety Protections.* Can a nation manage the health and safety risks involved in nuclear energy? Can worker safety be guaranteed? Will there be a government commitment to respond to health and safety risks?

In any cost-benefit analysis, these factors and others must be carefully considered in drawing conclusions about the advantages and disadvantages of going nuclear. One final major problem that also must be considered is what to do with nuclear wastes. This topic will be addressed in the next section.

Nuclear Waste Management

What can (or does) a nation do with the byproducts of the nuclear fuel cycle? How can (or does) a nation and its nuclear energy facilities dispose of or store the nuclear wastes that are created from the generation of electricity?

The U.S. Energy Department has chosen Yucca Mountain in southwestern Nevada as the nation's first permanent repository for high-level, commercial nuclear waste. The energy department is currently engaged in environmental analysis of the Yucca Mountain site and expects to finish its study in 1995. The department proposes to begin storing wastes there in 2003. The wastes will be "hot" for thousands of years because it takes centuries for the radiation captured in the wastes to dissipate. Factors that therefore affect the location of nuclear waste disposal sites include: (1) the geology of the area, (2) the level of the water table, (3) the presence of seismic activity, (4) the extent of underground pressure due to tectonic movements that could force water upward, and (5) the proximity of the waste site to population centers.

The nuclear industry in the United States has for many years been seeking a dump site for permanent storage of nuclear wastes. Alternatives to permanent storage have thus far proven to be scientifically unacceptable or have met major opposition from the states in which the storage sites might have been located and/or from vocal antinuclear pressure groups. Various alternatives to permanent storage have been proposed. For example, it has been suggested that nuclear wastes be sealed in containers and deposited on the ocean floor or that they be launched into outer space. But in 1987, the U.S. Congress passed legislation authorizing the underground disposal of commercial nuclear wastes in Nevada. Nevada, as of 1989, has raised objections to the depository decision.

The Nuclear Regulatory Commission is responsible for regulating the handling and disposal of nuclear waste through its Office of Nuclear Material Safety and Safeguards. The activities of this office include the regulation of all commercial high-level and low-level radioactive waste and uranium recovery facilities. Specific activities of this office include (U.S. Nuclear Regulatory Commission, *Annual Report,* 1987, p. 85):

1. Developing the criteria and the framework for high-level waste regulation, including the technical bases for the licensing of high-level waste respositories
2. Providing program management for Nuclear Regulatory Commission responsibilities under the Nuclear Waste Policy Act of 1982
3. Developing rules and guidance to assure a consistent national program of regulating and licensing low-level waste disposal facilities
4. Providing national program management for licensing and regulating uranium recovery facilities and associated mill tailings
5. Reviewing and concurring in significant Department of Energy decisions related to inactive mill tailings sites and the licensing of stabilized tailings piles for monitoring and maintenance programs

When considering waste disposal, it is also necessary to examine procedures for the dismantling of obsolete facilities. Because of a concern for safety and economics, nuclear plant licenses are granted for a period of only 40 years. As the equipment in nuclear power facilities ages it becomes less reliable. Hence, nuclear plants and their components may be dismantled because of the high cost of repairing and maintaining older equipment and the increased possibility of dangers resulting from the aging facilities. Although the nuclear power plant license expires after 40 years, the radioactivity in the equipment obviously does not cease to exist within that time period.

The Department of Energy and the Nuclear Regulatory Commission have developed three methods of decommissioning outmoded plants and equipment. The first is to "mothball" the site. In this process all nuclear fuel and fluids are removed and then the plant is locked and guarded for as long as the radioactivity of the facility and its components remains hazardous. Some analysts have estimated that it might be 200 years before the facility would no longer be considered hazardous (Nader and Abbotts, *The Menace of Atomic Energy*, 1979, p. 139). A second method of decommissioning plants is known as entombment, which involves sealing the facility and its components in concrete. This method of decommissioning would not require security measures as stringent as those required in the mothballing process. A third method is to dismantle the facility. All but the uncontaminated foundation structures would be removed and then stored in a repository for nuclear waste. After dismantling, the site would be restored to its original condition (Nader and Abbotts, *The Menace of Atomic Energy*, 1979, p. 140). This was the process used for the Shippingport Nuclear Plant, the largest nuclear unit and the only commercial reactor in the world to be taken out of service in this manner. Several other nuclear plants have been mothballed or entombed.

In December 1988, the Department of Energy entered into a $1 billion contract with the Bechtel Group, Inc., a large engineering, mining, and construction firm, to develop a comprehensive system to transport and store radioactive nuclear wastes. The contract requires Bechtel Corporation to evaluate the suitability of the Yucca Mountain nuclear waste storage site, which lies approximately 100 miles northwest of Las Vegas, Nevada. Bechtel is also responsible for designing, licensing, and managing all aspects of the transportation and storage of high-level nuclear wastes. Yucca Mountain is particularly appealing as a storage site because it is one of the driest areas in the United States and it is very much above the groundwater level (*San Francisco Chronicle*, January 13, 1988, p. A10).

Bechtel is not new to the nuclear power field. The corporation has previously managed $85 billion in nuclear-related contracts and, most recently, designed the new nuclear waste depository near Carlsbad, New Mexico. This disposal site was not intended for storage of commercial spent fuels but was instead designated for the storage of radioactive wastes from U.S. defense-related programs. The Carlsbad nuclear waste site is carved out of salt some 2,000 feet below ground level.

The subject of the storage of wastes that grow out of defense programs may be even more controversial than that of commercial production of electricity by nuclear power. For example, in 1988, a public interest group calling itself the Radioactive Waste Campaign issued a report that accused the U.S. Department of Energy of mismanaging defense-related radioactive waste disposal and storage sites. Some of the problems cited by the highly critical report included: (1) contamination of groundwater by routine pumping of wastes into the ground at the Hanford Nuclear Reservation in Washington; (2) the release of strontium-90—which can cause bone cancer and leukemia—into surface water at the Savannah River Nuclear Defense Plant in South Carolina; and (3) the contamination of aquifers at the Nevada Atomic Test Site as a result of numerous underground explosions.

The problems cited in the report focus on the lack of nuclear waste regulation by the Department of Energy, especially in defense-related development of nuclear weapons. But it should be recognized that there is presently no formal regulatory body responsible for overseeing nuclear weapons plants or the health and safety problems related to nuclear weapons production. In early 1989, the Department of Energy estimated it could take from $91 billion to $200 billion over the next 60 years just to clean up radioactive and chemical contamination at 45 government, civilian, and military nuclear plants in various locations in the United States. Dealing with this immense problem will probably require congressional action to fund and to begin the cleanup of contaminated sites at defense and weapons-related facilities.

Conclusion

The purpose of this book is to introduce the reader to the basic history, issues, problems, and prospects involved in the development of nuclear energy policy in the United States and to provide an introductory guide for reference and research. Nuclear power continues to offer a challenging opportunity to provide a significant portion of the electrical energy needs of the United States and of many other countries in the years ahead. Understanding the foundations of nuclear energy policy is thus a useful undertaking for layperson and specialist alike.

When a utility company in the United States wishes to construct a nuclear power plant, the company applies for a construction permit from the Nuclear Regulatory Commission, which regulates licensing and construction of such facilities. The construction permit requires the utility to provide a preliminary safety analysis report. This report addresses several points: (1) a safety plan for the facility, (2) a description of the facility and its design, (3) an analysis of the plant's safety systems and means to respond to and mitigate problems, (4) a description of the plant's quality assurance plan, (5) a plan for the utility's training and operations programs, and (6) a plan for responding to radioactive emergencies (Nader and Abbotts, *The Menace of Atomic Energy*, 1979, p. 324). After reviewing the application, the Atomic Safety and Licensing Board of the Nuclear Regulatory Commission schedules public hearings at which interested parties may challenge or question the applicant's proposal.

Once the construction permit has been granted, the utility must apply for an operating license. Such a license permits placement of nuclear fuel into the reactor and allows operation of the reactor for the purpose of producing electrical power. Actual application for the license occurs some two or three years before construction of the plant is scheduled for completion. The process for obtaining the operating license is similar to that utilized for the construction permit. The application is filed, then reviewed by the Nuclear Regulatory Commission staff and the Advisory Committee on Reactor Safeguards, and a safety evaluation report and an updated environment statement are issued. A public hearing is not required at this stage, but one may be held either if it is requested by members of the public or upon the initiative of the Nuclear Regulatory Commission (U.S. Nuclear Regulatory Commission, *Annual Report*, 1987, p. 12).

Once the nuclear power facility is licensed, it remains under review and monitoring and undergoes periodic inspection throughout its operating life. The Nuclear Regulatory Commission can require any changes or "backfitting" for any operator of a nuclear facility if the commission feels such measures are required for public health or safety reasons or for common defense and security.

The Nuclear Regulatory Commission also confirms standards for buildings and for materials used in the construction, design, maintenance, and operation of nuclear power facilities. For example, in 1988, the Nuclear Regulatory Commission was informed that bogus steam-valve parts had been found in a nuclear power plant in Michigan. As a consequence of this revelation, the Nuclear Regulatory Commission staff issued a special notice to all nuclear utilities to be on the alert for counterfeit valve parts of all types that might have been sold to unsuspecting buyers at power plants.

U.S. regulatory agencies have often been characterized as having difficulty actually regulating those under their jurisdiction because of the intimacy of relations between the regulators and those being regulated. For example, while the Nuclear Regulatory Commission attempts to regulate the nuclear power industry, it also plays the role of promoting and encouraging future development of nuclear generating facilities. An inherent irony in this role is that the Nuclear Regulatory Commission may risk bankrupting or shutting down a facility by requiring major improvements or changes in the facility's operating systems. Rancho Seco Nuclear Power Plant near Sacramento, California, is owned by the Sacramento Municipal Utilities District (SMUD). It has a net book value of $932 million, which includes $215 million worth of nuclear fuel. Between January 1985 and March 1988, Rancho Seco was shut down to correct problems related to overcooling. SMUD consequently lost tremendous income because of Rancho Seco's inability to produce electricity. Thus, while on the one hand encouraging development, on the other hand the Nuclear Regulatory Commission finds itself in the position of having to curb the practices of the very developments it has licensed. And even though there is a Nuclear Regulatory Commission employee onsite at every commercial nuclear power facility in the United States, this does not make it any easier for the commission to take corrective action before health and safety problems might occur.

On June 6, 1989, as a result of an effort by antinuclear groups, the voters of SMUD voted, with only 40 percent of the qualified electorate participating, to shut down the Rancho Seco plant. This may result in the loss of over 1,200 jobs and $96 million in annual payroll, a likely rate increase to consumers, and a great opportunity for the Pacific Gas and Electric Company to enhance its revenues. This is the first time that an operating nuclear energy plant has been decommissioned by a public vote. As Joe Buonaiuto, president of SMUD, put it, "After the antinuclear champagne bottles quit popping, this community's going to wake up with a severe hangover. . . .That's when they'll realize the economic consequences of the move" (*San Francisco Chronicle,* June 8, 1989, p. C-4).

The cost of building nuclear power plants is becoming more prohibitive each year. Moreover, the technology and construction of a plant will be much more complicated in the 1990s than it was in the 1970s. Future construction therefore becomes less feasible. Although online nuclear power facilities presently provide a substantial amount of electricity for public use at a reasonable cost, the aging of these facilities and of their thousands of pipes and electrical components will require major investments of money for sheer maintenance and preservation, let alone additional construction. In addition, safety issues are becoming a larger concern. The nonprofit research group Public Citizen Critical Mass Energy Project, for example, issued a report stating that the nation's nuclear power plants reported nearly 3,000 mishaps and at least 430 emergency shutdowns in 1987. Also in 1987, there were more than 104,000 incidents in which workers at nuclear plants were exposed to measurable doses of radiation. An accident at the Calvert Cliffs, Maryland, Nuclear Power Plant in 1988 took a worker's life. The Nuclear Regulatory Commission issues a semiannual report listing reactors that require constant monitoring. In 1988, 16 reactors were included in this list.

The tasks of the Nuclear Regulatory Commission are obviously extensive and wide-reaching. Its mission remains to develop short- and long-range goals, priorities, and plans as they relate to the benefits, costs, and risks of nuclear power at present—and presumably future—nuclear facilities in the United States.

In this brief introduction, we have attempted to provide the reader with an overview and a framework within which to examine nuclear energy policy. We conclude by reviewing the series of questions that have repeatedly presented themselves during the course of our discussion, as listed by Martocci and Wilson (*A Basic Guide to Nuclear Power,* 1987, p. 20).

1. Is nuclear power the safest and most efficient alternative to fossil fuels?
2. Are energy conservation and solar power feasible and realistic alternatives to the risks of using nuclear power?
3. In the face of increasing costs, is the construction of additional nuclear power plants justified?

4. What are the long-term effects of exposure to low levels of radiation?
5. Where should repositories for high-level waste be built?
6. Where should low-level waste be disposed of?
7. Can serious nuclear accidents be prevented by nuclear power industry diligence and self-monitoring?
8. Can the Nuclear Regulatory Commission effectively regulate the nuclear power industry?

The answers to these and related questions will help to shape a responsible nuclear energy policy in the years ahead.

Epilogue

As the final draft of this manuscript was being written in spring 1989, there came, on March 23, an announcement by two scientists at the University of Utah of a discovery that could transform the entire future of the nuclear power process in the United States and throughout the world. Professors B. Stanley Pons and Martin Fleischmann announced, by way of a news conference, that they had accomplished a "cold fusion" process by which, in an extremely simple way, cheap fusion—not fission— energy could be harnessed. If it proves valid, their discovery could utterly transform the nuclear energy industry and provide a safe, cheap, and virtually inexhaustible source of electrical power.

The apparatus used by the two scientists was extremely simple. An electric current was passed through two electrodes (made of platinum and palladium) that were immersed in so-called heavy water, a form of water in which hydrogen is replaced by deuterium (an element having an extra neutron in its nucleus). One of the submerged electrodes, made of the rare element palladium, draws deuterons (deuterium neutrons) into the structure of the palladium atoms. Because deuterons are charged positively, they are normally repelled from each other. Evidently, the palladium nuclei sufficiently shield the deuterons from their normal pattern of repelling each other and allow them to get close enough to form helium, in other words, allowing them to fuse. It is in this fusion process that energy and neutrons are released, and during which a form of hydrogen called tritium is also released. The scientists used common seawater at room temperature instead of a high-temperature nuclear furnace. The energy contained in one cubic foot of seawater is equivalent to the energy contained in ten tons of coal. Conventional nuclear fusion processes require temperatures of millions of degrees, close to the temperatures in the sun's interior, to create a reaction. Pons and Fleischmann said, however, that rather than using the traditional method they use an electrical charge that causes the palladium metal electrode to absorb and separate the heavy water's hydrogen ions, which carry an extra neutron. These hydrogen atoms then join together—they fuse—to create a helium atom and an extra proton. The fusion process could also create tritium, a radioactive form of hydrogen that contains two extra neutrons and a proton. Heat energy is generated in both instances.

The president of the University of Utah made it simple to understand. "The fuel is heavy water, driven by electric force into enormously compact concentrations in the holes inside this metal (palladium)," heating water in the surrounding container. "You boil water, and when you boil water you make steam, and when you make steam you run a turbine, and if you run a turbine you can create electricity. So this has the potential to create electricity" (*San Francisco Chronicle,* March 24, 1989, p. A11).

For a variety of reasons, skepticism immediately was expressed by many members of the scientific community. Scientists at the Lawrence Livermore National Laboratory and the Los Alamos National Laboratory, for example, suggested that they would have to examine all the data on which the experiment was based before any detailed evaluation could be made. Others were particularly critical of the method used to announce the work: a news conference instead of the publication of an article in a refereed professional journal, which would be subject to evaluation and criticism from one's scientific and professional peers. Still others suggested that it was really nothing particularly new. During the 1950s, for example, physicist Luis Alvarez discovered a similar process involving room-temperature fusion. According to Alvarez, "We had a short but exhilarating experience when we thought we had solved all of the fuel problems of mankind for the rest of time" (*U.S. News and World Report,* April 24, 1989, p. 66). But the reaction he discovered could not be sustained.

Edward Teller, however, who has long been involved in fusion research, was less skeptical: "My hunch is that these people have something. If it is real, then it will make a very real difference in what we are doing" (*San Francisco Chronicle,* March 25, 1989, p. A4). And one of the major engineering groups engaged in fusion research at the highly regarded Fusion Technology Institute of the University of Wisconsin took the announcement at face value and calculated the cost of constructing a power plant. Their calculations, quoted in the same newspaper article, indicated that the cost for palladium alone for each plant would be $1.6 billion. The Wisconsin scientists "estimated that a standard thousand-megawatt power plant would need 400 tons of palladium. Only 26,000 tons of palladium are believed to be in all the world's ore deposits, almost entirely in South Africa and the Soviet Union, and it currently costs $4 million per ton. . . .[I]f the discovery is confirmed, cheaper materials to do the job can be found" (*San Francisco Chronicle*, March 25, 1989, p. A4).

Since the initial announcement, scientists in such diverse locations as Stanford, Berkeley, MIT, Georgia, Texas, Hungary, Italy, and Yugoslavia, among others, have reported that their experiments have indicated a similar reaction, although none has claimed absolute certainty about the results. Experiments at some other places have not been so successful.

That the nuclear power industry—as currently constituted— has an uncertain future is hardly a profound observation. Indeed, this book is being written at the time of the tenth anniversary of the Three Mile Island accident in Pennsylvania. It is of some importance to note that not one nuclear power plant has been ordered in the United States since then and, possibly even more telling, plans for 65 others have been cancelled. One of the great ironies is that companies such as the Bechtel Group, Inc., now make a great deal of money from dismantling nuclear facilities instead of building them and in cleaning up the contamination caused by such incidents as that at Three Mile Island.

The industry counters with the observation that it does, in fact, have a fine safety record. It argues, among other things, that the accident at Three Mile Island actually has improved safety conditions at all existing nuclear power plants in the United States. It argues, too, that the industry is likely to face a resurgence in the 1990s. The mere demand for more electricity (presumably the country will require some 120 million to 220 million additional kilowatts, an increase of 15–30 percent, by the year 2000); the increasing concern over global warming and acid rain (nuclear energy does not cause carbon dioxide contamination as do such fuels as coal, oil, and natural gas, nor do nuclear plants emit sulfur dioxide into the atmosphere); and continued concerns about dependency on foreign oil will make the nuclear alternative much more attractive. The reduction of the size and complexity of nuclear plants, the lowering of costs (both for construction and production), and increased safety features will all add to the attractiveness of nuclear energy in the years ahead.

Nuclear fusion presents a stunning potential alternative to existing processes. Fusion as a source of energy has eluded scientists for nearly 50 years; the prospect of vast amounts of energy, literally squeezed from elements, that offers far less dangerous radiation or pollution serves as an alluring objective. Born in the research that led to the hydrogen bomb, fusion research for peaceful purposes began with Project Sherwood, launched by the U.S. government in 1951. The early assumption was that fusion energy could be produced within 10 to 20 years from that time. Nevertheless, the goal has escaped scientists at such pre-eminent institutions as the Lawrence Livermore Laboratory, Oak Ridge, Los Alamos, and others. Fusion Power Associates, a trade organization headquartered near Washington, D.C., has estimated that the United States has spent more than $8 billion on fusion research since 1951; the U.S. Department of Energy 1989 budget for fusion programs is $514 million. It should be noted, also, that nations such as the Soviet Union, Japan, and others in Europe are on the same quest.

And so the fascinating story of the development and utilization of nuclear energy continues to unfold. Would it not be the supreme irony if two comparatively lesser-known scientists, using some of their personal savings and materials that could be found in any undergraduate science laboratory, have achieved that which other scientists in the world's leading research institutions have been unable to achieve even after the expenditure of untold billions of dollars?

The authors hope that this book will provide a basic introduction to a discussion of that unfolding story, and that it will provide the basic facts and direction necessary for one to begin research in the field of nuclear energy policy.

References

Anderson, James E. *Public Policy-Making*. New York: Holt, Rinehart and Winston, 1979.

Bryerton, Gene. *Nuclear Dilemma*. New York: Ballantine Books, 1970.

Clary, Bruce B., and Michael E. Kraft. "Impact Assessment, Policy Failure, and the Nuclear Waste Policy Act." Paper presented at the meeting of the Western Political Science Association. San Francisco, March 10–12, 1988.

Cleveland, Harlan, ed. *Energy Futures of Developing Countries*. New York: Praeger, 1980.

Cochran, Clarke, T. R. Carr, N. Joseph Cayer, and Lawrence Mayer. *American Public Policy: An Introduction*. New York: St. Martin's Press, 1982.

Electric Power Research Institute. *Electricity: Today's Technologies, Tomorrow's Alternatives*. Pleasant Hill, CA: Innovative Technologies, Inc., 1987.

Holl, Jack M., Roger M. Anders, and Alice L. Buck. *United States Civilian Nuclear Power Policy, 1954–1984: A Summary History*. Washington, DC: U.S. Department of Energy, 1986.

Katz, James E., and Onker S. Marwah. *Nuclear Power in Developing Countries*. Lexington, MA: D. C. Heath and Company, 1982.

Kruschke, Earl R. "Toward a Brief Formulation of a Definition of Politics." *Social Science*. Spring 1973.

Kruschke, Earl R., and Byron M. Jackson. *The Public Policy Dictionary*. Santa Barbara, CA: ABC-CLIO, 1987.

Lawler, James, and William Parle. "Risk Communication and the NIMBY Syndrome in Hazardous Waste Decision-Making: Reconciling Technical Opinion and Citizen Participation." Paper presented at the meeting of the Western Political Science Association. San Francisco, March 10–12, 1988.

Lovins, Amory B., and L. Hunter. *Energy War: Breaking the Nuclear Link*. San Francisco: Friends of the Earth, 1980.

Martocci, Barbara, and Greg Wilson. *A Basic Guide to Nuclear Power*. Washington, DC: Edison Electric Institute, 1987.

Myers, Desaix, III. *The Nuclear Power Debate: Moral, Economic, Technical, and Political Issues*. New York: Praeger, 1977.

Nader, Ralph, and John Abbotts. *The Menace of Atomic Energy*. New York: W.W. Norton, 1979.

Pearman, William A., and Phillip Starr. *The American Nuclear Power Industry: A Handbook*. New York: Garland Publishers, Inc., 1985.

San Francisco Chronicle, January 13, 1988; March 24 and March 25, 1989; June 8, 1989.

Stobaugh, Robert, and Daniel Yergin, eds. *Energy Future*. New York: Ballantine Books, 1980.

U.S. Atomic Energy Commission. *The Safety of Nuclear Power Reactors and Related Facilities*. Washington, DC: U.S. Government Printing Office, 1973.

U.S. Congress. Office of Technology Assessment. *Nuclear Power in an Age of Uncertainty*. Washington, DC: U.S. Government Printing Office, 1984.

U.S. News and World Report, April 24, 1989.

U.S. Nuclear Regulatory Commission. *Annual Report*. Washington, DC: U.S. Government Printing Office, 1987.

Warkov, Seymour, ed. *Energy Policy in the United States*. New York: Praeger, 1980.

2

Chronology

THE TWENTIETH CENTURY HAS BEEN a century of phenomenal technological progress. Among the most important advances during the past 90 years have been the development of the airplane, the mass production of the automobile, the virtually universal use of electricity, the vast increase of large-scale mass production by industry, the incredible expansion of railroads, and the invention of the means of extracting fossil fuels to power these technological advancements. Even among this group, however, the leap to nuclear power stands out as a giant step forward that carries with it immense potential.

One of the most crucial concerns of the twentieth century has been meeting the needs for new and larger amounts of fuel and power resources. Wood long dominated as a source of heat and light for the world's peoples. As populations grew and became more urban, and as societies became more technologically sophisticated, there were new and greater energy demands. Thus, machines were invented to satisfy these demands.

The keen demand for kerosene to fuel lamps and for fuel oil for heating stimulated the widespread search for petroleum as a realistic source of fuel and energy in the early twentieth century. The year 1900 proved to be the watershed year for development of improved quality of petroleum products. It was during this same period—the last decade of the nineteenth century and the first decade of the twentieth—that the foundations of scientific investigation and experimentation in nuclear science were laid.

Following is a chronology of the history, legislation, and major events that were significant in the development of nuclear energy and the evolution of nuclear energy policy in the United States. The chronology runs from the late nineteenth century to the present.

1895   Wilhelm Roentgen, a German physicist noted for his work in thermology, mechanics, and electricity, discovers a shortwave ray, the Roentgen ray or *X-ray*, for which he will receive the Nobel Prize in physics in 1901. The use of the X-ray offers new insights into the structure of the atom.

1896   Antoine Henri Becquerel, a member of a famous French family of physicists who studied atmospheric polarization and the influence of the earth's magnetism on the atmosphere, discovers the radioactive properties of uranium.

1898   Pierre and Marie Sklodowska Curie, a famous French husband-wife scientific team, discover both polonium and radium. They isolate one gram of radium salts from about eight tons of pitchblende, and determine the atomic weights of radium and polonium. They refuse to patent or to profit from their highly significant discovery, which ultimately will have immense impact on research in radioactivity and nuclear science.

1903   Antoine Henri Becquerel shares the Nobel Prize in physics, with Pierre and Marie Curie, for the discovery of natural radioactivity.

1905   Dr. Albert Einstein, at the age of 26, makes what will be one of the major contributions to the world of science with the introduction of his theory of relativity. This idea discards the notion of absolute motion and deals only with relative motion between two systems. Thus, space and time are no longer viewed as separate and independent, but rather as a four-dimensional continuum known as space-time.

1908   Ernest Rutherford, a British physicist born in New Zealand who is known for his work in radioactivity and the discovery of the atomic nucleus, receives the Nobel Prize in chemistry for his discovery and naming (with Frederick Soddy) of alpha and beta radiation and for their theory of the radioactive transformation of atoms.

1932   James Chadwick, who had worked in the area of radioactivity under Ernest Rutherford at Manchester University, discovers the neutron. For this he will receive the Nobel Prize in 1935 and be knighted in 1945.

1934   Enrico Fermi, a physicist born in Italy, contributes to the theory of beta decay and the neutrino and to quantum statistics. He uses the neutron to bombard uranium; as a result, he reports the existence of a new element, neptunium. Fermi splits the atom, but the fact is ignored by the scientific community. He will be awarded the Nobel Prize in 1938.

1938   The German chemists Otto Hahn and Fritz Strassman produce the elements barium and krypton by bombarding uranium with neutrons.

1939   On January 26, Enrico Fermi announces in Washington, D.C., that each splitting of the atom releases a few neutrons. He predicts the possibility of a chain reaction.

With support and pressure from several leading scientists, Albert Einstein, on August 2, signs a letter to President Franklin D. Roosevelt alerting him to the feasibility of building an atomic bomb.

On October 21, the Uranium Committee, appointed by President Roosevelt, holds its first meeting to study the possibility of building an atomic bomb.

1941   President Franklin D. Roosevelt gives approval to a team of scientists led by Drs. Enrico Fermi, J. Robert Oppenheimer, and Ernest O. Lawrence to construct an atomic bomb. The Manhattan District Project, the code name for the atomic bomb project, gets underway.

1942   Under conditions of great uncertainty, the first self-sustaining nuclear chain reaction occurs in a laboratory at the University of Chicago.

1943   The Los Alamos Scientific Laboratory in New Mexico is constructed. With the combined talents of British and American scientists, the atomic bomb is designed and assembled in the laboratories of Los Alamos.

1943
cont. During this same year, the U.S. government acquires land in the Colorado Plateau, with the express goal of contracting with Union Mines, a subsidiary of Union Carbide Company, to mine uranium, the basic ore used in the fission process.

1945 On July 16, the first atomic bomb is tested at Alamogordo, New Mexico, by the U.S. Army's Manhattan Project scientists.

On August 6, the United States drops the first atomic bomb (a uranium bomb) on Hiroshima, Japan. The effects are incredibly devastating, and scientists will continue to study the long-range effects and consequences into the 1980s. The city is chosen because it is a military, not a civilian, target.

On August 9, the United States drops a second atomic bomb, this one a plutonium bomb, on Nagasaki, Japan. Japan soon surrenders unconditionally.

1946 On August 1, President Harry S Truman signs the Atomic Energy Act of 1946. This act establishes the Atomic Energy Commission (AEC), which has among its objectives the control of nuclear energy development and the exploration of peaceful uses of atomic energy. The Atomic Energy Act also establishes the Joint Committee on Atomic Energy (JCAE).

1947 The Atomic Energy Commission establishes the Reactor Safeguards Committee.

The Atomic Energy Commission appoints an Industrial Advisory Group under Chairman James W. Parker to investigate peaceful uses of atomic energy.

1949 The Atomic Energy Commission announces that a site in Idaho has been selected for the National Reactor Testing Station.

1951 Something of a milestone in nuclear energy development is reached when the first electricity is generated from atomic power in Arco, Idaho, by the Experimental Breeder Reactor 1.

1952 The National Research Experimental Reactor at Chalk River, Canada, goes out of control. A partial core meltdown is contained.

1953 President Dwight D. Eisenhower delivers his so-called Atoms for Peace speech before the delegates of the United Nations in New York.

1954   The Atomic Energy Act of 1954 is passed. This act is a revision of the 1946 act that provides for the private ownership of nuclear power and encourages the participation of private industry in the general development and use of nuclear energy.

The Joint Committee on Atomic Energy approves the AEC five-year program for reactor development. Construction begins on the first commercial nuclear power plant in the United States at the Shippingport Atomic Power Station near Pittsburgh, Pennsylvania.

1955   On January 10, the Atomic Energy Commission initiates the Cooperative Power Demonstration Program to stimulate construction of nuclear power facilities. Under this plan the Atomic Energy Commission offers assistance in technical research and a waiver of certain qualifying fees to any utility that desires to build an atomic power plant.

On August 8, the first United Nations International Conference on the Peaceful Uses of Atomic Energy is held in Geneva, Switzerland.

1956   On February 22, President Dwight D. Eisenhower directs the Atomic Energy Commission to make available to other nations, for sale or lease, 20,000 kilograms of uranium-235 for use in power and research reactors, as well as 20,000 kilograms for power reactors in the United States.

1957   The Brookhaven Report, "Theoretical Possibilities and Consequences of Major Accidents in Large Nuclear Plants," is released by the Atomic Energy Commission. The purpose of the report is to relieve fears and anxieties among members of the public and industries with respect to the possibilities of nuclear accidents.

On September 2, President Dwight D. Eisenhower signs the Price-Anderson Act, which encourages utilities to invest in nuclear power facilities and provides financial protection to the public and to Atomic Energy Commission licensees and contractors in the event of a major accident involving a nuclear power plant.

On October 1, the United Nations establishes the International Atomic Energy Agency to promote the peaceful uses of nuclear energy throughout the world.

1957
cont.
On December 2, the Shippingport (Pennsylvania) Nuclear Power Plant begins operation. Using a pressurized-water reactor, the Shippingport Power Station reaches full power three weeks later and begins to supply electricity to the Pittsburgh area.

1958
Construction begins on Commonwealth Edison's Dresden Nuclear Power Station, Unit 1, outside of Chicago, Illinois. It will not actually produce commercial power until June 1960.

1960
The Atomic Energy Commission publishes a ten-year plan of nuclear power development.

The first boiling-water reactor manufactured by General Electric goes online with the opening of Commonwealth Edison's Dresden Plant 1.

Yankee Nuclear Power Station in Massachusetts goes online and becomes the third nuclear reactor in the United States to produce commercial electrical power.

1961
In Idaho Falls, Idaho, a test reactor goes out of control, resulting in the death of three maintenance workers.

1962
President John F. Kennedy receives a report from the Atomic Energy Commission concerning the role of nuclear power in the economy. The report seeks Kennedy's support for a cooperative venture between the Federal Power Commission and the Department of the Interior to seriously consider the options provided by nuclear power for improving the nation's capacity to meet its future energy needs. This report is a landmark policy statement that encourages the development of breeder reactors to meet future electric power demands.

1964
President Lyndon B. Johnson signs the Private Ownership of Special Nuclear Materials Act, which allows the power industry to own fuel for power reactors. This makes possible the private ownership of fuels to operate nuclear reactors.

1966
On October 5, the Fermi fast breeder reactor outside of Detroit, Michigan, suffers a partial core meltdown. The reactor had been given clearance to start power generation by a Supreme Court decision in 1961, even though it had been the subject of controversy for many years. The Supreme Court decision overturned a U.S. Court of Appeals decision that halted construction of the Fermi fast breeder reactor in 1956.

1966
cont.   The AFL-CIO had attempted to stop construction of the nuclear facility because of technical difficulties, but the U.S. Supreme Court ruled that construction could continue while technical problems were being solved.

1969   Tarapur Atomic Power Station goes online in India. The facility was constructed by General Electric.

On January 1, President Lyndon Johnson signs the National Environmental Policy Act. The act requires government agencies to submit environmental inpact statements identifying the effects a proposed policy would have on the environment, but the requirement does not apply to the private sector.

On August 18, the Atomic Energy Commission establishes the Atomic Safety and Licensing Appeal Board, a three-member board responsible for technical review of the safety systems and measures required for the granting of a construction permit for a nuclear facility.

1970   On January 6, the Dresden-2 reactor near Chicago, Illinois, goes out of control and releases quantities of radioactive iodine.

1971   President Richard M. Nixon appropriates funds for, and announces as a national goal, the development of a liquid metal, fast breeder reactor demonstration plant in the United States.

By this year, a total of 22 commercial nuclear power stations are in operation in the United States.

1973   On June 29, President Richard M. Nixon proposes the creation of the Energy Research and Development Administration and the Nuclear Regulatory Commission to replace the Atomic Energy Commission.

The oil embargo by members of the Organization of Petroleum Exporting Countries (OPEC) begins against the United States. This results in the so-called energy crisis for the United States and furthers the cause of the development of nuclear energy as an alternate source of energy. The oil embargo will run from October 17, 1973, until March 17, 1974.

1974   On August 3, the federal government releases the results of a three-year reactor safety study that concludes that a meltdown in a power reactor would be extremely unlikely.

1974
cont.
On October 1, the Energy Reorganization Act is signed by President Gerald Ford. The act abolishes the Atomic Energy Commission and creates the Energy Research and Development Administration and the Nuclear Regulatory Commission.

On December 5, Daniel Ford and Henry Kendall, representing the Union of Concerned Scientists and Friends of the Earth, publish their findings that emergency core cooling systems in nuclear reactors might not work.

1975
The Nuclear Regulatory Commission orders the shutdown of 23 nuclear reactors because of cracking in the coolant pipes.

On March 4, the United States and Iran sign an agreement under which the United States will deliver eight nuclear reactors to Iran over the next ten years at a cost of $7 billion.

On March 22, a fire damages the reactor core at the Browns Ferry Nuclear Plant, a General Electric–built plant in Decatur, Alabama.

1976
By this year, 61 nuclear plants with a combined total capacity of 42,699 megawatts are producing some 8.3 percent of the electricity generated in the United States.

1977
On April 7, President Jimmy Carter announces that the United States will defer indefinitely its plans for reprocessing spent nuclear fuel. He also proposes that the Clinch River (Virginia) Breeder Reactor be terminated.

On August 4, President Carter signs the Energy Reorganization Act, which creates the Department of Energy (DOE) and combines the Energy Research and Development Administration and the Federal Energy Administration.

The Carolina Environmental Study Group, a citizens' organization represented by the Public Citizen Litigation Group, challenges the Price-Anderson Act as being unconstitutional, and a federal district court agrees. The court states that the act violates the Fifth Amendment to the Constitution because it allows destruction of life and property without the certainty that the victims would be justly compensated (*Carolina Environmental Study Group v. Atomic Energy Commission*, 431 F. Supp. 230, W.D.N.C. [1977]).

1978   The U.S. Supreme Court overturns the Federal District Court decision of June 1978, saving the nuclear power industry from the limited liability challenge.

1979   On March 28, there is an accident at the Three Mile Island Nuclear Power Plant near Harrisburg, Pennsylvania. It is the most serious accident to occur at a commercial nuclear power station in the United States. Causes of the accident will be attributed to human error and mechanical malfunction. No actual injuries are sustained, but radioactivity is released into the atmosphere.

The Nuclear Regulatory Commission imposes more stringent reactor safety standards and regulations and implements more rigorous inspection procedures to improve the safety of operations of nuclear reactor installations.

1980   On January 28, President Jimmy Carter presents the 1981 budget, which includes an appropriation of $1.26 billion for nonmilitary nuclear research.

France agrees to supply Iraq with weapons-grade uranium and a nuclear reactor.

The Nuclear Safety Research, Development, and Demonstration Act establishes a program within the Department of Energy to improve the safety of nuclear power plants.

1981   On October 8, President Ronald Reagan submits the Nuclear Power Policy Statement, which emphasizes the importance of nuclear power as a possible solution to the nation's energy needs.

1982   The Shippingport (Pennsylvania) Nuclear Power Station is shut down and decommissioned after 25 years of operation. Decommissioning is expected to take six years.

1983   On January 7, President Ronald Reagan signs into law the Nuclear Waste Policy Act. The act is designed to develop a program for the disposal of high-level radioactive waste and spent nuclear fuel from nuclear power plants.

On October 26, the Senate of the United States refuses further funding of the Clinch River Breeder Reactor, which effectively terminates the breeder reactor project.

1984   The Department of Energy establishes the Civilian Radioactive Waste Management Office.

1986   An explosion and accident that will have worldwide effects occur at the Chernobyl Nuclear Power Plant in the Ukraine in the Soviet Union. Thirty-five plant workers are killed. Nuclear contamination in Europe and, because of wind patterns, in other parts of the world will be substantial.

         The Federal Emergency Management Agency issues a report that concludes that the evacuation plans for the area surrounding the Pilgrim, Massachusetts, reactor are inadequate.

         A total of 430 plant shutdowns due to emergencies are reported to the Nuclear Regulatory Commission.

         The Nuclear Regulatory Commission cites 492 violations of nuclear safety regulations at U.S. power reactors.

1988   The Department of Energy estimates that 15 U.S. nuclear power plants will reach the end of their 30- to 40-year useful lifespan by the year 2000.

         The Department of Energy awards the Bechtel Group, Inc., a large engineering and mining firm, a $1 billion contract to develop a system to transport and store radioactive nuclear wastes.

References

Brown, Anthony, and Charles B. MacDonald. *The Secret History of the Atomic Bomb.* New York: Dell Publishing Co., 1977.

Electric Power Research Institute. *Electricity: Today's Technologies, Tomorrow's Alternatives.* Pleasant Hill, CA: Innovative Communications, Inc., 1987.

Epstein, William. *The Last Chance: Nuclear Proliferation and Arms Control.* New York: Collier MacMillan, 1976.

Freeman, Leslie J. *Nuclear Witnesses: Insiders Speak Out.* New York: W. W. Norton and Company, 1982.

Holl, Jack M., Roger M. Anders, and Alice M. Buck. *United States Civilian Nuclear Power Policy, 1954–1984: A Summary History.* Washington, DC: U.S. Department of Energy, 1986.

Katz, James E., and Onkar S. Marwah. *Nuclear Power in Developing Countries.* Lexington, MA: D. C. Heath and Company, 1982.

Martocci, Barbara, and Greg Wilson. *A Basic Guide to Nuclear Power.* Washington, DC: Edison Electric Institute, 1987.

Myers, Desaix, III. *The Nuclear Power Debate: Moral, Economic, Technical, and Political Issues.* New York: Praeger, 1977.

Pearman, William A., and Phillip Starr. *The American Nuclear Power Industry: A Handbook.* New York: Garland Publishers, Inc., 1985.

U.S. Department of Energy. *The History of Nuclear Energy.* Washington, DC: U.S. Government Printing Office, 1985.

3

Biographies

THE FOLLOWING ARE BIOGRAPHIES of individuals who have had varying degrees of influence on the development of nuclear energy policy in the United States. The list is not intended to be exhaustive, but it does provide the reader with relevant biographical and professional facts about a number of scientists and politicians who have been instrumental in the development of nuclear energy policy as it has unfolded to the present day.

Bernard Baruch (1870–1965)

Bernard Mannes Baruch was born in Camden, South Carolina, in 1870. Before he was 30, he became a millionaire through stock market speculation.

Wealthy, powerful, and influential in national politics, he was appointed chairman of the War Industries Board in 1918 by President Woodrow Wilson. In 1919, he served as an advisor on economic recovery at the Paris Peace Conference. He served through the 1920s and 1930s as a political strategist and publicist on national issues, such as price stabilization and economic recovery during the Great Depression. Much of Baruch's influence was felt in the New Deal programs of the Franklin Roosevelt administration.

Bernard Baruch may be particularly known for his promotion of appropriate control of atomic energy. Indeed, the Baruch Plan for International Control of Atomic Energy was an attempt to define a policy having international ramifications. The proposal was debated at the United Nations; thus, Baruch became significantly responsible for articulating U.S. atomic energy policy. President Harry S Truman appointed Baruch as U.S. representative to the United Nations Atomic Energy Commission.

At the United Nations, Baruch called on member nations to cooperate in the development of safe and peaceful uses of atomic energy. He suggested punishing nations that violated agreements on the uses of atomic energy. The national public mood at the time suggested that Americans would do best not to share the secrets of atomic energy with others. Many politicians were fearful of Soviet developments in atomic energy and thus did not wish to negotiate with the Soviets because the United States had a monopoly on nuclear weapons.

By the 1950s, the Baruch Plan was generally regarded as unworkable. The Soviets would not tolerate international control and development of atomic energy, claiming that the Baruch Plan preserved a U.S. monopoly on atomic bombs and did not allow the Soviet Union to develop its own nuclear weapons. These events contributed to the beginning of the arms race and the cold war.

PUBLICATIONS: *Baruch: My Own Story* (1957–1960); *The Public Years* (1960).

Niels Bohr (1885–1962)

Niels Henrik David Bohr was born in Copenhagen, Denmark, in 1885. He received his Ph.D. in 1911 from the University of Copenhagen. Generally recognized as one of the foremost physicists of modern times, he carried on research on the atom at Cambridge University under the guidance of Sir James J. Thomson and at Manchester University under Lord Ernest Rutherford. In 1919, Bohr became professor of theoretical physics at the University of Copenhagen, and in 1920, he became director of the Institute of Theoretical Physics.

Although Rutherford had discovered the nucleus of the atom in 1911, classical scientific theory had been unable to explain the stability of the nuclear model of the atom. Bohr was able to fill this void when, in 1913, he suggested that electrons move around the nucleus of the atom in restricted orbits. Thus, he combined the quantum theory with his own theory of atomic structure. Much of the knowledge of modern physics was made possible by Bohr's insistence that atomic processes cannot be understood by use of classical laws alone—a revolutionary assumption. He continued to be a leading figure in the development of quantum physics for at least the next 20 years, and won the Nobel Prize in physics in 1922.

Bohr had visited the United States in 1938 and 1939. During his visits, he pointed out to U.S. scientists that he believed, on the basis of work reported in Germany, that the uranium atom could be split. These ideas were later confirmed at Columbia University in New York.

Bohr fled from Nazi-occupied Denmark in 1943. He gave valuable advice to scientists at Los Alamos, New Mexico, in their efforts to develop the atomic bomb. In 1945 he returned to Denmark to do work on the peaceful uses of atomic energy.

Perhaps Bohr's greatest contributions in the field of nuclear energy were his bold, untraditional thinking and his work on atomic structure, which enabled later scientists to refine his theories and thus gain a greater understanding of quantum mechanics.

PUBLICATIONS: *Atomic Physics and Knowledge* (1958); *Atomic Theory and the Description of Nature,* (1961); and others.

Barry Commoner (1917–)

Barry Commoner is generally considered one of the country's leading biologists and environmentalists. Born in Brooklyn in 1917, he received his Ph.D. in biology from Harvard University. He is a member of the Scientists' Institute for Public Information and the founder of the St. Louis Committee for Environmental Information.

Commoner has written several books on environmental hazards caused by humans. In 1976, for example, he wrote *The Poverty of Power: Energy and the Economic Crisis.* This book raised serious questions about the energy future of the United States, the survival of the environment, and the costs of technology used to produce energy in this country. Commoner examines the partnership between the private and public sectors in the development of safe nuclear power and considers the risks associated with nuclear energy to be unacceptable to the citizens who must finally pay the price.

Commoner feels that the technology necessary for the operation of nuclear plants is too complicated and too risky—too large an investment is required to make a plant work properly. He does not see nuclear power as economically feasible or as providing the necessary safeguards from the perspective of health and safety standards.

PUBLICATIONS (in addition to those cited above): *The Closing Circle* (1971); *Alternative Technologies for Power Production* (1973); *Human Welfare: The End Use of Power* (1975); and *The Social Costs of Power Production* (1975).

Albert Einstein (1879–1955)

Albert Einstein was born in Ulm, Germany, of Jewish parents, in 1879. As a boy he lived in Munich and Milan; he graduated from the Federal Institute of Technology in Zurich, Switzerland, in 1900 and became a Swiss citizen. In 1905, he obtained his doctorate from the University of Zurich.

Einstein is generally recognized as one of the greatest physicists who ever lived. He evolved the special theory of relativity, explained the photoelectric effect, and studied the motion of atoms, by which he explained Brownian movement. He held professorships at the University of Zurich, the German University in Prague, and the Federal Institute of Technology in Zurich. His fame had by 1913 spread internationally, and in 1914 he was invited by the Prussian Academy of Sciences to come to Berlin to assume a position as professor of physics and director of theoretical physics at the Kaiser Wilhelm Institute. In 1921 he received the Nobel Prize in physics.

In 1933, Einstein accepted a position at the Institute for Advanced Study at Princeton University, and in 1934, while he was in the United States, the Nazis seized all of his property in Germany. Einstein became a U.S. citizen in 1940.

In 1939, at the request of a group of scientists that included Niels Bohr, Einstein signed a letter, which was sent to President Franklin D. Roosevelt, describing the possibilities of creating a new bomb and recommending to the president that the United States might consider developing it before the Germans became capable of producing the necessary technology to do so. The president took heed of Einstein's advice and ordered the development of the bomb by employing some of the most renowned physicists and engineers of the time. Einstein himself, however, remained an ardent pacifist.

He is best known for the development of the theory of relativity, which helped provide the basis for controlling the release of energy from the atom.

PUBLICATIONS: *Albert Einstein: Philosopher-Scientist* (1969); *Autobiographical Notes* (1979); and others.

Dwight D. Eisenhower (1890–1969)

Dwight David Eisenhower was born in Denison, Texas, in 1890. When he was two years old, his family moved to Abilene, Kansas, where he was raised. He entered West Point Military Academy, from which he graduated in 1915. He had an illustrious career as a military officer, particularly in Europe during the Second World War, and was also known in educational circles during his term as president of Columbia University. A national hero, he was persuaded by Republican liberals and internationalists to run for the presidency of the United States. He won the national election in 1952 and took office on January 20, 1953. He served two terms.

Although some historians have suggested that his presidency was not particularly distinguished, he is regarded as the U.S. president most directly responsible for the development of the atomic energy program in the United States. During his two terms of office (January 1953 to January 1961), the development of nuclear energy in the United States came to be regarded as a direct answer to many of the energy needs of both the United States and the world.

One of President Eisenhower's most memorable accomplishments was the delivery of his now famous "Atoms for Peace" speech at the United Nations. In that speech, Eisenhower suggested that nations pool their atomic information, materials, and research for peaceful purposes. The International Atomic Energy Agency was created in 1957 to further the ideals set forth in the Atoms for Peace speech; 62 countries signed the agency's charter.

It was during President Eisenhower's administration that the Atomic Energy Commission began encouraging the private development of nuclear power, and the first nuclear powered electricity for public use was produced in Idaho.

Thus, the two-term Eisenhower administration set the stage for the development and expansion of nuclear power in the United States.

PUBLICATIONS: *Eisenhower's Own Story of the War* (1946); *The White House Years* (1963); *The Eisenhower Diaries* (1981).

Enrico Fermi (1901–1954)

Enrico Fermi was born in Italy in 1901. He was a student at Pisa, Göttingen, and Leiden. For a time he taught physics at universities in Florence and Rome. It was Fermi who discovered element 93, known as neptunium. He was a major contributor to the theory of beta decay, the neutrino, and to quantum statistics. He also experimented with radioactivity, for which he received the Nobel Prize in physics in 1938.

Because Italy had been taken over by the Fascists, the Fermis did not return there after their journey to Stockholm to receive the Nobel Prize, but continued instead to the United States. From 1939 to 1945, Fermi was a professor of physics at Columbia University and from 1946 to 1954 he held a similar position at the University of Chicago. He became a U.S. citizen in 1944.

Fermi was responsible for the creation of the first uranium chain reaction at Chicago in 1942, and joined the illustrious team of scientists working on the development of the atomic bomb at Los Alamos, New Mexico. He also made contributions to the construction of the hydrogen bomb and, in addition, served on the General Advisory Committee of the Atomic Energy Commission, which awarded him its first special prize of $25,000 in 1954. The commission named the annual award in honor of Fermi himself; it is bestowed on a scientist who demonstrates scientific and technical achievement in the development, use, and control of atomic energy.

Enrico Fermi was a teacher, professor, theorist, scientist, and scholar. He is known not only for these attributes, but also for supervising Atomic Energy Commission laboratories at Los Alamos, Brookhaven, Oak Ridge, the Lawrence-Livermore Laboratory in Berkeley, and the Argonne Laboratory.

PUBLICATIONS: *Elementary Particles* (1951); *Thermodynamics* (1956); and *Molecules, Crystals, and Quantum Statistics* (1966).

Leslie Groves (1896–1970)

General Leslie Groves was a professional soldier. It became his task to organize and direct the scientists who were responsible for creating the atomic bomb at Los Alamos, New Mexico, the project known as the Manhattan Project. He was the most experienced and perhaps the most brilliant—and most abrasive—building construction officer in the U.S. Army.

General Groves was particularly concerned about the secrecy of the project. He required that certain scientists be monitored and followed. Thus, his relationship with the scientists became an adversarial one, but Groves' concern with security persevered. After World War II, General Groves served as director of atomic research laboratories and he remained an advocate of U.S. preparedness in nuclear armaments.

PUBLICATIONS: *Now It Can Be Told: The Story of the Manhattan Project* (1962).

Bourke B. Hickenlooper (1896–1971)

Bourke B. Hickenlooper, Republican senator from Iowa, was the first chairman of the Joint Committee on Atomic Energy. The joint committee was created by the Atomic Energy Act of 1946 and consisted of 18 members, 9 from the Senate and 9 from the House of Representatives. The Joint Committee on Atomic Energy had full jurisdiction over such subjects as bills, resolutions, and other matters in the House and Senate related to activities of the Atomic Energy Commission and the development, use, and control of atomic energy.

Senator Hickenlooper led a bipartisan effort in the Joint Committee on Atomic Energy to fund and expand the work of the Atomic Energy Commission. He was also instrumental in defining and clarifying the relationship between the U.S. Congress and the Atomic Energy Commission, through the work of the Joint Committee on Atomic Energy.

Senator Hickenlooper was much concerned with increasing the cooperation between the United States and friendly nations in the area of civilian applications of the military uses of atomic energy. In 1954, the so-called Cole-Hickenlooper bill was introduced in Congress to further this cause. Among the provisions of the bill was an effort to abandon government monopoly on special nuclear materials. The bill was passed that same year.

Hickenlooper was a strong advocate of bipartisan cooperation in the general area of nuclear power. He is widely remembered for his leadership and service in the field of nuclear energy because of his membership on the Joint Committee on Atomic Energy.

Henry M. Jackson (1912–1983)

Henry M. Jackson, U.S. senator from the state of Washington, had a long and distinguished career. During his years in public life, he acquired national recognition for his support of defense, civil rights, and labor legislation. Originally elected to the House of Representatives in 1940, Jackson was subsequently elected to the Senate in 1953. He served on the Joint Committee on Atomic Energy during his terms both in the House (1948) and in the Senate (1954).

In 1955, Senator Jackson encouraged President Dwight D. Eisenhower to stockpile uncommitted reserves of nuclear materials. Jackson's proposal included the development of a bank of nuclear materials for both military and civilian purposes. President Eisenhower eventually turned down the senator's plan.

Senator Jackson was highly influential in the development of a dual-purpose nuclear power reactor, which was capable of producing both plutonium and electric power, at the Atomic Energy Commission's Hanford (Washington) site. It is largely because of Senator Jackson's efforts that much of defense-related nuclear experimentation took place at Hanford. Jackson went so far in his support of nuclear energy that he proposed placing nuclear reactors in remote areas such as Antarctica. Throughout his public career, he was a strong proponent of nuclear energy and he worked to promote its development and use in the United States and elsewhere.

Ernest O. Lawrence (1901–1958)

Ernest Orlando Lawrence was born in Canton, South Dakota, in 1901. He graduated from the University of South Dakota in 1922 and received his Ph.D. from Yale University in 1925.

Lawrence started his career at the University of California in 1928, becoming professor of physics in 1930 and director of the radiation laboratory in 1936. This laboratory is now known as the Lawrence-Livermore Laboratory. While at the university, Lawrence was a colleague of J. Robert Oppenheimer.

Lawrence invented and developed the cyclotron, a device designed to accelerate the speed of atomic particles. For his research in atomic structure and transmutation, he received the Nobel Prize in physics in 1939. Using the cyclotron he was able to produce artificially radioactive elements and neutrons that could be used in research in such areas as chemistry and biology, as well as in nuclear physics. Among his other awards was the Enrico Fermi Award, which he received in 1957.

Because of his many accomplishments, Ernest O. Lawrence was recognized by the establishment of an award in his name—the Ernest O. Lawrence Memorial Award created by President Dwight D. Eisenhower in 1958. The award has since been given to those who have contributed to the development, use, and control of atomic energy.

David E. Lilienthal (1899–1981)

David Eli Lilienthal was born in Morton, Illinois, in 1899. He was admitted to the bar in 1923 and practiced law until Governor Philip La Follette appointed him to the Wisconsin Public Service Commission; President Franklin D. Roosevelt later appointed him as one of three directors of the Tennessee Valley Authority (TVA). As chairman of the TVA, Lilienthal engaged in bitter disputes with various private interests because of his insistence on nonpolitical administration of the agency.

In 1946, Lilienthal was appointed as the first chairman of the Atomic Energy Commission by President Harry S Truman. He thus became responsible for providing initial leadership and direction to the commission as defined under the Atomic Energy Act of 1946. He especially sought public accountability and criticism of the Atomic Energy Commission and its various programs. Among his major tasks were organization and management, evolution of an atomic reactor development program, and the inclusion of private industry and business in the development of nuclear energy.

In 1944, Senator Bourke B. Hickenlooper began a series of investigations into the security policies of the Atomic Energy Commission. He accused Chairman Lilienthal of mismanaging the agency's operations. Largely as a result of these charges, Lilienthal resigned in 1949.

As leader of the Atomic Energy Commission, Lilienthal was most interested in developing an atomic energy policy that met with and withstood public scrutiny. But during the late 1940s and the 1950s, American sensitivity to international communist subversion became acute. Thus, David Lilienthal's desire for an open information policy regarding Atomic Energy Commission activities ran counter to the prevailing political winds.

PUBLICATIONS: *This I Do Believe* (1949); *TVA: Democracy on the March* (1953); *Big Business: A New Era* (1953); *Change, Hope, and the Bomb* (1963); *The Journals of David Lilienthal* (1964); *Atomic Energy: A New Start* (1980).

Ralph Nader (1934–)

Ralph Nader was born in Winsted, Connecticut, in 1934. He practiced law in Connecticut and for a time in the early 1960s was a lecturer in history and government at the University of Hartford. His early reputation was made largely on the basis of his book *Unsafe at Any Speed,* which was an indictment of the U.S. auto industry; the U.S. Congress responded in 1966 by passing a stringent law that established safety standards for automobile production and manufacturing, such as impact requirements, seat belts, and placement of fuel tanks.

Ralph Nader has long been recognized as a leading consumer and public interest advocate. In more recent years, he has become particularly interested in the area of nuclear energy. In 1979, Nader and John Abbotts, a nuclear engineer, published the book *The Menace of Atomic Energy.* They offer a critical and incisive assessment of nuclear energy, its technology, the nuclear power industry in general, and the prospects for citizen action and response to existing, and proliferating, nuclear installations. Among other organizations he has established, Nader was responsible for the initiation of the Public Interest Research Group in Washington, D.C., which performs research, offers testimony, and takes legal action in certain selected public policy areas.

Ralph Nader's primary concern about nuclear energy is that serious unresolved questions remain, especially with respect to safety considerations. He also charges that the nuclear power industry has ignored the gravity of the problems related to the development of nuclear power. His objective is to bring these issues into an open forum for citizen action and debate.

PUBLICATIONS: *Unsafe at any Speed* (1972); *The Taming of the Giant Corporation* (1976); *The Menace of Atomic Energy,* with John Abbotts (1979); *The Lemon Book* (1980).

J. Robert Oppenheimer (1904–1967)

J. Robert Oppenheimer was born in New York City in 1904. He received his B.A. from Harvard University in 1925 and his Ph.D. from the University of Göttingen in 1927.

He taught at the University of California and the California Institute of Technology until his appointment as director of the Institute for Advanced Study at Princeton University in 1947. He served in this position until 1966, and throughout his term he actively advised and consulted with the U.S. government on nuclear energy matters.

Oppenheimer's early work involved quantum theory and nuclear physics. One of his most important papers, published in 1930, had to do with so-called antiparticles, which had not yet actually been discovered but were the subject of a great deal of speculation.

From 1942 to 1945, Oppenheimer was director of the atomic energy project at Los Alamos, New Mexico. There he made highly significant contributions to military uses of atomic energy. Yet, after the dropping of the atomic bomb on Hiroshima, Oppenheimer became an active proponent of civilian and international control over atomic energy and strongly opposed the development of the hydrogen bomb, on both technical and moral grounds.

He was the chairman of the general advisory committee of the U.S. Atomic Energy Commission from 1945 to 1952, and a leading consultant to the U.S. delegation of the United Nations Atomic Energy Committee.

In 1953, Oppenheimer was suspended by the Atomic Energy Commission as an alleged security risk. His case caused widespread controversy in legal, scientific, and academic circles. Shortly afterward, in 1954, he was unanimously reelected as the director of the Institute for Advanced Study at Princeton.

In 1963, the Atomic Energy Commission awarded Oppenheimer the Enrico Fermi Award for his work in nuclear physics. In addition, he had achieved a reputation as a great teacher, leaving his imprint on a generation of students at the University of California and at Princeton. He will be remembered, also, for raising critical questions about the uses of atomic energy and the nation's commitment to the peaceful applications of atomic science.

PUBLICATIONS: *Science: The Common Understanding* (1954); *The Open Mind* (1955); *Robert Oppenheimer: Letters and Recollections* (1980); *Uncommon Sense* (1984).

Dixy Lee Ray (1914–)

Dixy Lee Ray was the first female chair of the U.S. Atomic Energy Commission, her term running from 1973 to 1975.

Recognized as a strong proponent of atomic energy, Ray believed that nuclear power was quite safe. She once remarked that nuclear power was safer than eating, citing the statistic that 300 people choke to death each year simply trying to swallow food. But she was also aware of the difficulties that accompanied nuclear power, especially the safety problems. Indeed, she campaigned strenuously to eliminate defects in the construction and operation of nuclear power plants.

The Atomic Energy Commission was dissolved in 1974 when the Nuclear Regulatory Commission was created. Thus, Dixy Lee Ray was the last person to chair the "old" Atomic Energy Commission. Her tenure came in the midst of the energy crisis of 1973. This "crisis"—which is today seen largely as a contrived event rather than as a real crisis—raised major questions for energy policy in the United States.

Hyman G. Rickover (1900–1987)

Hyman George Rickover was born in Russia in 1900. He served in the U.S. Navy for 60 years, eventually rising to the rank of admiral. He was considered the father of the nuclear navy, and especially of the nuclear submarine.

During World War II, Admiral Rickover served as head of the electrical system of the navy's Bureau of Ships. Later, he was assigned to the atomic submarine project at Oak Ridge. It was at that time that he began to convince the navy that nuclear power for its ships was more than feasible. The first atomic-powered submarine, the *Nautilus,* was launched in 1954. Rickover later became chief of the Naval Reactors Branch of the Atomic Energy Commission and was in charge of the nuclear power propulsion division of the Bureau of Ships.

Admiral Rickover's tenure in office was marked by more than a little controversy. His outspoken style, his unwillingness to compromise on many issues, and his abrasiveness led to many an argument among policy makers. But he was convinced that the Soviet Union was intent on challenging the United States in the area of submarine production, and he insisted—eventually convincing others of the idea—that there was a need to upgrade the submarine forces of the United States by way of nuclear energy.

Admiral Rickover remained a powerful influence in the development of naval nuclear applications virtually until his death. In 1965, in recognition of his service to the navy and to the cause of nuclear power, he received the Enrico Fermi Award.

PUBLICATIONS: *Education and Freedom* (1959); *American Education, A National Failure* (1963).

Glenn T. Seaborg (1912–)

Glenn T. Seaborg is generally recognized as one of the great chemists of our time. In 1951, he shared the Nobel Prize in chemistry with Edwin McMillan, for work on the chemistry of transuranium elements.

Seaborg's research resulted in the development of the isotope Pu-239, which is recognized as a potential source of nuclear energy. In 1961, President John F. Kennedy appointed Seaborg as chairman of the Atomic Energy Commission, and he served in that position for ten years—the longest period for any Atomic Energy Commission chairman.

Dr. Seaborg believed that nuclear power could be made economically competitive and that it would be an effective energy source. One of his major contributions to nuclear energy policy was his 11 years of stable leadership of the Atomic Energy Commission. During this time, significant growth and development occurred in the Atomic Energy Commission, and Seaborg was regarded as an effective blend of both scientist and administrator.

Glenn T. Seaborg received the Enrico Fermi Award in 1959.

PUBLICATIONS: *Man and the Atom* (1971); *The Nuclear Milestones* (1972); *Kennedy, Khrushchev, and the Test Ban* (1981); *Stemming the Tide* (1987).

Lewis L. Strauss (1896–1974)

Lewis Lichtenstein Strauss was born in Charleston, West Virginia, in 1896. During World War I he served under Herbert Hoover on the Belgian Relief Commission; during World War II he served as special assistant to Secretary of the Navy James Forrestal. Strauss himself rose to the rank of rear admiral.

Strauss was appointed to the position of chairman of the Atomic Energy Commission in 1953 by President Dwight D. Eisenhower. He served simultaneously as President Eisenhower's special assistant for atomic energy matters. His term on the Atomic Energy Commission expired in 1958.

Strauss's term as chairman of the Atomic Energy Commission was controversial. He engaged in a series of disputes with the Joint Committee on Atomic Energy relevant to the proper role of the Atomic Energy Commission and its relationship with the Joint Committee on Atomic Energy. Another controversy involved a disagreement with J. Robert Oppenheimer, a scientist who opposed the development of the hydrogen bomb, while Strauss strongly supported it.

When Strauss left the Atomic Energy Commission, the relationship between the commission and the Joint Committee on Atomic Energy improved. Strauss had desired a more independent role for the Atomic Energy Commission. He also wanted to see only limited federal participation in the Power Reactor Demonstration Program. The program had been devised to build demonstration reactors to assist private industry in determining the most feasible reactor designs for commercial use. Strauss was well known for his advocacy of the private development of nuclear power. He did not believe that the government should play an active role in the subsidizing of nuclear development.

PUBLICATIONS: *Men and Decisions* (1963).

Edward Teller (1908–)

Edward Teller was born in Budapest, Hungary, in 1908, to a cultured, middle-class family. At any early age, he demonstrated a facility for mathematics. He studied chemical engineering in Germany as an undergraduate and later received his Ph.D. from the University of Leipzig. His reputation grew, and he soon received an assistantship in physics at the University of Göttingen. In 1932, he met Enrico Fermi in Rome. But as a Jewish scientist in Nazi Germany Teller had no future, so he fled Germany, spent a year in Copenhagen, and then moved on to University College in London. In 1935, Teller emigrated to the United States to join the growing list of émigré scientists seeking safe haven from the Nazis.

Edward Teller was among those scientists who worked on the Manhattan Project. After World War II, he became embroiled in the controversy over nuclear weapons and their future development. He was especially influential in bringing together a team of nuclear physicists to do research on thermonuclear weapons (the hydrogen bomb), of which he was regarded as the father. Thus,

Dr. Teller became immensely influential in the uses and development of nuclear weaponry. He worked closely with the Atomic Energy Commission and encouraged the U.S. government to support work in the thermonuclear area.

Dr. Teller had been associated with the Lawrence-Livermore Laboratory in the 1970s and 1980s, and he continues to serve as one of the leading proponents of the Strategic Defense Initiative (popularly known as Star Wars). Professor Teller has a reputation as a complex, brilliant, and opinionated man; he continues to have extensive influence over the direction of military uses of nuclear energy.

PUBLICATIONS: *Our Nuclear Future: Facts, Dangers, and Opportunities*, with Albert Latter (1958); *The Legacy of Hiroshima*, with Allen Brown (1962).

References

Commoner, Barry. *The Poverty of Power: Energy and the Economic Crisis.* New York: Alfred A. Knopf, 1976.

Davis, Nuell Pharr. *Lawrence and Oppenheimer.* New York: Simon and Schuster, 1968.

Del Sesto, Steven L. *Science, Politics, and Controversy: Civilian Nuclear Power in the United States, 1946–1974.* Boulder, CO: Westview Press, 1979.

Green, Harold, and Alan Rosenthal. *Government of the Atom.* New York: Atherton, 1963.

Hertsgaard, Mark. *Nuclear, Inc.: The Men and Money Behind Nuclear Energy.* New York: Pantheon Books, 1983.

Nader, Ralph, and John Abbotts. *The Menace of Atomic Energy.* New York: W. W. Norton, 1979.

Sylves, Richard. *The Nuclear Oracles.* Ames: Iowa State University Press, 1987.

Tyler, Patrick. *Running Critical: The Silent War, Rickover, and General Dynamics.* New York: Harper & Row, 1986.

4

Documents and Background Information

Speeches and Communications

The Einstein Letter

Albert Einstein
Old Grove Road
Naussau Point
Peconic, Long Island
August 2nd, 1939

F. D. Roosevelt
President of the United States
White House
Washington, D.C.

Sir:

Some recent work by E. Fermi and L. Szilard, which has been communicated to me in manuscript, leads me to expect that the element uranium may be turned into a new and important source of energy in the immediate future. Certain aspects of the situation which has arisen seem to call for watchfulness and, if necessary, quick action on the part of the Administration. I believe therefore that it is my duty to bring to your attention the following facts and recommendations.

In the course of the last four months it has been made probable—through the work of Joliot in France as well as Fermi and Szilard in America—that it may become possible to set up a nuclear chain reaction in a large mass of uranium by which vast amounts of power and large quantities of new radium-like elements would be generated. Now it appears almost certain that it could be achieved in the immediate future.

The new phenomenon would also lead to the construction of bombs, and it is conceivable—though much less certain—that extremely powerful bombs of a new type may thus be constructed. A single bomb of this type, carried by boat and exploded in a port, might very well destroy the whole port together with some of the surrounding territory. However, such bombs might very well prove to be too heavy for transportation by air.

The United States has only very poor ores of uranium in moderate quantities. There is some good ore in Canada and the former Czechoslovakia, while the most important source of uranium is the Belgian Congo.

In view of this situation you may think it desirable to have some permanent contact maintained between the Administration and the group of physicists working on chain reactions in America. One possible way of achieving this might be for you to entrust with this task a person who has your confidence and who could perhaps serve in an official capacity. His task might comprise the following:

(a) to approach Government Departments, keep them informed of the further developments, and put forward recommendations for Government action, giving particular attention to the problem of securing a supply of uranium ore for the United States,

(b) to speed up the experimental work, which is at present being carried on within the limits of the budgets of University laboratories, by providing funds, if such funds be required, through his contacts with private persons who are willing to make contributions for this cause, and perhaps also by obtaining the co-operation of industrial laboratories which have the necessary equipment.

I understand that Germany has actually stopped the sale of uranium from the Czechoslovakian mines which she has taken over. That she should have taken such early action might perhaps be understood on the ground that the son of the German Under-Secretary of State, von Weizsacker, is attached to the Kaiser-Wilhelm-Institut in Berlin where some of the American work on uranium is now being repeated.

Yours very truly,
A. Einstein

Source: Jack Dennis and faculty members of the Massachusetts Institute of Technology, eds., *The Nuclear Almanac: Confronting the Atom in War and Peace* (Reading, MA: Addison-Wesley Publishing Company, 1984), pp. 22–23.

Warning to Japan
Excerpts from Proposals for European Peace Settlement

Harry S Truman, President of the United States. Broadcast to the nation from Washington, D.C., August 9, 1945.

My fellow Americans: I have just returned from Berlin, the city from which the Germans intended to rule the world. It is a ghost city. The buildings are in ruins, its economy and its people are in ruins.

Our party also visited what is left of Frankfurt and Darmstadt. We flew over the remains of Kessel, Magdeburg and other devastated cities. German women and children and old men were wandering over the highways returning to bombed-out homes or leaving bombed-out cities, searching for food and shelter. . . .

We also saw some of the terrible destruction which the war had brought to the occupied countries of western Europe and to England.

How glad I am to be home again. And how grateful to Almighty God that this land of ours has been spared.

We must do all we can to spare her from the ravages of any future breach of the peace. That is why, though the United States wants no territory or profit or selfish advantage out of this war, we are going to maintain the military bases necessary for the complete protection of our interests and of world peace. . . .

The British, Chinese and United States governments have given the Japanese people adequate warning of what is in store for them. We have laid down the general terms on which they can surrender. Our warning went unheeded, our terms were rejected. Since then the Japanese have seen what our atomic bomb can do. They can foresee what it will do in the future.

The world will note that the first atomic bomb was dropped on Hiroshima, a military base. That was because we wished in this first attack to avoid, in so far as possible, the killing of civilians. But that attack is only a warning of things to come. If Japan does not surrender, bombs will have to be dropped on war industries and, unfortunately, thousands of civilian lives will be lost. I urge Japanese civilians to leave industrial cities immediately and save themselves from destruction. . . .

Our victory in Europe was more than a victory of arms.

It was a victory of one way of life over another. It was a victory of an ideal founded on the rights of the common man, on the dignity of the human being and on the conception of the state as the servant—not the master—of its people.

Source: *Vital Speeches of the Day,* Vol. XI, No. 21, August 15, 1945, pp. 642–645.

The Minimum Essentials to Control

Bernard M. Baruch, U.S. representative to the United Nations Atomic Energy Commission. Excerpts from speech delivered at Freedom House Award dinner, New York, October 8, 1946.

The peace we are enjoying—if that is the right word—threatens to become what a German historian said peace is: a brief interlude between wars.

Never were the opening words of the American [atomic] proposal so true as they are at this time: "We are here to make a choice between the quick and the dead. That is our business."

America asks nothing she is not willing to give. All of us must make contributions.

But I would be recreant to my trust if I dared to recommend the immediate abandonment of a major weapon in our arsenal—the bomb. How can any one ask destruction of existing bombs unless their further manufacture is effectively prohibited? Why should America alone be asked to make sacrifices by way of unilateral disarmament in the cause of international good-will? If equality of sacrifice be needed, then each should participate.

I firmly believe that the American proposals plead the cause and contain a rough approach to the abolition not only of one instrument of war but of war itself.

I now say that America stands ready to proscribe and destroy the atom bomb—to lift its use from death to life—if the world will join in a pact to insure the world's security from atomic warfare. But it must be a realistic working pact—not merely a pious expression of intent, wholly lacking in methods of enforcement.

Our proposals were submitted on June 14. Some weeks later came the frank, unqualified statement of [Soviet] Ambassador Gromyko, declaring the American plan . . . unacceptable to the Soviets, either in full or in part. He has repeated this position several times.

The Soviets protest that inspection violates national sovereignty. Better that than international disaster. America is willing to accept inspection as a control measure, and for some time America would be the most inspected.

I am at a loss to understand why national sovereignty should be made such a fetish. . . .

I say to you with all the weight of my experience that the American plan does not impair any country's national dignity or national security. It is a great forward motion toward international peace. Where there is a will, a way can be found.

Source: *Vital Speeches of the Day,* Vol. XIII, No. 2, November 1, 1946, pp. 59–61.

The Road to Survival
Balance Peaceful and Military Use of Atomic Energy

Bernard M. Baruch, author of the American Plan for International Control of Atomic Energy. Excerpts from speech delivered at the New York Herald Tribune *Forum, New York, October 18, 1948.*

There is no avoiding the tax of waste imposed by preparedness. To do so would risk the immensely greater destructions of actual war. Our problem is this: while preparing against war, to manage the peaceful resources left us so they swell our total substance. . . .

This struggle for a better balance in living streaks every aspect of existence. . . .

As old as the Biblical conflict between the forces of light and darkness, this struggle is also as new as atomic energy.

The problem of atomic energy is the problem of conservation. It is pre-eminently a wrestling between the fears which chain us to atomic development for destruction against the courage to seek its fullest peaceful release. It was to free atomic energy for usefulness that the American people took the bold and unprecedentedly generous action of offering to give up this, the most powerful weapon in history, on one condition—that no other nation be able to make the bomb. Since the Soviet leaders—not the Russian people, who have never known the American proposal, but the Soviet leaders—have vetoed the American dream of a world free of the threat of atomic destruction, we must continue manufacturing atomic weapons. But fear of war must not freeze peaceful atomic use. Our task is to strike a wise balance between peaceful and military development—the same balance needed all through life.

Source: *Vital Speeches of the Day,* Vol. XV, No. 2, November 1, 1948, pp. 46–48.

The Open Mind
Prospects for World Peace

J. Robert Oppenheimer, director, Institute for Advanced Study, Princeton. Excerpts from speech delivered at the Rochester Institute of International Affairs, Rochester, New York, December 11, 1948.

Perhaps, as much as anything, my theme tonight will have to do with enlisting time and nature in the conduct of our international affairs: in the quest for peace and a freer world. This is not meant mystically, for the nature which we must enlist is that of man; and if there is hope in it, that lies not least in man's reason. What elements are there in the conduct of foreign affairs which may be conducive to the exercise of that reason, which may provide a climate for the growth of new experience, new insight and new understanding? How can we recognize such growth, and be sensitive to its hopeful meaning, while there is yet time, through action based on understanding, to direct the outcome? . . .

You will not find it inappropriate that we fix attention on a relatively isolated, yet not a typical area of foreign affairs—on atomic energy. It is an area in which the primary intent of our policy has been totally frustrated. It is an area in which it is commonly recognized that the prospects for success with regard to this primary intent are both dim and remote. . . .

. . . [W]e need to start with the admission that we see no clear course before us that persuade the governments of the world to join with us in creating a more and more open world, and thus to establish the foundation on which persuasion might so largely replace coercion in determining human affairs. . . .With misgivings—and there ought to be misgivings—we are rearming, arming atomically, as in other fields.

Source: *Vital Speeches of the Day,* Vol. XV, No. 10, March 1, 1949, pp. 304–306.

Reactor Program of the Atomic Energy Commission
Outlook for Industrial Participation

Lawrence R. Hafstad, Atomic Energy Commission, Washington, D.C. Excerpts from speech delivered to a Joint Group Session of the Division of Refining and Marketing, Annual Meeting of the American Petroleum Institute, Los Angeles, November 15, 1950.

There are few subjects about which there has been so much talk and so little said as about atomic power. . . .

I will try my best, therefore, to give you a status report as to where we are now, will try to call your attention to trends which seem to me to be of significance and worth watching, and finally, to suggest the problems and issues which are emerging and will require attention at some future time.

We can classify most of our problems at the present time [with respect to atomic power] in two main categories, namely, technical, and economic. . . .

We need reactors—more accurately, there is an expressed

demand today for reactors—for the following purposes: (1) as a research tool, both by universities and by industry; (2) for mobile power, almost exclusively military; (3) for the production of fissionable material; and (4) for the generation of power. . . .

We note a trend toward complex multi-purpose reactors with civilian power probably emerging first as a by-product from production reactors and perhaps ultimately in its own right. Finally, we note an increasing interest on the part of the Commission to consider proposals for industrial participation.

Source: *Vital Speeches of the Day,* Vol. XVII, No. 8, February 1, 1951, pp. 249–253.

Are We Ready To Give the Atom to Private Enterprise? Disruption of Present Program Dangerous

Melvin Price, U.S. representative from Illinois. Excerpts from speech delivered in the House of Representatives, June 10, 1953.

Mr. Speaker, has the time arrived for private enterprise to enter atomic power development on an independent basis? . . .

As a member—for over 6 years—on the Joint Committee on Atomic Energy, I deem it my duty to speak on this important matter.

Let me begin by stating that I am heartily in favor of private enterprise participation in all phases of the atomic research and development program. I have vigorously supported the principle which has been followed by the Atomic Energy Commission, for example, contractual arrangements with college and private laboratories for research and development, contractual arrangements with industrial and business management concerns in the fields of plant construction and plant operation. This principle has been applied as a basic policy by the Atomic Energy Commission. . . .

Comprehensive hearings must be held to explore every phase of this important problem and the testimony of responsible representatives from all phases of affected business and finance must be heard. Scientists must be given the opportunity to publicly state their special knowledge regarding reactor development potentialities. The public interest can be served by legislation, only if it is based on a complete knowledge of the facts.

Source: *Vital Speeches of the Day,* Vol. XIX, No. 18, July 1, 1953, pp. 562–566.

Atoms for Peace

President Dwight D. Eisenhower. Excerpts from speech delivered to the United Nations General Assembly, December 8, 1953.

I know that the American people share my deep belief that if a danger exists in the world it is a danger shared by all, and, equally, that if hope exists in the mind of one nation that hope should be shared by all. . . .

Today the United States stockpile of atomic weapons . . . exceeds by many times the explosive equivalent of the total of all bombs and all shells that came from every plane and every gun in every theater of war in all the years of World War II. . . .

The Soviet Union has informed us that, over recent years, it has devoted extensive resources to atomic weapons. During this period, the Soviet Union has exploded a series of atomic devices, including at least one involving thermo-nuclear reactions. . . .

But let no one think that the expenditure of vast sums for weapons and systems of defense can guarantee absolute safety for the cities and citizens of any nation. . . .

I therefore make the following proposals:

The governments principally involved, to the extent permitted by elementary prudence, to begin now and continue to make joint contributions from their stockpiles of normal uranium and fissionable materials to an International Atomic Energy Agency. . . .

The Atomic Energy Agency could be made responsible for the impounding, storage, and protection of the contributed fissionable materials. The ingenuity of our scientists will provide special safe conditions under which such a bank of fissionable material can be made essentially immune to surprise seizure.

. . . encourage worldwide investigation into the most effective peacetime uses of fissionable material . . .

. . . begin to diminish the potential destructive power of the world's atomic stockpiles;

. . . allow all peoples of all nations to see that . . . the great powers . . . both of the East and of the West, are interested in human aspirations first, rather than in building up the armaments of war;

open up a new channel for peaceful discussion and initiate at least a new approach to the many difficult problems that must be solved in both private and public conversations, if the world is to shake off the inertia imposed by fear; and is to make positive progress toward peace.

Source: Jack Dennis and faculty members of the Massachusetts Institute of Technology, eds., *The Nuclear Almanac: Confronting the Atom in War and Peace* (Reading, MA: Addison-Wesley Publishing Company, 1984), pp. 355–356.

The Energy and Economic Crisis

President Gerald R. Ford. Excerpts from speech, Washington, D.C., January 13, 1975.

[W]e must wage a simultaneous three-front campaign against recession, inflation, and energy dependence. We have no choice. We need, within 90 days, the strongest and most far-reaching energy conservation program we have ever had. . . .

To get started immediately on an urgent national energy plan, I will use the presidential emergency powers to reduce our dependence on foreign oil. . . .

A more comprehensive program of energy conservation taxes on oil and natural gas to reduce consumption substantially must be enacted. . . .

My national energy conservation plan will urge Congress to grant a five-year delay on higher automobile pollution standards in order to achieve a 40-percent improvement in miles per gallon.

Stronger measures to speed the development of other domestic energy resources, such as coal, geothermal, solar, and nuclear power, are also essential. . . .

In my State of the Union and subsequent messages, I will not propose any new federal spending programs except for energy.

Source: Janet Podell and Steven Anzovin, eds., *Speeches of the American Presidents* (New York: H. W. Wilson Company, 1988), pp. 706–709.

Energy and National Goals

President Jimmy Carter. Excerpts from speech, Washington, D.C., July 15, 1979.

Ten days ago I had planned to speak to you again about a very important subject—energy. For the fifth time I would have described the urgency of the problem and laid out a series of legislative recommendations to the Congress. But as I was preparing to speak, I began to ask myself the same question I now know has been troubling many of you. Why have we not been able to get together as a nation to resolve our serious energy problem? . . .

So, I decided to reach out and listen to the voices of America.

I invited to Camp David people from almost every segment of our society—business and labor, teachers and preachers, governors, mayors, and private citizens. And then I left Camp David to listen to other Americans, men and women like you. It has been an extraordinary ten days, and I want to share with you what I've heard. . . .

It is a crisis of confidence. . . .

Energy will be the immediate test of our ability to unite this nation, and it can also be the standard around which we rally. On the battlefield of energy we can win for our nation a new confidence, and we can seize control again of our common destiny. . . .

The energy crisis is real. It is worldwide. It is a clear and present danger to our nation. These are facts and we simply must face them.

Source: Janet Podell and Steven Anzovin, eds., *Speeches of the American Presidents* (New York: H. W. Wilson Company, 1988), pp. 729–734.

Lando W. Zech, Jr., chairman of the U.S. Nuclear Regulatory Commission. Abstract of remarks presented at the 1987 Winter Meeting of the American Nuclear Society and the Nuclear Energy Forum, Los Angeles, November 16, 1987.

Mr. Zech made comments related to the NRC [Nuclear Regulatory Commission] and the nuclear industry as sharing a common goal, but having separate and complementary roles to achieve that goal. The goal is to bring the benefits of nuclear energy to American citizens while at the same time recognizing that a primary objective is the protection of the health and safety of Americans. Safe operation of nuclear facilities is at the heart of the future of nuclear energy in the United States.

Source: U.S. Nuclear Regulatory Commission, Office of Governmental and Public Affairs, Washington, DC 20555.

Kenneth M. Carr, U.S. Nuclear Regulatory Commission. Abstract of remarks at the USCEA Fuel Cycle 88 Conference, New Orleans, April 11, 1988.

Mr. Carr presented remarks related to factors shaping the nuclear fuel cycle, the regulatory progress being made on fuel cycle issues (such as licensing of uranium enrichment, spent fuel storage, and high-level waste), and the importance of communication with the public. His aspiration is that the American people will come to feel that the nuclear option is a significant part of the country's energy future.

Source: U.S. Nuclear Regulatory Commission, Office of Governmental and Public Affairs, Washington, DC 20555.

Frederick M. Bernthal, U.S. Nuclear Regulatory Commission. Remarks at the American Nuclear Society International Topical Meeting, "Safety of Next Generation Power Reactors," Seattle, May 2, 1988.

Mr. Bernthal presented a discussion of the disaster at Chernobyl in the Soviet Union, some of its consequences, and the role of the Nuclear Regulatory Commission in advanced reactor policy. He suggested that light-water reactor technology might be obsolete, and that there are many revolutionary designs on the drawing boards. He emphasized the need for public confidence in nuclear energy programs, and the need to maintain the NRC [Nuclear Regulatory Commission], not allow it to "wither away."

Source: U.S. Nuclear Regulatory Commission, Office of Governmental and Public Affairs, Washington, DC 20555.

Regulatory Approaches to the Setting of Exposure Standards for, and the Control of, Health Hazards from Nuclear Radiation

Harold R. Denton, director, Office of Governmental and Public Affairs, U.S. Nuclear Regulatory Commission. Abstract of remarks presented at the René Dubos Forum at the New York Academy of Medicine Only One Earth Forum on Managing Hazardous Materials, New York, May 15, 1988.

In this speech, Mr. Denton is concerned with the need by the Nuclear Regulatory Commission to constantly confront making judgments about the risks deriving from use of radioactive materials. He examines several questions related to risk factors which are now receiving attention throughout the world: research needed for dealing with hazardous materials; institutional and legislative changes needed to deal with such materials; the need and desire of the public to know about energy risks; and the highly visible nature of the debate on the subject.

Source: U.S. Nuclear Regulatory Commission, Office of Governmental and Public Affairs, Washington, DC 20555.

Lando W. Zech, Jr., chairman, U.S. Nuclear Regulatory Commission. Abstract of remarks before the IEEE Fourth Conference on Human Factors and Power Plants, Monterey, California, June 7, 1988.

This speech is an expression of his ideas related to human factors as they apply to nuclear power plant performance. He states that a high percentage of plant events is attributable to human error. Some events do not result in reports. His conclusion is that improvement is an essential factor for the conduct of safe plant operations and the success of nuclear power programs in the future. He suggests that training has constantly been improved but that plant leadership has to be increasingly concerned with doing things correctly the first time. He concludes that emphasis on the human factor in plant operation will make a positive contribution toward the reduction of human errors which have led to difficulties at nuclear power plant installations. He repeats the concept that nuclear power is a vital energy source for the future.

Source: U.S. Nuclear Regulatory Commission, Office of Governmental and Public Affairs, Washington, DC 20555.

Major Nuclear Energy Laws

Atomic Energy Act of 1946
60 Stat. 755 (Former 42 USCA Sections 1801–1819)

After the test of the atomic bomb in 1945 and its successful military employment shortly following, it was clear that laws were needed to control this dangerous energy source. Various bills were introduced into Congress; the compromises growing out of the political process resulted in the adoption of the Atomic Energy Act of 1946.

This act placed special emphasis on the common defense, security, and continuing supremacy of the United States in the area of nuclear energy, and also established the Atomic Energy Commission. The commission was given control over the production, distribution, and acquisition of fissionable materials; the ownership of production facilities; the licensing of manufacturers for nonmilitary purposes; and the making of atomic bombs, patents, and other areas. Eventually, given the passage of time and the course of events—both scientific and military—it became obvious that a major change in legislation was necessary.

Atomic Energy Act of 1954
68 Stat. 919 (42 USCA Sections 2011 et seq.)

This act was established with the main objectives of bringing the original 1946 act up-to-date with progress in atomic energy science and creating legislative controls that conformed with scientific, technical, economic, and political facts of the nuclear energy field. It widened cooperation with U.S. allies, improved procedures for the control and dissemination of information, and encouraged broad participation by private industry in the development of peaceful nuclear energy resources. The security and common defense of the United States remained the paramount concerns of the act.

The act contains provisions dealing with the Atomic Energy Commission; the disposition of energy; electric utility contracts; the production, acquisition, and distribution of materials; prospecting or mining leases; military applications; ownership of material and production facilities; establishment of the Joint Committee on Atomic Energy (later abolished); and other matters. Most directly, this act was designed to encourage commercial development of nuclear power in the United States.

Price-Anderson Act of 1957
P.L. 85-256. 71 Stat. 576 (42 USCA Section 2210)

This legislation recognized that private insurance companies would probably be hesitant in insuring utilities against nuclear power accidents, and absolved utilities of liability for such damages. The act set an upper limit of $560 million compensation for personal damages and established a fund in excess of $500 million of government money, which made up the major portion of the fund. Utilities were expected to make contributions to the fund. The act provides, essentially, for a type of "no-fault" insurance coverage for reactor accidents. In 1988, the liability limit per accident was raised to $7 billion. Pooled assessments of nuclear utilities help to contribute to the common fund.

EURATOM Cooperation Act of 1958
P.L. 85-846. 72 Stat. 1084 (42 USCA Sections 2291–2296)

This law was enacted to provide for a joint nuclear power program between the United States and the European Atomic Energy Commission (EURATOM), which included the governments of France, West Germany, Italy, Belgium, Holland, and Luxembourg.

The agreement was to be carried out in accordance with provisions of the Atomic Energy Act of 1954 that related to cooperation between the United States and other countries with respect to regional defense. The act also brought into operation in EURATOM countries power plants that used nuclear reactors and had a specified kilowatt capacity.

The Atomic Energy Commission was thus authorized to enter into contracts for research and development and contracts with reactor operators, to sell or lease specified quantities of uranium and plutonium, and to cooperate with any nation by distributing special nuclear material, all in conformity to the Atomic Energy Act of 1954.

Private Ownership of Special Nuclear Materials Act of 1964
P.L. 88-489. 78 Stat. 602 (42 USCA Sections 2012 *et seq.*)

This act once again emphasized that the development, use, and control of atomic energy was vital for the defense and security of the United States, and that the processing and utilization of source, byproduct, and special nuclear material must be regulated, both in the national interest and to promote the welfare of the public.

U.S. government regulation of the production and use of atomic energy and of the associated facilities was therefore deemed necessary. Other topics addressed included interstate damage from operation of nuclear facilities (resulting from the fact that nuclear materials were involved in interstate commerce), making available funds for damages, and related matters.

Energy Reorganization Act of 1974
P.L. 93-438. 88 Stat. 1233 (42 USCA Sections 5801 *et seq.*)

Because of the needs to increase machinery that would enhance the general welfare and the common defense and security; to enhance development and use of all energy sources to meet the needs of the present and future generations; to increase the productivity of the nation's economy and strengthen international trade; to enhance energy self-sufficiency and the quality of the environment; and to ensure the public health and safety, the Congress established the Energy Research and Development Administration to bring together and direct the various federal activities concerning research and development of the sources of energy and other matters.

Thus, the Atomic Energy Commission was split into the Nuclear Regulatory Commission (an independent panel appointed by the president to regulate the nuclear industry) and the Energy Research and Development Council.

Nuclear Non-Proliferation Act of 1978
P.L. 95-242. 92 Stat. 120 (22 USCA Sections 3201 *et seq.*)

The USCA states: "The Congress finds and declares that the proliferation of nuclear explosive devices or of the direct capability to manufacture or otherwise acquire such devices poses a grave threat to the security interests of the United States and to continued international progress toward world peace and development" (22 USCA 3201).

U.S. policy therefore pursues "mechanisms for fuel supply assurances and the establishment of more effective international controls over the transfer and use of nuclear materials and equipment . . . ;" the capacity to meet "its commitments to supply nuclear reactors and fuel to nations which adhere to effective non-proliferation policies . . . ; encourages nations which have not ratified the Treaty on the Non-Proliferation of Nuclear Weapons to do so . . . ;" and attempts to "cooperate with foreign nations in identifying and adapting suitable technologies for energy production and, in particular, to identify alternative options to nuclear power . . ." (ibid.).

Uranium Mill Tailings Radiation Control Act of 1978
P.L. 95-604. 92 Stat. 3021 (42 USCA Sections 2014, 2021)

The nuclear industry creates, essentially, three types of waste, one of which is uranium mill tailings, a byproduct of uranium mining. These waste products represent relatively straightforward disposal problems. Mill tailings contain about 85 percent of the radioactivity contained in the original uranium ore, and have been extensively used in construction materials. It is possible that they have contributed to a number of diseases and even deaths.

The Uranium Mill Tailings Radiation Control Act put in place a remedial program to stabilize the disposal sites. The U.S. government, under the act, covered 90 percent of the costs and state governments were responsible for the remaining 10 percent. The act emphasized cooperative arrangements between the Nuclear Regulatory Commission and the various state regulatory offices. It also charged the U.S. Environmental Protection Agency and the Nuclear Regulatory Commission with establishing and enforcing standards in this area of nuclear energy.

Low Level Waste Policy Act of 1980
P.L. 96-573. 94 Stat. 3347 (42 USCA Sections 2014, 2021)

The problem with low-level nuclear wastes is their comparatively huge volume. By the year 2000, it is estimated that there will be some one billion cubic feet of low-level nuclear wastes, such as medical products and industrial wastes, in the United States. Land disposal sites are already filling up and there has been illegal dumping of such wastes. States that have disposal sites are increasingly reluctant to accept wastes from other states. The U.S. Low Level Waste Policy Act made the disposal of such low-level wastes the responsibility of the individual states, subject to federal laws and regulations.

Nuclear Waste Policy Act of 1982
P.L. 97-425. 96 Stat. 2201 (42 USCA Section 10101)

This law was a reaction to the inability of the federal and state governments, the nuclear industry, and various environmental groups to arrive at an agreement about the disposal of nuclear wastes. The Nuclear Waste Policy Act was signed by President Reagan on January 7, 1983.

The law established a timetable for creating a permanent, underground repository for nuclear wastes. The act also required the Department of Energy to select five possible underground repository sites and recommend three of these to the president by January 1, 1985. The president was to submit his choice for the first repository site to Congress by 1987, and the site was to receive nuclear waste no later than January 31, 1998.

There was to be one site in the East and one site in the West. The government has since contracted with the Bechtel Corporation, effective in December of 1988, to develop and plan the sites.

Government Hearings, Documents, Reports

Brown, Omer F., II. **Insurance-Indemnity Coverage for Nuclear Transportation: An Overview.** Prepared by Sandia National Laboratories, Albuquerque, New Mexico, and Livermore, California, for the U.S. Department of Energy. Printed January 1986. Available from National Technical Information Service, U.S. Department of Commerce, 5285 Port Royal Road, Springfield, Virginia 22161.

The summary states, in part: "This report provides a comprehensive overview of insurance-indemnity coverage for various nuclear transportation activities. It examines public liability coverage under the present provisions of the Price-Anderson Act, liability insurance policies issued by the nuclear insurance pools, conventional liability insurance policies containing the 'Broad Form Nuclear Energy Liability Exclusion Endorsement,' and Public Law 85-804. It also outlines (in the appendix) some of the issues Congress has been considering for the last two years in deciding whether to extend the Price-Anderson Act beyond its present 1987 expiration."

Coffman, F. E., M. R. Murphy, D. W. Kearney, K. R. Schultz, and B. L. Scott. **Fusion Power by Magnetic Confinement: Questions and Answers.** Energy Research and Development Administration, Division of Magnetic Fusion Energy, May 1977. Available from National Technical Information Service, U.S. Deparment of Commerce, 5285 Port Royal Road, Springfield, Virginia 22161.

Glasstone, Samuel. **Fusion Energy.** Washington, DC: U.S. Department of Energy, Technical Information Center, 1980.

An excellent brief summary of explanations of the fusion energy process and the procedures and configurations being developed to bring fusion energy into fruition. Because of the rapid developments in the area of fusion energy, the booklet has not been updated; nevertheless, it provides a fundamental understanding of the scientific efforts underway in this area. It stands as a basic source of information about fusion.

Mullen, Sarah A., Miriam J. Welch, and Bradford W. Welles. **HM-164: Radioactive Materials: Routing and Driver Training Requirements.** Contractor Report. Prepared by Sandia National Laboratories, Albuquerque, New Mexico, and Livermore, California, for the U.S. Department of Energy. Printed March 1986. Available from National Technical Information Service, U.S. Department of Commerce, 5285 Port Royal Road, Springfield, Virginia 22161.

The abstract states: "This report summarizes the history and comments on HM-164 from January 1976 to January 1986. HM-164 was created by the U.S. Department of Transportation in response to proliferating state and local laws prohibiting or restricting highway movement of radioactive materials and establishes a nationally consistent highway routing system for radioactive materials. Upheld by the U.S. Supreme Court in 1984, HM-164 has formed the basis for a number of state and local laws to be judged inconsistent with federal laws."

U.S. Congress. **Nuclear Power in an Age of Uncertainty.** Washington, DC: U.S. Congress, Office of Technology Assessment, February 1984. OTA-E-216.

This is clearly one of the best overviews of the uncertain financial and economic future of the nuclear energy industry in the United States. It deals with such matters as alternative reactor systems, the management of nuclear enterprises, the regulation of nuclear power, public attitudes toward nuclear energy, various policy options available to the United States, and the survival of the nuclear energy industry in the United States and in foreign countries. It contains a list of acronyms and a glossary.

U.S. Congress. House. Committee on Energy and Commerce. **Soviet Nuclear Accident at Chernobyl.** Briefing and Hearing before the Subcommittee on Energy Conservation and Power of the Committee on Energy and Commerce, House of Representatives, Ninety-ninth Congress, second session, May 1 and 7, 1986. Washington, DC: U.S. Government Printing Office, 1987.

U.S. Congress. House. Committee on Government Operations. Subcommittee on Environment, Energy, and Natural Resources. **Nuclear Safety—Three Years after Three-Mile Island.** Joint Hearings before certain Subcommittees of the Committee on Government Operations and Interior and Insular Affairs, House of Representatives, Ninety-seventh Congress, second session, March 12, 1982. Washington, DC: U.S. Government Printing Office, 1982.

U.S. Congress. House. Committee on Interior and Insular Affairs. Subcommittee on Energy and the Environment. **Implementation of the Nuclear Waste Policy Act (Site Selection Program).** Oversight Hearing before the Subcommittee on Energy and the Environment of the Committee on Interior and Insular Affairs, House of Representatives, Ninety-ninth Congress, second session, on implementation of the Nuclear Waste Policy Act (Site Selection Program), July 31, 1986. Washington, DC: U.S. Government Printing Office, 1987.

U.S. Congress. House. Committee on Interior and Insular Affairs. Subcommittee on Energy and the Environment. **Nuclear Overview.** Oversight Hearings before the Subcommittee on Energy and the Environment of the Committee on Interior and Insular Affairs, House of Representatives, Ninety-ninth Congress, second session, June 10 and 17, 1986.

U.S. Congress. House. Committee on Science and Technology. Subcommittee on Energy Research and Production. **Nuclear Waste Policy Act: Current Status and Future Options.** Hearing before the Subcommittee on Energy Research and Production of the Committee on Science and Technology, House of Representatives, Ninety-ninth Congress, second session, July 22, 1986.

U.S. Congress. House. Committee on Science and Technology. Subcommittee on Energy Research and Production. **Regulatory Policy for Advanced Nuclear Reactors.** Report prepared by the Subcommittee on Energy Research and Production. Transmitted to the Committee on Science and Technology, House of Representatives, Ninety-ninth Congress, second session. Washington, DC: U.S. Government Printing Office, 1986.

U.S. Congress. House. Committee on Science and Technology. Subcommittee on Investigations and Oversight. **Decommissioning Nuclear Power Plants: The Shippingport Project.** Hearing before the Subcommittee on Investigations and Oversight and the Subcommittee on Energy Research and Production of the Committee on Science and Technology, House of Representatives, Ninety-ninth Congress, second session, July 30, 1986. Washington, DC: U.S. Government Printing Office, 1987.

U.S. Congress. Senate. Committee on Energy and Natural Resources. **The Chernobyl Accident.** Hearing on the Chernobyl accident and implications for the domestic nuclear industry before the Committee on Energy and Natural Resources, Senate, Ninety-ninth Congress, second session, June 19, 1986. Washington, DC: U.S. Government Printing Office, 1986.

U.S. Congress. Senate. Committee on Environment and Public Works. Subcommittee on Nuclear Regulation. **Nuclear Powerplant Shutdowns.** Hearing before the Subcommittee on Nuclear Regulation of the Committee on Environment and Public Works, Senate, Ninety-sixth Congress, first session, March 6, 1979. Washington, DC: U.S. Government Printing Office, 1979.

U.S. Congress. Senate. Committee on Environment and Public Works. Subcommittee on Nuclear Regulation. **Report of the President's Commission on the Three Mile Island Accident.** Joint Hearing before the Subcommittee on Nuclear Regulation of the Committee on Environment and Public Works, Senate, and the Subcommittee on Energy and the Environment of the Committee on Interior and Insular Affairs, House of Representatives, Ninety-sixth Congress, first session, October 31, 1979.

U.S. Department of Energy. **Magnetic Fusion Energy Research: A Summary of Accomplishments.** Washington, DC: U.S. Department of Energy, Office of Energy Research, Office of Program Analysis, 1986.

Alvin W. Trivelpiece, director of the Office of Energy Research, writes in the foreword: "Fusion energy is the internal power source of the sun and the stars. Resisting natural forces of separation, lighter elements, such as hydrogen and helium, are forcibly joined together to form the nucleus of a heavier element of slightly less mass than the sum of its original parts. In accord with Einstein's now familiar equation, this small difference in mass is converted into an enormous amount of energy, which we ultimately observe as heat and light from the sun." This brief document summarizes some of the most important research that was required to establish the basis for fusion energy production.

U.S. Department of Energy. **Transportation Institutional Plan.** Washington, DC: U.S. Department of Energy, Office of Civilian Radioactive Waste Management, August 1986.

This document is considered a foundation for the creation of a system of transporting spent fuel and high-level radioactive waste under the requirements of the Nuclear Waste Policy Act. It discusses background information, purposes, and policy guidance for the transportation system, the major participants who must be involved in the plan, and the mechanisms for interaction that will provide planning, implementation, development, and operation of a transportation system.

U.S. Department of Energy. Office of Civilian Radioactive Waste Management. Washington, DC: November 1986.

Overview: Nuclear Waste Policy Act

Nuclear Waste Disposal

What Will a Nuclear Waste Repository Look Like?

What Is Spent Nuclear Fuel?

Can Nuclear Waste Be Transported Safely?

Radiation and Nuclear Waste: How Are They Related?

How Much High-Level Nuclear Waste Is There?

This is a series of brief but highly informative one- to four-page publications put out by the Office of Civilian Radioactive Waste Management. Each is intended to deal briefly and succinctly with a specific issue concerning the management of the nation's nuclear waste. The reports contain illustrations that are helpful in explaining the particular topic they cover. They are written in lay language and provide excellent introductions to the topics concerned.

U.S. Department of Energy. Office of Energy Research. **Magnetic Fusion Program Plan.**

The executive summary states, in part: "The goal of the National Energy Policy Plan is to foster an adequate supply of energy at reasonable costs. As an element in this Plan, the goal of the magnetic fusion program is to establish the scientific and technological base required for fusion energy.... [F]our key issues" are involved in reaching the program goal. "These are magnetic confinement systems, properties of burning plasmas, materials for fusion systems and nuclear technology of fusion systems."

U.S. Department of Energy. Office of Energy Research. Office of Fusion Energy. Division of Planning Projects. **Proceedings of the Summit Working Group on Magnetic Fusion Energy.** Published June 1984. Available from National Technical Information Service, U.S. Department of Commerce, 5285 Port Royal Road, Springfield, Virginia 22161.

This document presents a summary of the conclusions of the Versailles Summit Follow-on Meeting on Fusion held in Washington, D.C., on September 29–30, 1983; international agreements for cooperation in magnetic fusion research and development; and statements by representatives from Canada, the European Economic Community, the Federal Republic of Germany, and Japan.

U.S. Environmental Protection Agency. **Final Rule for High-Level and Transuranic Radioactive Wastes.** Washington, DC: U.S. Environmental Protection Agency, Office of Radiation Programs, 1985.

This is a technical but highly useful document related to current regulatory programs and strategies; the quantities, sources, and characteristics of spent nuclear fuel and high-level transuranic wastes; planned disposal programs; radiation dosimetry; estimations of risk of health effects; and risk of disposal in mined geologic repositories, among other subjects. It contains a description of computer codes related to doses and risks from radiation exposure and a glossary of terms and acronyms.

U.S. Environmental Protection Agency. **Radiation Protection Guidance to Federal Agencies for Occupational Exposure: Recommendations Approved by the President.** Washington, DC: U.S. Environmental Protection Agency, Office of Radiation Programs, January 1987.

This document transmits recommendations updating previous guidelines to federal agencies dealing with protection of workers exposed to ionizing radiation. The recommendations are based on current scientific understanding of the effects of ionizing radiation, recommendations of national and international organizations, federal guidance and public comment, and experience of federal agencies in general in the area of controlling occupational exposure to ionizing radiation.

U.S. General Accounting Office. **Security at Nuclear Powerplants—At Best, Inadequate.** Nuclear Regulatory Commission. Report to the Congress by the Comptroller General of the United States. Washington, DC: U.S. General Accounting Office, 1977.

U.S. Nuclear Regulatory Commission. **1988 Annual Report.** Washington, DC: U.S. Government Printing Office, June 1989.

This is a very useful summary of the activities of the Nuclear Regulatory Commission for the preceding year. It contains, for example, information related to nuclear reactor regulation, cleanup efforts at Three Mile Island, operational experience, nuclear materials regulation, safeguard activities, nuclear regulatory research, proceedings and litigation, and other subjects related to the issue of nuclear regulations.

Wolff, Theodore A. **The Transportation of Nuclear Materials.** Prepared by Sandia National Laboratories, Albuquerque, New Mexico, and Livermore, California, for the U.S. Department of Energy, December 1984. Available from National Technical Information Service, U.S. Department of Commerce, 5285 Port Royal Road, Springfield, Virginia 22161.

The abstract states: "This report contains basic information about the transportation of radioactive materials. It is a reference document for transportation information and factors that can be used to assess the impacts of transporting nuclear materials. Because the report is general in nature, it should be used in conjunction with site-specific analyses." The report contains an excellent bibliography and highly useful figures and tables dealing with such matters as design concepts for truck casks, source and components of pollutants, sources of federal regulations, estimated emissions of air pollutants, and many other relevant topics. It has a good glossary and list of acronyms on the subject.

Significant Court Cases

City of West Chicago v. Kerr-McGee
677 F.2d 571 (7th Cir. 1982)

This case involved a public nuisance complaint by the city of West Chicago against the Kerr-McGee Corporation. The city alleged that the company had permitted dangerous conditions to exist, e.g., open pits filled with chemical and other refuse, holes in floors, and falling roofing. In this case, the 7th Circuit Court ruled that the Atomic Energy Act did not preempt the public nuisance complaint because the city was attempting to regulate nonradiation hazards and thus its action was permissible.

Commonwealth Edison Co. v. NRC
819 F.2d 750–764 (7th Cir. 1987)

The Commonwealth Edison Company sued for a declaratory judgment to the effect that making the license-fee ceilings of the Nuclear Regulatory Commission applicable to work that had been done before the date of the current ceilings was illegal.

Commonwealth Edison argued that the NRC impermissibly used a retroactive application of the 1984 version of fees for inspection work carried out at Edison's Byron (Illinois) and Braidwood (Illinois) plants.

In a subsequent petition for rehearing, the court reversed its earlier decision, stating that it had jurisdiction to review the merits of the NRC rule challenge made within 60 days of the application of the rule to the aggrieved party.

The court rejected Commonwealth Edison's claim of illegal retroactivity. Therefore, the court held that the 1984 fee schedule did properly control the amount of the license application fee that Commonwealth Edison owed for its Byron and Braidwood plants. The court also applied penalties and interest on the unpaid fees due the NRC from the company.

County of Suffolk v. Long Island Lighting Company
728 F.2d 52 (2nd Cir. 1984)

In this case the county attempted to acquire a court order to allow an inspection of a nuclear power plant under construction. There had been claims of negligence, breach of contract, and misrepresentation and concealment in the design and construction of the plant. The court ruled that such an inspection was preempted because inspection of nuclear power plants falls within the areas of construction and operation of nuclear facilities, reserved to the NRC.

Critical Mass Energy Project v. NRC
No. 86-5647 (D.C. Cir. September 29, 1987),
remanded in part, 644 F. Supp. 344 (D.D.C. 1986)

Plaintiff here sought access to documents of the Institute of Nuclear Power Operations (INPO) that had been withheld under Exemption 4 of the Freedom of Information Act.

The plaintiff lost in the District Court and appealed. The D.C. Circuit Court upheld the agency's view. The case was remanded to the District Court for better development of the factual record.

The D.C. Circuit Court held that the INPO documents were "commercial" and then established a two-part legal test to determine whether they were also "confidential." "To be considered 'confidential' the information at issue 'would customarily not be released to the public by the person from whom it was obtained.'" (The INPO documents met this test.) In addition, the agency had to show that release of the information would "impair [its] ability to obtain necessary information in the future." The court found itself unable to make a determination on the confidentiality of the records at issue because it found the factual record on these matters to be inconclusive.

"Then, breaking new FOIA [Freedom of Information Act] ground, the court held that, as an alternative to impairment of the NRC's ability to obtain the documents, impairment of other NRC interests could also justify withholding under Exemption 4. . . ."

Eddleman v. NRC
825 F.2d 46 (4th Cir. 1987)

On January 2, 1987, Wells Eddleman and several other persons filed a petition to review the Nuclear Regulatory Commission's licensing of the Shearon Harris Nuclear Power Plant.

In a unanimous decision, the U.S. Circuit Court of Appeals for the Fourth Circuit upheld the agency's grant of a license for the facility. The court stated that the petitioners had no rights to notice and hearing before the decision to license was made. The court also stated that petitioners did not have a right, under the Atomic Energy Act, to a hearing on a petition that had been considered and rejected by the commission as part of its immediate effectiveness review.

In addition, the court upheld the agency's decision to grant the applicant's request for an exemption from the scheduling requirements of a full-scale emergency planning exercise, which theretofore had been required one year prior to licensing.

Ohio Citizens for Responsible Energy v. NRC
803 F.2d 258 (6th Cir. 1986); Ohio v. NRC, 814 F.2d 258 (6th Cir. 1987)

These suits were aimed at the licensing of the Perry plant by the Nuclear Regulatory Commission. The initial suit raised questions of earthquake considerations because of a quake that had occurred only ten miles from the Perry plant site in January 1986. The Nuclear Regulatory Commission had denied a motion to reopen the proceedings related to licensing and emergency planning procedures.

The Sixth Circuit Court upheld the NRC on the merits in March 1987, finding no abuse of discretion in NRC's refusal to reopen the record in regard to seismic contentions. Thus the court held that there was no basis on which to overturn the full-power operating license that had been granted to the Perry plant.

Pacific Gas and Electric Company (PG&E) v. State Energy Resources Conservation and Development Commission
103 S. Ct. 1713 (1983)

In this case the U.S. Supreme Court was asked to consider whether a California State statute that made the construction of nuclear plants contingent on federal requirements concerning disposal of high-level nuclear waste was preempted by the Atomic Energy Commission. The court held that California was not preempted, stating that the Nuclear Regulatory Commission's prime area of interest in licensing is that of national security and public health and safety. (The Nuclear Regulatory Commission replaced the Atomic Energy Commission in this respect in 1974, when the Atomic Energy Commission was abolished.) The court reasoned that because California had enacted its law for economic, not safety reasons, the statute was outside the field of nuclear safety regulations.

Silkwood v. Kerr-McGee Corporation
104 S. Ct. 615 (1984)

The state of Oklahoma had awarded punitive damages to Karen Silkwood for injuries suffered because of a leak at a federally licensed plutonium processing plant. Kerr-McGee argued that such an award was preempted because it was tantamount to making a regulation about radiation hazards. Kerr-McGee also argued that the allowance of punitive damage awards for radiation injury conflicted with the promotional objectives of the Atomic Energy Act.

The court rejected both arguments, saying that the awarding of punitive damages was not preempted and that the provisions of the

Atomic Energy Act specifically require that atomic energy be developed and used only to the extent that it is consistent with the protection of the health and safety of the public. The court argued that Congress had not intended to promote nuclear energy at the expense of those who are injured by its use.

State of Wisconsin v. Northern States Power Company
No. 85-CV-0032 (Cir. Ct., Dane Co., Wis., June 6, 1985)

The circuit judge in this case ruled that a utility's spent nuclear fuel shipments are not subject to regulatory control under state statutes. In other words, federal law preempts state attempts to impose restrictions on transportation of nuclear materials.

Union of Concerned Scientists v. NRC
824 F.2d 108 (D.C. Cir. 1987)

This was a suit filed by the Union of Concerned Scientists against the Nuclear Regulatory Commission with the aim of declaring the commission's "backfitting" rule null and void. The scientists' union sought to force the commission to establish a regulation that would conform to the specific requirements of the Atomic Energy Act.

In 1987, the court struck down the backfit rule on the grounds that it took into account costs in establishing the "adequate protection standard." The court ruled, among other things, that the adequate protection standard must be based exclusively on health and safety grounds without reference to cost.

However, the court determined that where a plant already meets the adequate protection standard, the Nuclear Regulatory Commission may take cost factors related to safety improvement into account during the course of deciding whether the plant should be made even safer.

The court thus rejected the claim by the Union of Concerned Scientists that the Atomic Energy Act prohibits the Nuclear Regulatory Commission from ever taking into account costs in decisions related to backfitting.

United States of America and Trustees of Columbia University
v. City of New York
463 F. Supp. 604 (S.D.N.Y. 1978)

The court here held that the licensing requirement imposed by the city for a nuclear reactor was preempted because the license conditions pertained to health and safety factors.

Vermont Yankee Nuclear Power Corp. v. NRDC
435 U.S. 519 (1978)

This case arose out of two actions by the Nuclear Regulatory Commission. The NRC Appeals Board required the Licensing Board to report on the transportation of nuclear fuel but not on its processing or storage; the NRC then granted a license. The NRC subsequently initiated a rule-making proceeding in which cross-examination of witnesses was not permitted and, ultimately, it ruled that the impact of processing and storage of fuel was not highly significant.

The Natural Resources Defense Council sought review of these actions. The appellate court found that the NRC's procedures had been inadequate to ensure complete consideration of the issues involved.

The Supreme Court, however, reversed and remanded the ruling of the Circuit Court. In general, the conclusion of the Supreme Court was that unless a statute required something else, rule-making procedures were up to the agency; procedural requirements were not to be increased by the courts. Thus, reviewing courts were forewarned to lean more toward the "deference to agency action" of the "deference versus close scrutiny" continuum.

Excerpts from Illustrative Treaties

Statute of the International Atomic Energy Agency (IAEA)
Opened for signature on October 26, 1956.
Entered into force on July 29, 1957.

Article III. Functions.

A. The Agency is authorized: . . .

5. To establish and administer safeguards designed to ensure that special fissionable and other materials, services, equipment, facilities, and information made available by the Agency or at its request or under its supervision or control are not used in such a way as to further any military purpose; and to apply safeguards, at the request of the parties, to any bilateral or multilateral arrangement, or at the request of a State, to any of that State's activities in the field of atomic energy. . . .

Article XII. Agency Safeguards.

. . . B. The Agency shall, as necessary, establish a staff of inspectors. The staff of inspectors shall have the responsibility of examining all operations conducted by the Agency itself to determine whether the Agency is complying with the health and safety measures prescribed by it for application to projects subject to its approval, supervision or control, and whether the Agency is taking adequate measures to prevent the source and special fissionable materials in its custody or used or produced in its own operations from being used in furtherance of any military purposes. The Agency shall take remedial action forthwith to correct any non-compliance or failure to take adequate measures.

C. . . . The inspectors shall report any non-compliance to the Director General who shall thereupon transmit the report to the Board of Governors.

Source: *Statute* (Vienna: IAEA, March 1967).

The Antarctic Treaty
Signed at Washington on December 1, 1959.
Entered into force on June 23, 1961.

Recognizing that it is in the interest of all mankind that Antarctica shall continue forever to be used exclusively for peaceful purposes and shall not become the scene or object of international discord;
   . . . Convinced also that a treaty ensuring the use of Antarctica for peaceful purposes only and the continuance of international harmony in Antarctica will further the purposes and principles embodied in the Charter of the United Nations;
   [the signatory parties] Have agreed as follows:

Article I

1. Antarctica shall be used for peaceful purposes only. There shall be prohibited, inter alia, any measures of a military nature, such as the establishment of military bases and fortifications, the carrying out of military maneuvers, as well as the testing of any type of weapons. . . .

Article V

1. Any nuclear explosions in Antarctica and the disposal there of radioactive waste material shall be prohibited.

2. In the event of the conclusion of international agreements concerning the use of nuclear energy, including nuclear explosions and the disposal of radioactive waste material . . . the rules established under such agreements shall apply in Antarctica.

Source: *Treaty Series,* Treaties and International Agreements Registered or Filed and Recorded with the Secretary of the United Nations, Vol. 402 (New York: United Nations, 1962).

Treaty Banning Nuclear Weapon Tests in the Atmosphere, in Outer Space, and Under Water
Signed at Moscow on August 5, 1963.
Entered into force October 10, 1963.

The Governments of the United States of America, the United Kingdom of Great Britain and Northern Ireland, and the Union of Soviet Socialist Republics . . .

Have agreed as follows:

Article I

1. . . . to prohibit, to prevent, and not to carry out any nuclear weapon test explosion, or any other nuclear explosion at any place under its jurisdiction or control:

(a) in the atmosphere; beyond its limits, including outer space; or under water, including territorial waters or high seas; or

(b) in any other environment if such explosion causes radioactive debris to be present outside the territorial limits of the State under whose jurisdiction or control such explosion is conducted. . . .

2. . . . to refrain from causing, encouraging, or in any way participating in, the carrying out of any nuclear weapon test explosion, or any other nuclear explosion, anywhere which would take place in any of the environments described, or have the effect referred to, in paragraph 1 of this Article.

Source: *Treaty Series,* Treaties and International Agreements Registered or Filed and Recorded with the Secretary of the United Nations, Vol. 480 (New York: United Nations, 1963).

Treaty for the Prohibition of Nuclear Weapons in Latin America
Signed at Mexico, Federal District, on February 14, 1967.

Article 1. Obligations.

1. The Contracting Parties hereby undertake to use exclusively for peaceful purposes the nuclear material and facilities which are under their jurisdiction, and to prohibit and prevent in their respective territories:

(a) The testing, use, manufacture, production or acquisition by any means whatsoever of any nuclear weapons, by the Parties themselves, directly or indirectly, on behalf of anyone else or in any other way, and

(b) The receipt, storage, installation, deployment and any form of possession of any nuclear weapons, directly or indirectly, by the Parties themselves, by anyone on their behalf or in any other way.

2. The Contracting Parties also undertake to refrain from engaging in, encouraging or authorizing, directly or indirectly, or any way participating in the testing, use, manufacture, production, possession or control of any nuclear weapon. . . .

Article 17. Use of Nuclear Energy for Peaceful Purposes.

Nothing in the provisions of this Treaty shall prejudice the rights of the Contracting Parties, in conformity with this Treaty, to use nuclear energy for peaceful purposes, in particular for their economic development and social progress.

Article 18. Explosions for Peaceful Purposes.

1. The Contracting Parties may carry out explosions of nuclear devices for peaceful purposes—including explosions which involve devices similar to those used in nuclear weapons—or collaborate with third parties for the same purpose, provided that they do so in accordance with the provisions of this article and the other articles of the Treaty, particularly articles 1 and 5.

Source: *Treaty Series,* Treaties and International Agreements Registered or Filed and Recorded with the Secretary of the United Nations, Vol. 634 (New York: United Nations, 1970).

Treaty on the Non-Proliferation of Nuclear Weapons
Signed at London, Moscow, and Washington, D.C., on July 1, 1968.
Entered into force on March 5, 1970.

Article I

Each nuclear-weapon State Party to the Treaty undertakes not to transfer to any recipient whatsoever nuclear weapons or other nuclear explosive devices or control over such weapons or explosive devices directly, or indirectly; and not in any way to assist, encourage, or induce any non-nuclear-weapon State to manufacture or otherwise acquire nuclear weapons or other nuclear explosive devices, or control over such weapons or explosive devices.

Article II

Each non-nuclear-weapon State Party to the Treaty undertakes not to receive the transfer from any transferor whatsoever of nuclear weapons or other nuclear explosive devices or of control over such weapons or explosive devices directly, or indirectly; not to manufacture or otherwise acquire nuclear weapons or other nuclear explosive devices; and not to seek or receive any assistance in the manufacture of nuclear weapons or other nuclear explosive devices.

Article III

... 2. Each State Party to the Treaty undertakes not to provide: (a) source or special fissionable material, or (b) equipment or material especially designed or prepared for the processing, use or production of special fissionable material, to any non-nuclear-weapon State for peaceful purposes, unless the source or special fissionable material shall be subject to the safeguards required by this article.

Source: *United States Treaties and Other International Agreements,* Vol. 21, Part 1 (Washington, DC: U.S. Department of State, 1979).

Treaty between the United States of America and the Union of Soviet Socialist Republics on Underground Nuclear Explosion for Peace Purposes Signed at Moscow and Washington, D.C., on May 28, 1976.

[from the Preamble:]

The United States of America and the Union of Soviet Socialist Republics ...

Proceeding from a desire to implement Article III of the Treaty between the United States of America and the Union of Soviet Socialist Republics on the Limitation of Underground Nuclear Weapon Tests, which calls for the earliest possible conclusion of an agreement on underground nuclear explosions for peaceful purposes,

Reaffirming their adherence to the objectives and principles of the Treaty Banning Nuclear Weapon Tests in the Atmosphere, in Outer Space and Under Water, the Treaty on the Non-Proliferation of Nuclear Weapons, and the Treaty on the Limitation of Underground Nuclear Weapon Tests, and their determination to observe strictly the provisions of these international agreements,

Desiring to assure that underground nuclear explosions for peaceful purposes shall not be used for purposes related to nuclear weapons,

Desiring that utilization of nuclear energy be directed only toward peaceful purposes,

Desiring to develop appropriately cooperation in the field of underground nuclear explosions for peaceful purposes,

Have agreed. ...

Article I. . .

2. This Treaty shall govern all underground nuclear explosions for peaceful purposes conducted by the Parties after 31 March 1976.

Source: *Disarmament Conference Documents* CCD/496, 23 June 1976; and CCD/496/Corr. l, 5 August 1976.

Guidelines for Nuclear Transfers
Agreed to on September 21, 1977, by the Nuclear Supplier Group, and attached to communications addressed January 11, 1978, to the director general of IAEA.

1. The following fundamental principles for safeguards and export controls should apply to nuclear transfers to any non-nuclear-weapon State for peaceful purposes. In this connection, suppliers have defined an export trigger list and agreed on common criteria for technology transfers.

Prohibition on nuclear explosives . . .

Physical protection . . .

Safeguards . . .

Safeguards triggered by the transfer of certain technology . . .

Special controls on sensitive exports . . .

Special controls on export of enrichment facilities, equipment and technology . . .

Controls on supplied or derived weapons-usable material . . .

Controls on retransfer . . .

Physical security . . .

Support for effective IAEA safeguards . . .

Sensitive plant design features . . .

Consultations.

Source: IAEA document INFCIRC/254.

Convention on the Physical Protection of Nuclear Material
Signed at Vienna and New York on March 3, 1980.
Entered into force February 8, 1987.

States parties shall identify and make known to each other directly or through the International Atomic Energy Agency their central authority and point of contact having responsibility for physical protection of nuclear material and for co-ordinating recovery and response operations in the event of any unauthorized removal, use or alteration of nuclear materials or in the event of credible threat thereof.

In the case of theft, robbery or other unlawful taking of nuclear material or of credible threat thereof, states parties shall, in accordance with their national law, provide cooperation and assistance to the maximum extent feasible in their recovery and protection of such material to any state that so requests.

Source: William Sweet, *The Nuclear Age: Atomic Energy, Proliferation, and the Arms Race* (Washington, DC: Congressional Quarterly, Inc., 2nd Edition, 1988), p. 193.

Operating Nuclear Power Plants

Nuclear Electric Generating Units
in Operation or under Construction
(as of December 31, 1988)

Alabama

Decatur	Browns Ferry Nuclear Power Plant Unit 1
Decatur	Browns Ferry Nuclear Power Plant Unit 2
Decatur	Browns Ferry Nuclear Power Plant Unit 3
Dothan	Joseph M. Farley Nuclear Plant Unit 1
Dothan	Joseph M. Farley Nuclear Plant Unit 2
Scottsboro	Bellefonte Nuclear Plant Unit 1
Scottsboro	Bellefonte Nuclear Plant Unit 2

Arizona

Wintersburg	Palo Verde Nuclear Generating Station Unit 1
Wintersburg	Palo Verde Nuclear Generating Station Unit 2
Wintersburg	Palo Verde Nuclear Generating Station Unit 3

Arkansas

Russellville	Arkansas Nuclear One Unit 1
Russellville	Arkansas Nuclear One Unit 2

California

Clay Station	Rancho Seco Nuclear Generating Station Unit 1
Diablo Canyon	Diablo Canyon Nuclear Power Plant Unit 1
Diablo Canyon	Diablo Canyon Nuclear Power Plant Unit 2
San Clemente	San Onofre Nuclear Generating Station Unit 1
San Clemente	San Onofre Nuclear Generating Station Unit 2
San Clemente	San Onofre Nuclear Generating Station Unit 3

Colorado

Platteville	Fort St. Vrain Nuclear Generating Station Unit 1

Connecticut

Haddam Neck	Haddam Neck Generating Station
Waterford	Millstone Nuclear Power Station Unit 1
Waterford	Millstone Nuclear Power Station Unit 2
Waterford	Millstone Nuclear Power Station Unit 3

Florida

Florida City	Turkey Point Station Unit 3
Florida City	Turkey Point Station Unit 4
Fort Pierce	St. Lucie Plant Unit 1
Fort Pierce	St. Lucie Plant Unit 2
Red Level	Crystal River Plant Unit 3

Georgia

Baxley	Edwin I. Hatch Plant Unit 1
Baxley	Edwin I. Hatch Plant Unit 2
Waynesboro	Alvin W. Vogtle, Jr., Plant Unit 1
Waynesboro	Alvin W. Vogtle, Jr., Plant Unit 2

Illinois

Braidwood	Braidwood Unit 1
Braidwood	Braidwood Unit 2
Bryon	Bryon Station Unit 1
Bryon	Bryon Station Unit 2
Clinton	Clinton Nuclear Power Plant Unit 1
Cordova	Quad-Cities Station Unit 1
Cordova	Quad-Cities Station Unit 2
Morris	Dresden Nuclear Power Station Unit 2
Morris	Dresden Nuclear Power Station Unit 3
Seneca	LaSalle County Nuclear Station Unit 1
Seneca	LaSalle County Nuclear Station Unit 2
Zion	Zion Nuclear Plant Unit 1
Zion	Zion Nuclear Plant Unit 2

Iowa

Pala	Duane Arnold Energy Center Unit 1

Kansas

Burlington	Wolf Creek

Louisiana

St. Francisville	River Bend Station Unit 1
Taft	Waterford Steam Electric Station

Maine

Wiscasset — Maine Yankee Atomic Power

Maryland

Lusby	Calvert Cliffs Nuclear Power Plant Unit 1
Lusby	Calvert Cliffs Nuclear Power Plant Unit 2

Massachusetts

Plymouth	Pilgrim Station Unit 1
Rowe	Yankee Nuclear Power Station

Michigan

Big Rock Point	Big Rock Point Nuclear Plant
Bridgman	Donald C. Cook Plant Unit 1
Bridgman	Donald C. Cook Plant Unit 2
Laguna Beach	Enrico Fermi Atomic Power Plant Unit 2
South Haven	Palisades Nuclear Power Station

Minnesota

Monticello	Monticello Nuclear Generating Plant
Red Wing	Prairie Island Nuclear Generating Plant Unit 1
Red Wing	Prairie Island Nuclear Generating Plant Unit 2

Mississippi

Port Gibson	Grand Gulf Nuclear Station Unit 1
Port Gibson	Grand Gulf Nuclear Station Unit 2

Missouri

Fulton — Callaway Plant Unit 1

Nebraska

Brownville	Cooper Nuclear Station
Fort Calhoun	Fort Calhoun Station Unit 1

New Hampshire

Seabrook — Seabrook Nuclear Station Unit 1

New Jersey

Salem	Hope Creek Generating Station Unit 1
Salem	Salem Nuclear Generating Station Unit 1
Salem	Salem Nuclear Generating Station Unit 2
Toms River	Oyster Creek Nuclear Power Plant Unit 1

New York

Brookhaven	Shoreham Nuclear Power Station
Indian Point	Indian Point Station Unit 2
Indian Point	Indian Point Station Unit 3
Ontario	R. E. Ginna Nuclear Power Plant Unit 1
Scriba	James A. FitzPatrick Nuclear Power Plant
Scriba	Nine Mile Point Nuclear Unit 1
Scriba	Nine Mile Point Nuclear Unit 2

North Carolina

Bonsal	Shearon Harris Plant Unit 1
Cowans Ford Dam	Wm. B. McGuire Nuclear Station Unit 1
Cowans Ford Dam	Wm. B. McGuire Nuclear Station Unit 2
Southport	Brunswick Steam Electric Plant Unit 1
Southport	Brunswick Steam Electric Plant Unit 2

Ohio

Oak Harbor	Davis-Besse Nuclear Power Station Unit 1
Perry	Perry Nuclear Power Plant Unit 1
Perry	Perry Nuclear Power Plant Unit 2

Oregon

Prescott	Trojan Nuclear Plant Unit 1

Pennsylvania

Berwick	Susquehanna Steam Electric Station Unit 1
Berwick	Susquehanna Steam Electric Station Unit 2
Goldsboro	Three Mile Island Nuclear Station Unit 1
Peach Bottom	Peach Bottom Atomic Power Station Unit 2
Peach Bottom	Peach Bottom Atomic Power Station Unit 3
Pottstown	Limerick Generating Station Unit 1
Pottstown	Limerick Generating Station Unit 2
Shippingport	Beaver Valley Power Station Unit 1
Shippingport	Beaver Valley Power Station Unit 2

South Carolina

Broad River	Virgil C. Summer Nuclear Station Unit 1
Hartsville	H. B. Robinson S.E. Plant Unit 2
Lake Wylie	Catawba Nuclear Station Unit 1
Lake Wylie	Catawba Nuclear Station Unit 2
Seneca	Oconee Nuclear Station Unit 1
Seneca	Oconee Nuclear Station Unit 2
Seneca	Oconee Nuclear Station Unit 3

Tennessee

Daisy	Sequoyah Nuclear Power Plant Unit 1
Daisy	Sequoyah Nuclear Power Plant Unit 2
Spring City	Watts Bar Nuclear Plant Unit 1
Spring City	Watts Bar Nuclear Plant Unit 2

Texas

Bay City	South Texas Nuclear Project Unit 1
Bay City	South Texas Nuclear Project Unit 2
Glen Rose	Commanche Peak Steam Electric Station Unit 1
Glen Rose	Commanche Peak Steam Electric Station Unit 2

Vermont

Vernon	Vermont Yankee Generating Station

Virginia

Gravel Neck	Surrey Power Station Unit 1
Gravel Neck	Surrey Power Station Unit 2
Mineral	North Anna Power Station Unit 1
Mineral	North Anna Power Station Unit 2

Washington

Richland	WPPSS No. 1 (Hanford) Supply System
Richland	WPPSS No. 2 (Hanford) Supply System
Satsop	WPPSS No. 3 Supply System

Wisconsin

Kewaunee	Kewaunee Nuclear Power Plant
Two Creeks	Point Beach Nuclear Plant Unit 1
Two Creeks	Point Beach Nuclear Plant Unit 2

Source: U.S. Nuclear Regulatory Commission, *Annual Report 1988*, pp. 233–239.

Major Nuclear Reactor Incidents

November 1955

An experimental breeder reactor at the National Reactor Testing Station in Idaho Falls, Idaho, partially melted down because of operator error.

October 1957

The Windscale plutonium production reactor, north of Liverpool, England, caught fire. It spread about 20,000 curies of radioactive iodine throughout Britain and Northern Europe.

May 1958

In Chalk River, Ontario, Canada, the fuel elements in an experimental reactor burst. Although actual pollution to the environment was slight, the reactor itself was significantly contaminated.

January 1961

Because the SL-1 experimental reactor at Idaho Falls went out of control, the building was ruptured. The damaged core emitted radiation at the rate of more than 500 rems per hour, although actual pollution of the environment was low.

October 1966

At the Enrico Fermi experimental breeder reactor near Detroit, the sodium cooling system failed, resulting in a partial metldown of the core. A runaway reaction was prevented, but the reactor was permanently disabled.

October 1969

In Saint-Laurent, France, a partial meltdown occurred in a gas-graphite commercial reactor because of a fuel-loading error.

November 1973

A fire, caused by a sodium-water explosion, occurred at the fast breeder reactor at Shevchenko, on the Caspian Sea in the Soviet Union.

March 1975

In Decatur, Alabama, a technician using a candle to look for air leaks caused a fire under the control room at the Browns Ferry reactor.

Electrical controls were burned out, and the water level fell to a dangerous low.

March 1978

Because a technician dropped a light bulb into the control panel, the main electrical supply at Rancho Seco, near Sacramento, California, was short-circuited and the inputs from instruments to the plant's computer were severely scrambled. The reactor was barely under control for about one hour.

March 1979

At Harrisburg, Pennsylvania, both equipment failure and human error resulted in an accident at Three Mile Island's Unit 2 reactor. The actual cause and sequence of events continue to remain imperfectly understood.

April 1986

Unit 4 of the Chernobyl reactor near Kiev, Russia, experienced runaway reactions that resulted in a series of tremendous explosions that ruptured the containment structures and sent huge amounts of radiation throughout Europe and the northern hemisphere. The entire area was eventually evacuated, and troops were brought in to fight the fire and to help stop the reactions in the melted core. Negligence on the part of the managers was found to be the cause of the disaster, which was perhaps the worst in the history of nuclear incidents.

The Pros and Cons of Nuclear Power

The Case for Nuclear Power

1. Nuclear power is reliable, and its reliability is growing.

2. Nuclear energy is less expensive than other forms of energy for the generation of electricity.

3. Current technology can assure safe procedures for the disposal of radioactive waste materials. All other countries having nuclear power routinely recycle their nuclear wastes.

4. Radiation is one of those facts of life with which humans must live; it would occur with or without the existence of nuclear power facilities. Watching color television, receiving a chest X-ray, and natural background radiation each expose a human to more radiation than would living next to a nuclear plant for a full year. And states with high levels of natural radiation have lower cancer rates than those with low levels of natural radiation.

5. The supply of uranium in the United States could fuel reactors well into the next century.

6. Opposition to the development of nuclear energy is in reality political, not scientific. The scientific community generally supports development of nuclear energy.

The Case against Nuclear Power

1. Nuclear plants are, on the average, only 75 to 80 percent reliable.

2. The costs of generating electricity by the use of nuclear energy are rising, and these costs do not include the billions of dollars spent by the government to help develop commercial nuclear energy in the United States.

3. Although it is true that much of the nuclear waste produced can be recycled, the waste that cannot be recycled will have to be stored somewhere for at least 100 years, and probably much longer. Nuclear waste may remain "hot" for thousands of years.

4. Although radiation may be a fact of life, nuclear power plants release additional radiation that is potentially harmful to public health. We don't know everything we need to know about the effects of low-level radiation; because of that we should be cautious—harmful effects of nuclear plant radiation might not be evident for 20 or more years.

5. There are other forms of energy—such as solar and coal—that might be used instead of nuclear energy. Technology already exists for the sophisticated development of these alternatives.

6. The problems linked to the disposal of nuclear waste are largely insoluble.

Technical and Statistical Information

The texts and charts in this section have been reproduced directly from original sources, preserving their appearance as well as their content. Information is included about the licensing and construction of nuclear power plants; the roles of federal and state governments, the utility companies, other interested groups, and the public in decision making; and options and strategies for the future, including the possibilities of fusion reactors.

The Nuclear Licensing Process

Obtaining an NRC construction permit—or a limited work authorization (see discussion below) prior to a decision on issuance of a construction permit—is the first objective of a utility or other company seeking to operate a nuclear power reactor or other nuclear facility under NRC licensing authority. The process is set in motion with the filing and acceptance of the application, generally comprising 10 or more large volumes of material covering both safety and environmental factors, in accordance with NRC requirements and guidance. The second phase consists of safety, environmental, safeguards and antitrust reviews undertaken by the NRC staff. Third, a safety review is conducted by the independent Advisory Committee on Reactor Safeguards (ACRS); this review is required by law. Fourth, a mandatory public hearing is conducted by a three-member Atomic Safety and Licensing Board (ASLB), which then makes an initial decision as to whether the permit should be granted. This decision is subject to appeal to an Atomic Safety and Licensing Appeal Board (ASLAB) and could ultimately go to the Commissioners for final NRC decision. The law provides for appeal beyond the Commission in the Federal courts.

As soon an initial application is accepted, or "docketed," by the NRC, a notice of that fact is published in the Federal Register, and copies of the application are furnished to appropriate State and local authorities and to a local public document room (LPDR) established in the vicinity of the proposed site, as well as to the NRC public document room in Washington, D.C. At the same time, a notice of a public hearing is published in the Federal Register and local newspapers which provides 30 days for members of the public to petition to intervene in the proceeding. Such petitions are entertained and adjudicated by the ASLB appointed to the case, with rights of appeal by the petitioner to the ASLAB.

The NRC staff's safety, safeguards, environmental and antitrust reviews proceed in parallel. With the guidance of the Standard Format (Regulatory Guide 1.70), the applicant for a construction permit lays out the proposed nuclear plant design in a Preliminary Safety Analysis Report (PSAR). If and when this report has been made sufficiently complete to warrant review, the application is docketed and NRC staff evaluations begin. Even prior to submission of the report, NRC staff conducts a substantive review and inspection of the applicant's quality assurance program covering design and procurement. The safety review is performed by NRC staff in accordance with the Standard Review Plan for Light-Water-Cooled Reactors, initially published in 1975 and updated periodically. This plan sets forth the acceptance criteria used in evaluating the various systems, components and structures related to safety and in assessing the proposed site; it also describes the procedures to be used in performing the safety review.

The NRC staff examines the applicant's PSAR to determine whether the plant design is safe and consistent with NRC rules and regulations; whether valid methods of calculation were employed and accurately carried out; whether the applicant has conducted his analysis and evaluation in sufficient depth and breadth to support staff approval with respect to safety. When the staff is satisfied that the acceptance criteria of the Standard Review Plan have been met by the applicant's preliminary report, a Safety Evaluation Report is prepared by the staff which summarizes the results of its review regarding the anticipated effects of the proposed facility on public health and safety.

Following publication of the staff Safety Evaluation Report, the ACRS completes its review and meets with staff and applicant. The ACRS then prepares a letter report to the Chairman of the NRC presenting the results of its independent evaluation and recommending whether or not a construction permit should be issued. The staff issues a supplement to the Safety Evaluation Report incorporating any changes or actions adopted as a result of ACRS recommendations. A public hearing can then be held, generally in a community near the proposed facility site, on safety aspects of the licensing decision.

In appropriate cases, the NRC may grant a Limited Work Authorization to an applicant in advance of the final decision on the construction permit in order to allow certain work to begin at the site, saving as much as seven months time. The authorization will not be given, however, until NRC staff has completed environmental impact and site suitability reviews and the appointed ASLB has conducted a hearing on environmental impact and site suitability with a favorable finding. To realize the desired saving of time, the applicant must submit the environmental portion of the application early.

The environmental review begins with an assessment of the acceptability of the applicant's Environmental Report (ER). If the ER is judged sufficiently complete to warrant review, it is docketed, and an analysis of the consequences to the environment of the construction and operation of the proposed facility at the proposed site is begun. Upon completion of this analysis, a Draft Environmental Statement is published and distributed with specific requests for review and comment by Federal, State and local agencies, other interested parties and members of the public. All of their comments are then taken into account in the preparation of a Final Environmental Statement. Both the draft and the final statements are made available to the public at the time of respective publication. During this same period, the NRC is conducting an analysis and preparing a report on site suitability aspects of the proposed licensing action. Upon completion of these activities, a public hearing—with the appointed ASLB presiding—may be held on environmental and site suitability issues related to the proposed licensing action. (Or a single hearing on both safety and environmental matters may be held, if that is indicated.)

The antitrust reviews of license applications are carried out by the NRC and the Attorney General in advance of, or concurrent with, other licensing reviews. If an antitrust hearing is required, it is held separately from those on safety and environmental aspects.

About two or three years before construction of a plant is scheduled to be completed, the applicant files an application for an operating license. A process similar to that for the construction permit is followed. The application is filed, the NRC staff and the ACRS review it, a Safety Evaluation Report and an updated Environmental Statement are issued. A public hearing is not mandatory at this stage, but one may be held if requested by affected members of the public or at the initiative of the Commission. Each license for operation of a nuclear reactor contains technical specifications which set forth the particular safety and environmental protection measures to be imposed upon the facility and the conditions that must be met for the facility to operate.

Once licensed, a nuclear facility remains under NRC surveillance and undergoes periodic inspections throughout its operating life. In cases where the NRC finds that substantial, additional protection is necessary for the public health and safety or the common defense and security, the NRC may required "backfitting" of a licensed plant, i.e., the addition, elimination or modification of structures, systems or components of the facility.

Source: U.S. Nuclear Regulatory Commission, *1987 Annual Report* (Washington, D.C.: U.S. Government Printing Office, 1988), p. 12.

NRC Responsibilities in Nuclear Powerplant Licensing

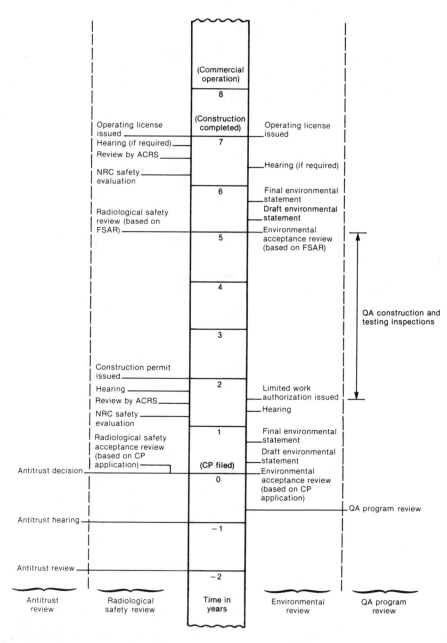

Source: *Nuclear Power in an Age of Uncertainty* (Washington, D.C.: U.S. Congress, Office of Technology Assessment, OTA-E-216, February 1984), p. 146.

Utility Responsibilities in Nuclear Powerplant Licensing and Construction

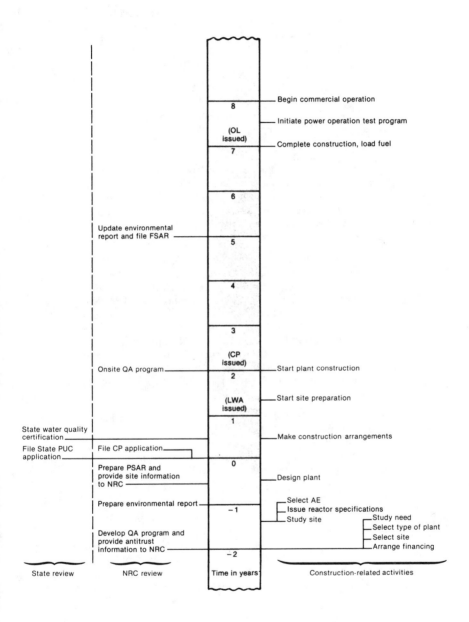

Source: *Nuclear Power in an Age of Uncertainty* (Washington, D.C.: U.S. Congress, Office of Technology Assessment, OTA-E-216, February 1984), p. 147.

Nuclear Regulatory Commission Regulations and Guides

NRC standards are primarily of two types:

- Regulations, setting forth requirements that must be met by NRC licensees in Title 10, Chapter I, of the *Code of Federal Regulations.*

- Regulatory Guides, usually to describe methods acceptable to the NRCstaff for implementing specific portions of NRC regulations.

When NRC proposes new or amended regulations, they are normally published in the *Federal Register* to allow interested persons time for comment before they are adopted. This is required by the Administrative Procedure Act. Following the public comment period, the regulations are revised, as appropriate, to reflect the comments received. Once adopted by the NRC, they are published in the *Federal Register* in final form, with the date they became effective. After that publication, rules are codified and included annually in the *Code of Federal Regulations.*

Some Regulatory Guides describe techniques used by the staff to evaluate specific situations. Others provide guidance to applicants concerning the information needed by the staff in its review of applications for permits and licenses. Many NRC guides refer to or endorse national standards (also called ''consensus standards'' or voluntary standards) that are developed by recognized organizations, often with NRC participation. The NRC makes use of a national standard in the regulatory process only after an independent review by the NRC staff and after review of public comment on NRC's planned use of the standard.

The NRC encourages comments and suggestions for improvements in Regulatory Guides and, before staff review is completed, issues them for comment to many individuals and organizations, along with the value/impact statements that set forth the objectives of each guide and its expected effectiveness and impact.

Source: U.S. Nuclear Regulatory Commission, *1987 Annual Report* (Washington, D.C.: U.S. Government Printing Office, 1988), p. 110.

The Seven Sides of the Nuclear Debate

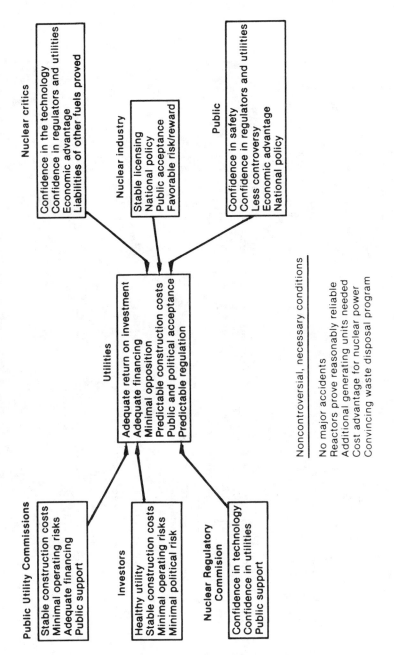

Public Utility Commissions

Stable construction costs
Minimal operating risks
Adequate financing
Public support

Investors

Healthy utility
Stable construction costs
Minimal operating risks
Minimal political risk

Nuclear Regulatory Commision

Confidence in technology
Confidence in utilities
Public support

Utilities

Adequate return on investment
Adequate financing
Minimal opposition
Predictable construction costs
Public and political acceptance
Predictable regulation

Nuclear critics

Confidence in the technology
Confidence in regulators and utilities
Economic advantage
Liabilities of other fuels proved

Nuclear industry

Stable licensing
National policy
Public acceptance
Favorable risk/reward

Public

Confidence in safety
Confidence in regulators and utilities
Less controversy
Economic advantage
National policy

Noncontroversial, necessary conditions

No major accidents
Reactors prove reasonably reliable
Additional generating units needed
Cost advantage for nuclear power
Convincing waste disposal program

Source: *Nuclear Power in an Age of Uncertainty* (Washington, D.C.: U.S. Congress, Office of Technology Assessment, OTA-E-216, February 1984), p.7.

Major National Groups Influencing Public Opinion For and Against Nuclear Power

Groups supporting nuclear power	Groups opposing some aspects of nuclear power
Category 1: Large organizations with a focus on nuclear energy targeting a broad audience. — U.S. Committee for Energy Awareness — Atomic Industrial Forum — American Nuclear Society *Category 2:* Lobbying organizations with a primary or secondary focus on nuclear energy. — Americans for Nuclear Energy — American Nuclear Energy Council — Americans for Energy Independence *Category 3:* Trade and professional associations that support commercial nuclear energy. — Edison Electric Institute — American Public Power Association — National Rural Electric Cooperative Association — Institute of Electrical and Electronics Engineers — American Association of Engineering Societies — Health Physics Society — Scientists and Engineers for Secure Energy *Category 4:* Industry research organizations indirectly influencing public opinion. — Electric Power Research Institute — Institute for Nuclear Power Operations — Nuclear Safety Analysis Center	*Category 1:* Groups with a focus on nuclear energy and alternatives to it. — Union of Concerned Scientists — Critical Mass Energy Project of Public Citizen, Inc. — Nuclear Information and Resource Service — Safe Energy Communications Council *Category 2:* Large environmental groups that participate in lobbying and public criticism of nuclear energy. — Sierra Club — National Audubon Society — Natural Resources Defense Council — Friends of the Earth — Environmental Policy Center — Environmental Defense Fund — Environmental Action, Inc.

Source: *Nuclear Power in an Age of Uncertainty* (Washington, D.C.: U.S. Congress, Office of Technology Assessment, OTA-E-216, February 1984), p. 215.

Unresolved Safety Issues

Issue/Description

Water hammer: Since 1969 there have been over 150 reported incidents involving water hammer in BWRs and PWRs. The incidents have been attributed to rapid condensation of steam pockets, steam-driven slugs of water, pump startup with partially empty lines, and rapid valve motion. Most of the damage has been relatively minor.

Steam generator tube integrity: PWR steam generators have shown evidence of corrosion-induced wastage, cracking, reduction in tube diameter, and vibration-induced fatigue cracks. The primary concern is the capability of degraded tubes to maintain their integrity during normal operation and under accident conditions with adequate safety margins.

Mark I containment long-term program: During a large-scale testing program for an advanced BWR containment system, new suppression pool loads associated with a loss of coolant accident were identified which had not been explicitly included in the original design of the Mark I containment systems. In addition, experience at operating plants has identified other loads that should be reconsidered. The results of a short-term program indicate that, for the most probable loads, the Mark I containment system would maintain its integrity and functional capability.

Reactor vessel material toughness: Because the possibility of pressure vessel failure is remote, no protection is provided against reactor vessel failure in the design of nuclear facilities. However, as plants accumulate service time, neutron irradiation reduces the material fracture toughness and initial safety margins. Results from reactor vessel surveillance programs indicate that up to 20 operating PWRs will have materials with only marginal toughness after comparatively short periods of operation.

Fracture toughness of steam generator and reactor coolant pump supports: Questions have been raised as to the potential for lamellar tearing and low fracture toughness of steam generator and reactor coolant pump support materials in the North Anna nuclear powerplants. Since similar materials and designs have been used on other plants, this issue will be reassessed for all PWRs.

Systems interactions in nuclear powerplants: There is some question regarding the interaction of various plant systems, both as to the supporting roles such systems play and as to the effect one system can have on other systems, particularly with regard to the effect on the redundancy and independence of safety systems.

Determination of safety relief valve pool dynamic loads and temperature limits for BWR containment: Operation of BWR primary system pressure relief valves can result in hydrodynamic loads on the suppression pool retaining structures or structures located within the pool.

Seismic design criteria: While many conservative factors are incorporated into the seismic design process, certain aspects of it may not be adequately conservative for all plants. Additional analysis is needed to provide assurance that the health and safety of the public is protected, and if possible, to reduce costly design conservatism.

Containment emergency sump performance: Following a loss of coolant accident in a PWR, water flowing from a break in the primary system would collect on the floor of containment. During the injection mode, water for core cooling and containment spray is drawn from a large supply tank. When the tank water is depleted, a recirculation mode is established by drawing water from the containment floor or sump. This program addresses the safety issue of the adequacy of the sump and suppression pool in the recirculation mode.

Station blackout: The loss of A.C. power from both offsite and onsite sources is referred to as a station blackout. In the event this occurs, the capability to cool the reactor core would be dependent on the availaility of systems which do not require A.C. power supplies and the ability to restore A.C. power in a timely manner. There is a concern that a station blackout may be a relatively high probability event and that this event may result in severe core damage.

Shutdown decay heat removal requirements: Many improvements to the steam generator auxiliary feedwater system were required after the accident at Three Mile Island. However, an alternative means of decay heat removal in PWRs might substantially increase the plants' capability to deal with a broader spectrum of transients and accidents and thus reduce the overall risk to the public.

Seismic qualification of equipment in operating plants: The design criteria and methods for the seismic qualification of equipment in nuclear plants have undergone significant change. Consequently, the margins of safety provided in existing equipment to resist seismically induced loads may vary considerably and must be reassessed.

Safety implications of control systems: It is generally believed that control system failures are not likely to result in the loss of safety functions which could lead to serious events or result in conditions that cannot be handled by safety systems. However, indepth plant-by-plant studies have not been performed to support this belief. The purpose of this program is to define generic criteria that may be used for plant-specific reviews.

Hydrogen control measures and effects of hydrogen burns on safety equipment: Reactor accidents which result in degraded or melted cores can generate large quantities of hydrogen and release it to the containment. Experience gained from the accident at Three Mile Island indicates that more specific design provisions for handling large quantities of hydrogen releases may be appropriate, particularly for smaller, low-pressure containment designs.

Pressurized thermal shock: Neutron irradiation of reactor pressure vessel weld and plate materials decreases fracture toughness. This makes it more likely that, under certain conditions, a crack could grow to a size that might threaten vessel integrity.

Source: *Nuclear Power in an Age of Uncertainty* (Washington, D.C.: U.S. Congress, Office of Technology Assessment, OTA-E-216, February 1984), p. 91.

Criteria for Environmental Impact Statements (EISs)

An EIS is a detailed document outlining:

. Anticipated environmental impacts of a proposed action;

. Alternatives to a proposed action;

. Any adverse environmental impacts;

. Any irreversible and irretrievable commitments of resources that would be involved in the implementation of a proposed action; and

. The relationship between local short-term uses of the environment through such proposed action and the maintenance and enhancement of long-term productivity.[14]

Under provisions of NEPA, federal agencies determine whether their proposed actions require the preparation of an EIS. Generally, federal agencies have established classification guidelines for certain agency activities that either require some type of environmental review under NEPA or constitute categorical exclusions for which no environmental review is required.

Should the proposed action not fall within the established classifications, or in the event of a challenge to a classification, the agency will normally prepare an environmental assessment (EA). The EA is a concise public document that provides sufficient evidence and analysis for the determination of whether to prepare an EIS or a finding of no significant impact (FNSI). As well, the EA (1) serves to facilitate an agency's compliance with NEPA provisions when an EIS is not required; (2) provides a basic outline of issues to be addressed in an EIS, when required by the proposed action; and (3) presents brief discussions of the need for the proposal, alternatives to the proposed action (as required under Section 102(2)(E) of NEPA), environmental impacts of the proposed action and alternatives to it, and a list of agencies and persons consulted while preparing the EA. Upon completion of the EA, the agency then proceeds to appropriate environmental review under the provisions of NEPA for the preparation of either EIS or FNSI documents and associated public review and participation.

---

[14] 42 U.S.C. §4332(2)(C).

Under NEPA regulations, the recommended format for an EIS includes:

- A brief statement of the need for and purpose of the proposed action;

- A detailed comparison of alternatives to the proposed action;

- A description of the environmental area to be affected by the proposed action;

- A complete discussion of the environmental consequences of the proposed action (including mitigation measures, direct and indirect effects, depletable resource requirements, and possible conflicts with state or local land-use plans);

- A list of the names and qualifications of individuals primarily responsible for EIS preparation; and

- An index.

For an FNSI, the agency will briefly present the reasons that an action, not otherwise excluded, will not have a significant impact on the human environment and the reasons that an EIS will not be prepared. An FNSI includes the EA, or a summary of it, and references any other related environmental documents.

Figure 2-1 is a flow chart depicting the generic environmental impact statement process.

Moreover, by the terms of the Presidential Directive under which the CEQ published the original guidelines in 1970, those standards for agency implementation were confined to Subsection 102(2)(C) of NEPA -- the requirement for EIS preparation. The CEQ concluded that this limitation impaired the consideration of the other important provisions for agency planning and decision-making contained in Section 102(2).

Basically, the CEQ believed that EIS preparation had become "an end in itself," rather than a means to making better decisions by establishing a link between what is learned through the NEPA process and how this information can contribute to decisions that further national environmental policies and goals. Therefore, to more generically and consistently apply the policies and procedures for environmental review outlined in NEPA, the CEQ published regulations that are binding on all federal agencies (although some question exists as to their impact on independent regulatory agencies when they are of a substantive, rather than procedural, nature). The CEQ regulations effectively replace more than 70 different sets of agency regulations with uniform standards for environmental review at the federal level. They address all nine subdivisions of Section 102(2) of NEPA, rather than just the one outlining EIS

preparation. The CEQ also included formal guidance on the requirements of NEPA in the regulations for use by federal courts inter-
preting the law during review of agency actions under the Administrative Procedures Act (APA).

Source: *Analysis of NEPA/CEQ Requirements With Respect to Nuclear Materials Transportation,* Final Report. International Energy Associated Limited. Prepared by Sandia National Laboratories, Albuqeurque, New Mexico and Livermore, California, for the United States Department of Energy under Contract DE-AC04-76DP00789. Printed May 1985. Available from National Technical Information Service, U.S. Department of Commerce, 5285 Port Royal Road, Springfield, Virginia, 22161. Pp. 12–14.

Environmental Impact Statement Process

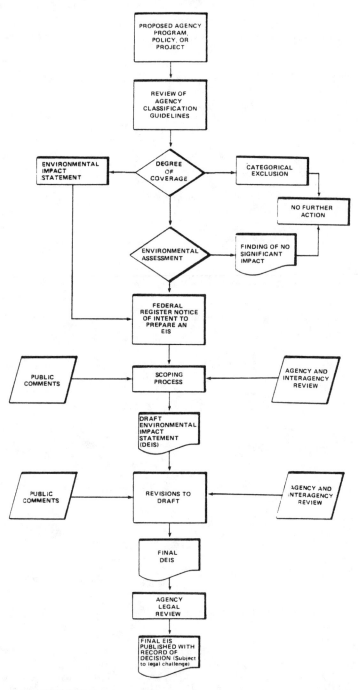

Source: *Analysis of NEPA/CEQ Requirements With Respect to Nuclear Materials Transportation,* Final Report, p. 15. For full documentation, see source for preceding entry.

State Agreements Program

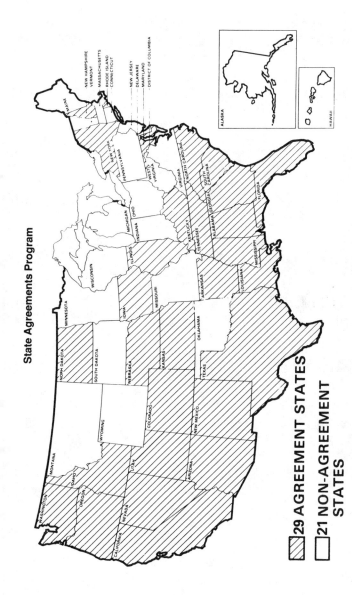

☒ **29 AGREEMENT STATES**

☐ **21 NON-AGREEMENT STATES**

By formal agreement with the NRC, a total of 29 States have assumed regulatory responsibility over byproduct and source materials and small quantities of special nuclear material. The latest (29th) agreement, with Illinois, became effective on June 1, 1987. Negotiations for an Agreement with the State of Maine are under way. At the end of fiscal year 1987, there were about 15,000 radioactive material licenses in these Agreement States; they represent about 65 percent of all the radioactive materials licenses in the United States. (See map of Agreement States in this chapter.)

Source: U.S. Nuclear Regulatory Commission, *1987 Annual Report* (Washington, D.C.: U.S. Government Printing Office, 1988), pp. 97–98.

State Siting Laws

State	Lead agency PUC[a]	Lead agency Ind.[b]	Env.[c]	Forecasting plans required[d] (years) Utility	Forecasting plans required[d] (years) State	One-stop licensing	Statutory decision time (months)	Preemption authority	Need for power determination	Legislation adopted Original	Legislation adopted Amended	Title of legislation or agency created
Arizona		x		10		No	—	No	Yes	71		Power Plant Siting Committee
Arkansas	x			2		No	—	Yes	Yes	73		Utility Facility Environmental Protection Act (two stop)
California			x		5-10-20	Yes	25-36[e]	No	Yes	74		Energy Resources Conservation and Development Commission
Connecticut			x	10		Yes	10	Yes	Yes	71	73	Public Utilities Environmental Standards Act (Power Facility Evaluation Council
Florida			x	10		No	14	No	Yes	73	75	Electric Power Plant Siting Act (1973)
Iowa		x		None		No	[f]	No	Yes	76		State Commerce Commisson
Kansas		x		None		No	—	Yes	Yes	76		Corporation Commission
Kentucky			x	None		No	—	No	Yes	74		Power Plant Siting Act
Maine						No	—	Yes	Yes	71		Power Plant Siting Act
Maryland			x		10	No	—	Yes	Yes	71		Energy Facilities and Siting Council (1975)
Massachusetts			x		10	Yes	6[h]	Yes	Yes	73	75	Power Plant Siting Act
Minnesota	x			15		No	—[i]	Yes	Yes	73		Utility Siting Act
Montana	x			10		No	—	No	Yes	73		Public Service Commission
Nevada	x			None		Yes	—	No	Yes	71		Electric Power Plant Siting Act
New Hampshire	x			10-15		Yes	14[j]	Yes	Yes	73		Coastal Area Facility Review Act
New Jersey			x		4	No	—	N/A	N/A			

State		Forecast period		Time (months)			Year	Agency
New Mexico	x	None	No	—	No	No	71	Public Utilities Commission
New York	x	15	Yes	—	Yes	Yes	72	Board of Electric Generation Siting and the Environment
North Dakota	x	10	Yes	—	No	Yes	75	Energy Conversion and Transmission Facilities Siting Act
Ohio	x	10	Yes	—	Yes	Yes	72	Power Siting Commission
Oregon	x	10	Yes	24[k]	Yes	Yes	71, 75	Energy Facility Siting Council (1975)
South Carolina	x	10	No	—	Yes	Yes	71	Public Service Commission
Vermont	x	None	Yes	—[m]	Yes	Yes	75	Public Service Board
Washington	x	10	Yes	12[h]	Yes	Yes	70, 76	Energy Facility Site Evaluation Council (1976)
Wisconsin	x	10	No	18	Yes	Yes	75	Public Service Commission (two stop)
Wyoming	x	5	yes	—	No	Yes	75	Industrial Development and Siting Act

[a] Public Utility Commission
[b] Independent.
[c] Environmental.
[d] Indicates the period of time which utility or state prepared forecasts must cover (e.g., Arizona utilities are required to submit a 10-year forecast).
[e] California allows extended time upon mutual agreement by Commission and applicant.
[f] Statute specifies that "the Commission shall expeditiously render a written decision with complete determination . . ."
[g] Only available information is given.
[h] A 1976 amendment provides for the time period to be nonbinding if "compliance with said requirements will prevent the Council from rendering a decision upon the application . . ."
[i] The Minnesota statute contains an emergency certification provision for "demonstrable emergency." The provision authorizes certification "no later than 195 days "following acceptance of an application."
[j] A 1976 amendment allows the state legislature opportunity to disaffirm findings by the siting council 45 days after council certification of nuclear power facility.
[k] Nine months for combustion and/or geothermal generation.
[m] Certification of nuclear power facilities is contingent upon approval by the Vermont General Assembly.
[n] Allows for extended time upon mutual agreement by the Energy Facility Site Evaluation Council and applicant. A 1977 amendment also provides for "expedited processing" of an application upon request by "any person."

Source: *Nuclear Power in an Age of Uncertainty* (Washington, D.C.: U.S. Congress, Office of Technology Assessment, OTA-E-216, February 1984), p. 152.

Summary of Policy Options

	Strategy[a]	Congressional role
A. Reduce capital costs and uncertainties		
1. Revise the regulatory process for predictable licensing	One	Oversight, legislation
2. Develop a standardized, optimized design	One	Moderate R&D funding (design)
	Two	Major R&D funding (demonstration)
3. Promote the revision of rate regulation	Two	Inquiry; FERC regulation
B. Improve reactor operations and economics		
1. R&D programs to improve economics of operations	Base Case	Minor R&D funding
2. Improve utility management of nuclear operations	One	NRC oversight
3. Resolve occupational exposure liability	Two	Legislation
C. Reduce the risk of accidents that have public safety or utility financial impacts		
1. Improve confidence in safety	Base Case	NRC oversight; minor R&D funding
2. Certify utilities and contractors	Two	Legislation
3. Develop alternative reactors	Two	Major R&D funding
4. Revise institutional management of nuclear operations	Two	Inquiry, oversight
D. Alleviate public concerns and reduce political risks		
1. Accelerate studies of alternative energy sources	Base Case	Minor R&D funding
2. Address the concerns of the critics	One	Oversight, legislation
3. Control the rate of nuclear construction	One	Legislation
4. Maintain nonproliferation policies	Two	Oversight of legislation
5. Promote regional planning for electric growth	Two	Legislation

[a]Strategies incorporating these policy options are described later in the chapter: Base Case, Strategy One, and Strategy Two.

Source: *Nuclear Power in an Age of Uncertainty* (Washington, D.C.: U.S. Congress, Office of Technology Assessment, OTA-E-216, February 1984), p. 252.

Major Policy Strategies (and the policy options included in each)

Strategy	Policy Options Included
Base Case: No change in Federal nuclear policy: *Three noncontroversial policies that would be useful even in the absence of more orders*	

Goals	*Policy Options*
Improve reactor economics	(B1) R&D to improve fuel burnup
Reduce accident risk	(C1) Improve analysis of reactor safety
Alleviate public concern	(D1) Accelerate studies of alternative energy sources

Variation: Sharpen market competition of nuclear power
This strategy, not analyzed in detail, would include some or all of steps towards: reduction or removal of Federal subsidies for nuclear and alternatives; marginal cost pricing; deregulation; full costing of external impacts

Strategy One: Remove obstacles to more nuclear orders: *Three policies above plus five others*

Goals	*Policy Options*
Reduce capital cost barrier	(A1) Revise regulation
	(A2) Assist funding of standardized optimized LWR design
Improve reactor economics	(B2) Improve utility management
Alleviate public concerns	(D2) Address concerns of critics
	(D3) Control the rate of nuclear construction

Strategy Two: Provide a moderate stimulus to more nuclear orders: *Eight policies above plus eight others*

Goals	*Policy Options*
Reduce capital cost barrier	(A2) Assist funding of a demonstration of new LWR designs
	(A3) Promote the revision of rate regulation
	(B3) Solve occupational exposure liability
Improve reactor economics	(C2) Certify utilities and contractors
Reduce accident risk	(C3) Develop alternative reactors
	(C4) Revise institutional management of nuclear operations
Alleviate public concern	(D4) Maintain nonproliferation policies
	(D5) Promote regional planning for electric growth

Variation: Support the U.S. nuclear industry in future world trade
This strategy, not analyzed in detail, would support industry and utility R&D and export financing policies aimed at obtaining a major share of the future world market in nuclear and other advanced electrotechnologies.

Source: *Nuclear Power in an Age of Uncertainty* (Washington, D.C.: U.S. Congress, Office of Technology Assessment, OTA-E-216, February 1984), p. 264.

Key Technical Issues for Magnetic Fusion

Magnetic Confinement Systems

A variety of magnetic fields can be used to confine and insulate a fusion plasma. However, the confined plasma interacts with different confining magnetic fields in ways that affect the heating and confinement efficiency of the system. The unique nature of this interaction creates the scientific richness of fusion plasma physics. The nature of the fusion reactor will also be profoundly affected by the particular magnetic configuration. The size of the reactor, the ease of operation, and the cost of construction all depend on understanding the scientific principles of the interactions of the fusion plasma with the magnetic confinement configuration.

There are only two basic magnetic structures which have been shown to confine plasmas of fusion interest: the magnetic mirror and the magnetic torus. However, each of these magnetic confinement systems has several variations. These confinement systems differ in practice by emphasizing particular principles of fusion science to improve plasma confinement or to simplify the technical requirements for producing the magnetic fields. Historically, the tokamak, a toroidal confinement concept, embodied a set of principles which was comparatively easy to implement in the laboratory. As a result, most of the scientific progress has been made with this concept. Today tokamaks are unique in the ability to produce the most fusion reactor-like plasmas for scientific study.

The rapid scientific and technological development of the fusion program in the last decade, resulting in large part from successful tokamak experiments, has contributed to overcoming many of the technical difficulties of other magnetic confinement concepts. We are fortunate to have a number of concepts which are now beginning to catch up with the tokamak. In addition, the tokamak concept itself has begun to evolve rapidly because of discoveries in tokamak research and ideas generated by research in these other concepts.

Properties of Burning Plasmas

Resolution of the confinement issue depends on a fundamental scientific understanding of several magnetic confinement principles. All of these principles are now under investigation, with the exception of those associated with a burning plasma. The new physical phenomena in the burning state will also require study. A fusion plasma is said to burn when the heat released within the plasma by the fusion reaction is sufficient to maintain the plasma temperature in face of heat loss from the system. In order to attain this state, one must solve scientific problems of magnetic confinement which are prerequisites to achieving the necessary insulation. Only the tokamak confinement system is approaching the point at which this condition might be achieved. Identification of the conditions required for ignition is expected to occur in the United States experiment, Tokamak Fusion Test Reactor, within two years. Initial experiments with significant fusion reactions are planned for following years. At the same time, studies are proceeding to specify a cost-effective experiment to investigate the physics of burning plasmas.

Fusion Materials

The ultimate economics of fusion energy, like most other energy systems, will depend on the materials required for the system. Fusion materials research separates naturally into two classes of problems: those associated with interaction of plasma with the materials and those associated with the interaction of fusion neutrons with the materials. Both involve basic and applied research. However, the former are near-term problems which must be solved to advance plasma confinement research. The latter problems are more fundamental to the ultimate success of fusion as an energy source.

The last decade of research, using available nuclear test facilities, has revealed that there are materials which could withstand the nuclear environment of a fusion reactor with reasonable system economics and relatively modest waste disposal requirements. However, studies have also shown that it is important to improve the economics of these systems and to reduce the need for long-term waste disposal of fusion materials even further through the development of specialized materials. The future fusion materials program must include both the basic research on fundamental new materials and the development of the new technology required for testing those materials.

Fusion Nuclear Technology

In a fusion reactor, most of the energy is recovered from a structure surrounding the fusion plasma. This structure is known as a fusion blanket and must perform several functions besides converting the energy released by the fusion plasma into useful heat. The blanket must also use the energetic neutrons emitted from the plasma to create part of the fuel for the fusion reactor and allow recovery of this fuel. It is even possible that the blanket might be used to produce nuclear fuel for use in fission reactors. The blanket also shields the outside world from radiation, but in doing so becomes radioactive. It is clear that as the major radioactive component of a fusion system, the blanket is the main focus of interest for safety and environmental concerns.

There are several technical options, based on combinations of different materials and technologies, to perform the various blanket functions. Moreover, different confinement concepts may impose different limitations on these technologies and on overall blanket design. These individual technologies can be evaluated on their ability to satisfy the blanket function in the most acceptable way. However, each of the blanket functions is so interrelated in practice that an integrated research and development approach is required.

Source: U.S. Department of Energy, Office of Energy Research, *Magnetic Fusion Program Plan* (Washington, D.C.: February 1985), p. 6.

Magnetic Fusion Program Plan

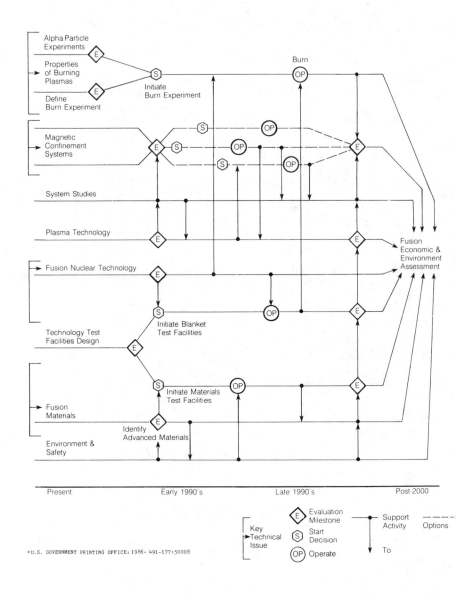

| Present | Early 1990's | Late 1990's | Post-2000 |

Key
►Technical Issue

⬡E Evaluation Milestone
Ⓢ Start Decision
⑳P Operate

● Support Activity
---- Options
↓ To

Source: U.S. Department of Energy, Office of Energy Research, *Magnetic Fusion Program Plan* (Washington, D.C.: February, 1985), p. 15

118

5

Directory of Organizations

American Nuclear Energy Council (ANEC)
410 First Street, SE
Washington, DC 20003
(202) 484-2670

A trade organization that represents the U.S. nuclear industry. It is interested in promoting the peaceful uses of nuclear energy and advocates further development of nuclear power. It represents these views before Congress, reviews legislation involving nuclear energy, and publishes a weekly newsletter for members.

American Nuclear Society (ANS)
555 North Kensington Avenue
La Grange Park, IL 60525
(312) 352-6611

An organization established by physicists, mathematicians, life scientists, educators, and other professionals in nuclear science and engineering to promote peaceful use of nuclear power. It works with government, educational institutions, regulatory agencies, and other groups to disseminate information, enhance research, and conduct meetings. It publishes various monthly, bimonthly, and semiannual journals related to nuclear science and engineering.

Americans for Nuclear Energy
2525 Wilson Boulevard
Arlington, VA 22201
(703) 528-4430

Composed of individuals favoring expansion of the use of nuclear energy. It lobbies Congress and the state legislatures, sponsors conferences and speakers, works in campaigns promoting nuclear power, and issues a monthly publication.

Arms Control and Disarmament Agency
320 21st Street, NW
Department of State Building
Washington, DC 20451
(202) 632-0392

Concerned with arms control and disarmament policies that will lead to increased security of the United States. It engages in negotiations and conferences on matters of strategic arms limitations, mutual force reductions, and the prevention of the spread of nuclear weapons. It plays a leading role in implementing the nonproliferation policy of the United States and attempts to monitor the flow of arms in countries throughout the world.

Association of European Atomic Forums (FORATOM)
Hirschenplatz 7
CH-6004 Lucerne
Switzerland
Tel. 41 513013

A multinational organization that represents utilities, nuclear plant and component manufacturers, research organizations, and other groups in Western European countries. Its primary objective is achieving increased development of peaceful uses of nuclear energy by identifying, studying, and proposing solutions to problems faced by the nuclear industry and by promoting public understanding of the use of nuclear power to generate electricity. The organization publishes various annual and periodic reports.

Atomic Energy Levels Data Center
Atomic & Plasma Radiation Division
National Bureau of Standards
A167 Physics Building
Gaithersburg, MD 20899
(301) 921-2011

Although not involved with the making of nuclear energy policy, this office compiles data dealing with atomic spectra and answers questions related to that topic. The office also provides consulting and reference services and has publications for distribution.

Atomic Industrial Forum
7101 Wisconsin Avenue
Bethesda, MD 20814
(301) 654-9260

An organization that collects materials related to radiation and radioisotopes, nuclear health and safety standards, legislation on nuclear energy, nuclear insurance and indemnity, and related matters. It is concerned with the development and use of nuclear energy for constructive and applied purposes. Its library is open to members and publishes monthly periodicals.

Australian Nuclear Association
P.O. Box 445
Sutherland, NSW 2232
Australia
Tel. 2 5433313

An organization aimed at promoting knowledge of safe and peaceful uses of nuclear energy and technology. It is composed of individuals having interests in nuclear power and its related fields (e.g., nuclear medicine, nuclear fuel cycle, etc.), and is concerned with broader applications of nuclear science and technology in Australia. It publishes periodicals and monographs.

Center for Nuclear Information (CNI)
Rua General Severiano 90
22294 Rio de Janeiro, RJ
Brazil
Tel. 21 2958545

A Brazilian organization maintained by the National Commission for Nuclear Energy of Brazil. Its primary function is to furnish information to scientists, technical experts, and the national and international clients it serves. It produces monthly and annual publications, and maintains ties to the International Atomic Energy Agency and the Organization of American States.

Citizens' Energy Project
1110 Sixth Street, NW
Washington, DC 20001
(202) 289-4999

Gathers information and conducts research in such areas as nuclear power, renewable energy, solar energy, and related subjects. It provides reference services, distributes publications related to its areas of interest, and sometimes conducts seminars.

Controlled Fusion Atomic Data Center (CFADC)
Building 6003
Oak Ridge National Laboratory
Oak Ridge, TN 37831
(615) 574-4701

The CFADC answers requests for information related to fusion; produces annotated bibliographies of fusion-related data and maintains computer files for online searching; and compiles cross-section and reaction-rate data on specific collision processes of interest to the fusion energy program. Its files include extensive bibliographies on heavy particle collisions, charged particles, electron collisions, photon collisions, general theory, and related materials.

Edison Electric Institute
1111 19th Street
Washington, DC 20036
(202) 828-7582

A trade association that represents investor-owned electric utilities. It provides information on all aspects of energy, including nuclear energy. Statistical information, research, and other services are provided to members, and a list of its publications is available to the public.

Energy Information Administration
U.S. Department of Energy
1000 Independence Avenue, SW
Washington, DC 20585
(202) 252-2363

Collects, processes, and publishes data on energy reserves and on energy technology, production, demand, consumption, and distribution.

European Atomic Energy Community (EURATOM)
Commission of European Communities
Rue de la Loi 200
B-1049 Bruxelles
Belgium
Tel. 32 2 235 11 11

This organization supervises a common market involving nuclear materials, seeks to eliminate import and export duties on nuclear products, operates a safeguard system, implements and monitors protection standards, forecasts energy consumption, and assures an adequate supply of nuclear materials. The organization traces its origins to the creation of the European Coal and Steel Community.

European High Temperature Nuclear Power Stations Society (EURO-HKG)
Industriestrasse 10
D-4700 Hamm 1
Federal Republic of Germany
Tel. 2388 615

Concerned with the exchange of scientific and technical data and information about high-temperature nuclear reactors. Its multinational membership is composed of utilities and operators of nuclear power stations.

European Nuclear Society (ENS)
Postfach 2613
CH-3001 Berne
Switzerland
Tel. 31 216111

Attempts to promote the interests of the European nuclear industry and is involved in efforts to represent the industry before European and international government organizations. It seeks progress in scientific and technological advancement for the peaceful uses of nuclear energy and keeps its members informed about developments in the nuclear field. It provides scholarships and awards and publishes periodical newsletters and other materials.

Federal Emergency Management Agency (FEMA)
500 C Street SW
Washington, DC 20472
(202) 646-2500

Provides information about what to do if there is a nuclear attack or some other chemical or natural disaster occurs. The office can be reached 24 hours a day through either personal consultation or by message center. Provides a citizens' handbook for distribution.

Fusion Energy Foundation (FEF)
P.O. Box 1438
Radio City Station
New York, NY 10101

An organization concerned with educating Americans about nuclear energy and laser technology. It publishes reports that deal with the subjects of hydrogen fusion, hydrogen bombs, thermal nuclear explosives, and the analysis of laser energy for defense and other purposes.

Fusion Power Associates (FPA)
Two Professional Drive, Suite 248
Gaithersburg, MD 20879
(30l) 258-0545

A group interested in the development of fusion energy. Members include representatives from private industry, utility companies, universities, and private laboratories. It promotes the development of fusion energy as a viable energy alternative for the future, asserting that fusion energy is inexhaustible and safe. Presents testimony before congressional committees and provides information of various types related to fusion energy. Publishes monthly, quarterly, and biennial reports.

German Nuclear Forum (GNF)
Heussallee 10
D-5300 Bonn 1
Federal Republic of Germany
Tel. 228 5070

Composed of members of the scientific community, utilities, businesses, and government agencies. It distributes information about nuclear energy to the public and encourages the development and peaceful uses of nuclear technology and energy. It publishes weekly and monthly journals.

Grand Junction Projects Office
Idaho Operations Office
U.S. Department of Energy
P.O. Box 2567
Grand Junction, CO 81502
(303) 242-8621, ext. 201

Agency concerned with remedial action programs involving uranium mine and mill tailing operations having an impact on the environment. Also concerned with managing uranium leases under the control of the U.S. Department of Energy. It participates in international technical exchanges.

Ground Zero
P.O. Box 15559
Washington, DC 20003
(202) 638-7402

A nonpartisan public interest group funded by foundations and private individuals that is concerned with educating the public on the effects of nuclear war. It attempts to involve citizens in matters related to national security and has published a variety of booklets, slides, guides for teachers, and similar materials. Its library is open to the public.

Health and Energy Institute
236 Massachusetts Avenue, NE, No. 506
Washington, DC 20002
(202) 543-1070

An institute supported by foundations and the public, it is concerned mainly with the effects of nuclear energy on health and the environment. It is involved with radiation law, food irradiation, special radiation risks incurred by women, and development of nuclear energy in the area of electricity. It provides speakers, maintains a small library, and supplies information to the public.

House Committee on Energy and Commerce
2125 Rayburn House Office Building
Washington, DC 20515
(202) 225-2927

Has jurisdiction over interstate and foreign commerce, petroleum and natural gas, railroads, communications, waterways, power transmission, securities and exchanges, public health and health facilities, and other areas. Subcommittee on Energy and Power, (202) 226-2500; Subcommittee on Transportation, Tourism, and Hazardous Materials, (202) 225-9304; Subcommittee on Health and Environment, (202) 225-4952.

House Committee on Interior and Insular Affairs
1324 Longworth House Office Building
Washington, DC 20515
(202) 225-2761

Jurisdiction over such areas as forests and national parks, geologic survey, irrigation and reclamation, insular possessions, mining and minerals, petroleum conservation on public lands, and the domestic nuclear energy industry, among other things. Subcommittee on Energy and Environment, (202) 225-8331; Subcommittee on Water and Power Regulation, (202) 225-4952.

House Committee on Science, Space, and Technology
2321 Rayburn House Office Building
Washington, DC 20515
(202) 225-6371

Jurisdiction over astronautical matters, the Bureau of Standards, the metric system, the National Aeronautics and Space Administration, the National Science Foundation, outer space, and energy (including nuclear, but not for defense purposes), among other areas. Subcommittee on Energy Research and Development, (202) 225-8056; Subcommittee on Science, Research, and Technology, (202) 225-8844.

Institute of Nuclear Materials Management
60 Revere Drive, Suite 500
Northbrook, IL 60062
(312) 480-9080

An organization of members of government, industry, EURATOM, public utilities, insurance agencies, academic institutions, and others in the field of nuclear energy who are concerned with applying the techniques of chemistry, engineering, and statistics to the management of nuclear materials. Provides speakers and publishes a quarterly journal.

Institute of Nuclear Power Operations (INPO)
1820 Water Place
Atlanta, GA 30339
(404) 953-3600

An organization composed of electric utilities either operating or constructing a nuclear power plant installation. It conducts evaluations and analyses relevant to nuclear power plants, publishes reports, and offers seminars.

Inter-American Nuclear Energy Commission (IANEC)
General Secretariat of the Organization of American States
Washington, DC 20006
(202) 789-3368

Composed of the 21 members of the Organization of American States, the commission's objectives are the coordination of research, exchange of scientific and technical information, establishment of public health safeguards, organization of conferences, and related matters in the field of nuclear energy. It meets every two years and publishes reports of its sessions, symposia, and other specialized conferences.

International Atomic Energy Agency (IAEA)
United Nations Vienna International Centre
Wagramerstrasse 5
Postfach 100
A-1400 Vienna
Austria
Tel. 222 2360

An organization established in 1957 under the auspices of the United Nations to enhance the peaceful uses of atomic energy. It provides health and safety standards for the uses of atomic energy and applies these in terms of the provisions of the Treaty on Non-Proliferation of Nuclear Weapons. It maintains an extensive library, issues monthly and quarterly publications, and publishes the proceedings of its conferences, seminars, symposia, and other gatherings. It is authorized to purchase and sell fissionable materials for peaceful purposes.

International Energy Agency (IEA)
2 Rue Andre-Pascal
75775 Paris Cedex 16
France
Tel. 33 1 45 24 82 00

The IEA is an autonomous body established in 1974 within the framework of the Organisation for Economic Co-operation and Development. It carries out a comprehensive cooperative program among 21 nations. Its basic objectives include reducing excessive dependence on oil through conservation; developing alternative energy sources, which includes supporting research and development efforts; exchanging information; engaging in consultation; establishing a stable international energy trade; and preparing participating countries against major disruption of oil supplies.

International Energy Information Center
909 M Street, NW
Washington, DC 20001
(202) 737-2073

An organization concerned with fossil and nuclear energy, mining, and transportation of energy. It provides consulting services, responds to inquiries regarding subjects within its purview, and provides publications on subjects about which it has data or expertise.

International Nuclear Information System (INIS)
Head, INIS Section, International Atomic Energy Association
P.O. Box 100
Vienna International Center
Wagramerstrasse 5
A-1400 Vienna
Austria
Tel. 43 222 2883

An organization established in 1970 by the International Atomic Energy Agency. It collects and prepares information supplied by cooperating member states and international organizations and redistributes this information to national centers in 75 IAEA member states. Data collection activities include all aspects of the peaceful uses of nuclear science and technology. Publishes *INIS Atomindex,* cumulative indexes to *INIS Atomindex,* and the INIS Reference Series.

International Nuclear Law Association (INLA)
Square de Meeus 29
B-1040 Bruxelles
Belgium
Tel. 32 2 513 68 45

This organization arranges for and promotes the study of legal problems related to the peaceful utilization of nuclear energy. It advocates the protection of both humankind and the environment from nuclear pollution, and cooperates on a scientific basis with associations and institutions having similar interests. It organizes conferences, congresses, discussions, lectures, and seminars. Membership consists of qualified legal experts.

Israel Agency for Nuclear Information (IANI)
P.O. Box 581
Karkur 37105
Israel
Tel. 63 79538

An organization concerned primarily with the hazards of nuclear energy as they pertain to Israel. It distributes information on various aspects of the nuclear energy production process and publishes a bimonthly newsletter.

National Energy Information Center (NEIC)
Forrestal Building, 1F-048
1000 Independence Avenue, SW
Washington, DC 20585
(202) 586-8800

A branch of the Energy Information Administration (EIA) of the U.S. Department of Energy, the NEIC provides information on historical and future-oriented energy data. Among its many services are information on EIA and DOE programs, energy sources, energy reserves, production, consumption, and imports and exports. It provides publications, fact sheets, catalogs, computer models, and other information about its programs. People may visit its reading room and public inquiries may be made by writing or telephoning.

National Nuclear Data Center (NNDC)
Building 197 D
Brookhaven National Laboratory
Upton, NY 11937
(516) 282-2901

Concerned mainly with the acquisition, storage, retrieval, and dissemination of data about neutrons and nuclear structures. It reviews and evaluates data dealing with neutron and nonneutron information on fission and fusion reactors and related subjects, and publishes a newsletter and other reports. Its use is restricted to the United States and Canada.

Netherlands Atomic Forum (NAF)
Scheveningseweg 112
The Hague
Netherlands
Tel. 70 825804

An organization founded in 1968 that consists of utilities and industries in the Netherlands concerned with the development of the peaceful uses of nuclear energy. It publishes brochures and holds a periodic conference on issues related to its objectives.

Nordic Liaison Committee for Atomic Energy (NKA)
Postboks 49
DK-4000 Roskilde
Denmark
Tel. 2 37 1212

A coalition of Denmark, Finland, Iceland, Norway, and Sweden, this organization coordinates peaceful uses of nuclear energy among the member nations. Its primary committee function is Nordic nuclear safety; it publishes periodic reports.

Nuclear and Alternative Fuels Division
Energy Information Administration
U.S. Department of Energy
Mailstop 2F021-E153
1000 Independence Avenue, SW
Washington, DC 20585
(202) 252-6363

Collects information related to industries involved with uranium, mining, milling, and the generation of nuclear power. The office will supply forecasting data and other publications.

Nuclear Regulatory Commission (NRC)
1717 H Street, NW
Washington, DC 20555
(301) 492-7715

Dispenses information related to the licensing of commercial nuclear power plants and the various uses of nuclear materials in private industry, medicine, education, and general research. The agency is also concerned with assuring that licensed activities are carried on in compliance with government regulations and involved in safety activities with respect to nuclear facilities and materials. It issues press releases, responds to inquiries, and will refer questions to the appropriate office as necessary.

Nuclear Safety Information Center (NSIC)
Oak Ridge National Laboratory
P.O. Box Y
Oak Ridge, TN 37830
(615) 574-0391

An agency concerned mainly with providing information about the safety of nuclear facilities, from the perspectives of design, licensing, and construction, as well as operation once completed. The office retains all summaries of licensee event reports on unusual reactor experiences in the United States and collects all foreign documents in the NRC Light Water Reactor Foreign Exchange Program. Distributes all foreign reports, by way of microfiche, to the official organizations on its distribution list.

Nuclear Standards Program Information Center (NSPIC)
Nuclear Standards Management Center
Oak Ridge National Laboratory
Mail Stop 10, Building 9204-1
P.O. Box Y
Oak Ridge, TN 37830
(615) 574-7886

The center receives, stores, develops, and distributes information related to nuclear standards. It maintains a large database on matters related to program standards and issues newsletters, guides, indexes, summaries, and requirements information. Its information is not available to foreign organizations or for distribution to foreign organizations or individuals.

Nuclear Task Force
Nuclear Energy
U.S. Department of Energy
1000 Independence Avenue, SW, Room 7B084
Washington, DC 20585
(202) 252-4710

This office helps to plan construction of nuclear power plants by implementing, integrating, and planning policy and programs.

Oak Ridge Associated Universities
P.O. Box 117
Oak Ridge, TN 37831
(615) 576-3150

A group of 49 universities working under a contract with the U.S. Department of Energy to conduct research, education, and training in science and science education. One of its major functions is the distribution of information related to U.S. energy programs. It publishes various technical reports related to energy, health, and the environment on a periodic basis.

OECD Nuclear Energy Agency (NEA)
38 bd Suchet, F-75016
Paris
France
Tel. 33 1 45 24 82 00

A semiautonomous agency of the Organization for Economic Cooperation and Development (OECD) that promotes the cooperation of member governments in safety and regulatory matters related to nuclear power and the development of nuclear energy. It attempts to reconcile conflicting government regulations, reviews matters related to the nuclear fuel cycle, deals with matters of supply and demand, and coordinates and exchanges scientific and technical information related to nuclear energy issues. It publishes periodic and annual reports.

Office of Air Quality and Nuclear Energy
Louisiana Department of Environmental Quality
P.O. Box 14690
Baton Rouge, LA 70898-4690
(318) 925-4518

A government department concerned with radioactive waste, nuclear emergency planning, peaceful uses of nuclear energy, and general matters related to radiation problems. It provides information, distributes reports, and makes referrals to other agencies.

Office of Assistant Secretary for Nuclear Energy
U.S. Department of Energy
1000 Independence Avenue, SW
Washington, DC 20585
(202) 252-6450

Concerned with all aspects of nuclear energy power systems, research and development of technologies related to nuclear power, and nuclear safety technology. It provides reference materials, publications, and general assistance for inquiries.

Office of Civilian Radioactive Waste Management
Nuclear Energy
U.S. Department of Energy
Germantown, G-451
Washington, DC 20545
(301) 353-4288

Researches the problems related to civilian nuclear waste management, particularly with respect to alternatives for the permanent disposition of high-level radioactive wastes. It conducts research and development studies and expedites new reactor storage technology in an attempt to create an integrated waste management system.

Office of Coal, Nuclear, Electric, and Alternate Fuels
U.S. Department of Energy
1000 Independence Avenue, SW
Washington, DC 20585
(202) 353-3498

This office is concerned with preparing analyses relevant to the transportation and distribution of nuclear and alternate energy supplies, managing data on nuclear power and alternate systems of energy, and making projections concerning the energy supply in the future.

Office of Energy Research
U.S. Department of Energy
1000 Independence Avenue, SW
Washington, DC 20585
(202) 783-3238

Provides information on the Energy Department's research and development programs, university training activities, and various forms of financial assistance. The main concerns of the office include high energy physics, basic energy sciences, nuclear physics, fusion energy, and support for universities.

Office of Fusion Energy
Energy Research
U.S. Department of Energy
1000 Independence Avenue, SW, ER-50 Room J204
Washington, DC 20585
(301) 353-3347

This agency supplies information relevant to the latest technology for the safe, economical, and environmentally compatible development of fusion power to generate electricity. It supervises plant construction and operation of fusion energy programs and publishes statistical data about fusion reactors and related subjects.

Office of International Nuclear Nonproliferation
International Affairs
U.S. Department of Energy
1000 Independence Avenue, SW, Room 76-049
Washington, DC 20585
(202) 252-1883

This office deals with information related to U.S. nuclear nonproliferation policy, cooperative efforts with other countries, and nuclear export policy.

Office of Nuclear Energy
U.S. Department of Energy
1000 Independence Avenue, SW
Washington, DC 20585
(202) 252-8728

Supplies information to the public regarding nuclear energy and nuclear energy programs. The office is able to answer questions of a general nature and will refer more technical inquiries to appropriate sources. Provides pamphlets, data sheets, and booklets related to virtually all aspects of nuclear energy.

Office of Nuclear Export Policy
Bureau of Oceans and International Environmental and Scientific Affairs
U.S. Department of State
2201 C Street, NW, Room 7828
Washington, DC 20520
(202) 632-7036

Will provide information on U.S. nuclear export laws and regulations, national nonproliferation policy, and international organizations concerned with the peaceful development of nuclear energy.

Office of Reactor Deployment
Office of Nuclear Energy
U.S. Department of Energy
DOE-NE-40
1000 Independence Avenue, SW
Washington, DC 20545
(301) 353-3773

This office deals with high-temperature reactor technology, light-water reactor research in the areas of safety and development and evaluation of plant system technology, component evaluation, development and testing, and fuel fabrication technology, among other things. It publishes an annual statistical report comparing utilities on a state and regional basis.

Office of Remedial Action and Waste Technology
Nuclear Energy
U.S. Department of Energy
GTN, NE-20, Room E435
Washington, DC 20585
(301) 353-5006

This office is concerned with planning, developing, and executing programs for the treatment of civilian nuclear waste and for low-level waste management. It also is concerned with the decontamination and decommissioning of legislatively authorized, nongovernment facilities. It helps to develop beneficial uses of nuclear waste byproducts.

Office of Technology Support Programs
Nuclear Energy
U.S. Department of Energy
GTN, NE-46, Room H404
Washington, DC 20585
(301) 353-3609

An agency that conducts and coordinates the civilian reactor technology support program and coordinates and cooperates with federal agencies in developing and executing international efforts in the field of nuclear power reactor development. It is the principal contact in the federal government for the National Liquid Metal Fast Breeder Reactor Program.

Professional Reactor Operator Society
P.O. Box 181
Mishicot, WI 54228
(414) 863-6996

A group composed of licensed and certified nuclear reactor operators, their supervisors, nonlicensed and retired operators, manufacturers, and utilities. It seeks to develop communication among reactor operators, government, Congress, and industrial firms to promote the safe and efficient operation of nuclear installations. The organization publishes a newsletter and holds an annual convention.

Radioactive Waste Campaign (RWC)
625 Broadway, 2nd Floor
New York, NY 10012
(212) 473-7390

Concerned with informing individuals about nuclear waste disposal dangers and the new technology available to deal with waste disposal, and with aiding individuals in fighting nuclear waste dumps in their areas. Supplies speakers, conducts research, and publishes fact sheets and a quarterly newspaper.

Research and Analysis Division
Legislative Affairs
U.S. Department of Energy
1000 Independence Avenue, SW, 8E070
Washington, DC 20585
(202) 252-8687

This agency keeps a daily tally on all energy legislation being dealt with by the Congress and can provide information on the status of such legislation.

Senate Committee on Energy and Natural Resources
358 Dirksen Senate Office Building
Washington, DC 20510
(202) 224-4971

Has jurisdiction over energy policy, nonmilitary nuclear energy policy, hydroelectric power, and other areas. Subcommittee on Energy Regulation and Conservation, (202) 224-4971; Subcommittee on Energy Research and Development, (202) 224-4971; Subcommittee on Water and Power, (202) 224-4971.

Senate Committee on Environment and Public Works
410 Dirksen Senate Office Building
Washington, DC 20510
(202) 224-6176

Has jurisdiction over environmental policy, solid waste, water resources, air and noise pollution, fisheries and wildlife, among other things. Subcommittee on Environmental Protection, (202) 224-6691; Subcommittee on Hazardous Wastes and Toxic Substances, (202) 224-5031; Subcommittee on Nuclear Regulation, (202) 224-4039.

Society for the Advancement of Fission Energy (SAFE)
336 Coleman Drive
Monroeville, PA 15146
(412) 374-2222

An association of individuals interested in future electrical supplies, particularly in terms of encouraging the use of nuclear energy sources. The organization conducts seminars and publishes a kit for persons who wish to establish local energy organizations interested in nuclear energy. May be currently inactive.

Spanish Nuclear Society (SNS)
Department of Nuclear Energy
ETS Ingenieros Industriale
Universidad Politrecnica de Madrid
Paseo de la Castellana 80
Madrid 6
Spain
Tel. 1 4114064

An organization involved in the development of discussions and participation in educational programs concerning nuclear energy. It is made up largely of nuclear scientists interested in developing the nuclear industry in Spain. Publishes a monthly and an annual periodical.

Transportation System Development Center
Sandia National Laboratories
P.O. Box 5800
Albuquerque, NM 87185
(505) 844-4296

The national center for the research of nuclear waste transportation and development programs and of waste storage and disposal. It serves as an office to integrate U.S. Department of Energy programs on this subject with those of other national government agencies and of private industry.

Union of Concerned Scientists
26 Church Street
Cambridge, MA 02238
(617) 547-5552

An interest group concerned with, among other subjects, the impact of nuclear power on society, nuclear plant safety, arms control policy, nuclear waste disposal, the nuclear arms race, and energy policy alternatives. It carries on educational programs and distributes research results to the public. Has a speakers bureau and library, publishes books and periodicals on the subject of nuclear energy, and engages in legislative lobbying.

U.S. Department of Energy
1000 Independence Avenue, SW
Washington, DC 20585
(202) 252-5000

A department of the national government of the United States responsible for creating a comprehensive national energy program. It is also responsible for research and development in energy technology in all areas, including nuclear energy, and is concerned with energy conservation, marketing federal power, nuclear weapons, regulation of energy production and its use, and waste programs. It has a vast data collection and analysis program that deals with virtually all aspects of energy, both domestic and international.

U.S. Department of Energy Historian
Chief Historian, Office of the Secretary
U.S. Department of Energy
1000 Independence Avenue, SW, Room MSG033
Washington, DC 20585
(202) 252-5235

The energy historian is responsible for producing the official history of the U.S. Department of Energy and its predecessor offices. The historian decides which records and documents to retain and provides policy and analysis information. Helpful in all aspects of the energy area, including the development of nuclear energy and its current ramifications.

U.S. Environmental Protection Agency (EPA)
401 M Street, SW
Washington, DC 20460
(202) 382-4355

Objectives are to protect and enhance the present environment for today's citizens as well as for future generations. Under legislation enacted by Congress, EPA is involved in controlling and abating water and air pollution and pollution from solid waste materials, radiation, toxic substances, and noise.

Uranium Mill Tailings Remedial Actions Project Office
Albuquerque Operations Office
U.S. Department of Energy
P.O. Box 5400
Albuquerque, NM 87115

Functions as a cleanup agency at 24 uranium mill tailings sites in 11 states and the Navajo Indian Reservation in New Mexico. These sites, although privately owned, sold uranium oxide milled there to the former Atomic Energy Commission. The U.S. Environmental Protection Agency has set standards that must be met by the AEC and its successor agencies.

Utility Nuclear Waste Management Group
1111 19th Street, NW
Washington, DC 20036
(202) 778-6512

An organization of electric utilities that promotes solutions to the problem of radioactive nuclear waste management. It develops task forces and inquiry groups to research and investigate specific problems related to the nuclear waste issue. It monitors high- and low-level waste management efforts and publishes a newsletter.

Western Interstate Energy Board
6500 Stapleton Plaza
3333 Quebec Street
Denver, CO 80207
(303) 377-9459

A group of 16 western states that assists governors and legislators in influencing the national government on matters affecting their region with respect to the orderly development of energy resources. Among its interests are topics related to high-level radioactive wastes, uranium, alternative fuels, energy conservation, and uranium mining. It publishes a newsletter and an annual report and analyzes various energy problems.

World Information Service on Energy (WISE)
Postbus 5627
NL-1007
AP Amsterdam
Netherlands
Tel. 20 853857

Distributes information related to nuclear power, nuclear weapons, alternative energy sources, and related areas. It is largely a networking organization for antinuclear groups throughout the world. It maintains a library and publishes biweekly reports and books.

6

Reference Materials

THE FOLLOWING LIST of reference materials is intended to help the reader understand the development of nuclear energy policy from the 1930s to the present. Thus, several early bibliographies and references are listed that some readers might feel are dated. These references are intended to provide exposure to some of the early literature in the field. Wherever possible, page numbers and ISBN numbers have been provided.

Articles

Asselstine, James K. **"The Future of Nuclear Power after Chernobyl."** *Virginia Journal of Natural Resources Law* 6:2 (Spring 1987), 239–261.

This article discusses the consequences of the Chernobyl accident and the impact of the accident on U.S. nuclear policy. The continuing credibility of the Nuclear Regulatory Commission is examined, and the conclusion is that public confidence needs to be improved if nuclear plants are to have a future in the United States.

Ausness, Richard. **"High Level Radiation Waste Management: The Nuclear Dilemma."** *Wisconsin Law Review* 1979, 707–767.

This is an excellent overview of radioactive waste and its many hazards. Among topics treated are high-level waste management; treatment, reprocessing, and transportation of waste; and the problems of disposal. The article discusses goals for high-level waste management and the need for the development of a responsible waste management program.

Barron, Jillian. **"After Chernobyl: Liability for Nuclear Accidents under International Law."** *Columbia Journal of Transnational Law* 25:3 (1987), 647–672.

This article discusses the extent of the spread of radiation; judicial decisions and national practice related to such matters; conventions, declarations, and codifications of international law; the existing standards of liability; government civil liability for nuclear damages; and a proposal for a liability standard, among other topics.

Brandt, Debra Branom. **"Fueling the Fire of Nuclear Debate: It's Time To Plan for the Scrapping of Nuclear Power Plants."** *Southern Illinois University Law Journal* 1978:1, 536–555.

This article emphasizes the steps that must be taken to prepare for the decommissioning of the nation's nuclear reactors. It treats the legal framework for nuclear regulation; the basics of the National Environmental Policy Act of 1969; the problems of nuclear power plant disposal; taking action for disposal of nuclear plants; and the role of the states in planning for decommissioning, with an emphasis on Illinois. The article emphasizes that inasmuch as nuclear plants are designed with a planned lifetime of about 40 years, their decommissioning must be planned out long in advance.

Cavers, David E. **"State Responsibility in Regulation of Atomic Reactors."** *Kentucky Law Journal* 50 (1961–1962), 29–51.

This article discusses the division of authority between the federal and state governments with respect to nuclear reactors. It treats such matters as whether the states should be authorized to license reactors and gives examples of what has transpired in various states. Also discusses state laws and cases on the subject.

Clancy, Kevin. **"Unresolved Safety Issues in Nuclear Power Plant Licensing: Reasonable Assurance of Safety or Nuclear Shell Game?"** *Columbia Journal of Environmental Law* 7:1 (Fall 1980), 99–119.

This article treats the problems inherent in the Nuclear Regulatory Commission's power to formulate standards and license nuclear facilities in the United States. It discusses licensing procedures, the Three Mile Island incident, the analysis of risk in individual determinations, and the problems involved in judicial review and concludes that courts will in the future pay less deference to the Nuclear Regulatory Commission.

Cole, Sterling. **"The Power and the Prize—The Development of Civilian Nuclear Power in the United States."** *The George Washington Law Review* 25:4 (April 1957), 471–491.

This article encompasses a broad discussion of the legislative framework for the development and use of atomic energy; the roles of both government and industry; the policy of the Atomic Energy Commission; the status and development of atomic energy; the development of atomic energy both in the United States and other countries; problems faced by Congress in the atomic energy field; and the future of nuclear energy policy. This is a good early review.

Daub, William. **"Meeting the Challenge to Nuclear Energy Head-On."** *Atomic Energy Law Journal* 15:4 (Winter 1974), 238–264.

This article addresses the energy crisis of the 1970s and "what can or should be done to streamline the process to license and build commercial nuclear reactors . . . to help meet our energy requirements" (p. 238). It discusses industry responsibility, short-term nuclear projects, delays, long-term views, standardization, and related matters. A good overview.

Dean, Gordon. **"The Impact of Atomic Energy on the Law."** *The Journal of the Bar Association of the District of Columbia* 19:7 (July 1952), 282–292.

This article is the text of the address given by Gordon Dean at the Bar Association. It addresses a summary of the Atomic Energy Act of 1946 and emphasizes the duality of atomic energy—its application to both defense and human welfare—and the limitations placed upon private enterprise in the area of atomic energy, while at the same time stimulating private industry to engage in peaceful development of nuclear facilities. The legal aspects are addressed in a general way.

Dean, William Tucker. **"The Atomic Energy Act of 1946."** *The Journal of the Bar Association of the State of Kansas* 15:3 (February 1947), 255–260.

This is a good brief summary of the major provisions of the Atomic Energy Act of 1946. For persons totally unfamiliar with the act, this will provide a useful introduction. The article concludes with the suggestion that effective administration of the act will require skill and understanding by lawyers and that the act will require amendments in the future.

Gorove, Stephen. **"Distinguishing 'Peaceful' from 'Military' Uses of Atomic Energy: Some Facts and Considerations."** *Ohio State Law Journal* 30:3 (Summer 1969), 495–501.

This article discusses international control arrangements related to atomic energy, the difficulties involved in distinguishing between the peaceful and military uses of atomic energy, the fact that the difficulty is more than just a lexical one, the issue of interpretation, and the notion that reinterpretation of the problem is continually necessary. It emphasizes the immense complexity of distinguishing one application of atomic energy from another.

Grammer, Elisa J. **"The Uranium Mill Tailings Act of 1978 and NRC's Agreement State Program."** *Natural Resources Lawyer* 13:3 (1981), 469–522.

This article provides a good overview of uranium milling and the consequences of inadequate tailings management. It also provides a detailed discussion of the Uranium Mill Tailing Radiation Control Act of 1978, and the effects of the act upon the Agreement State Program.

Green, Harold P. **"Safety Determinations in Nuclear Power Licensing: A Critical View."** *Notre Dame Lawyer* 43:5 (June 1968), 633–656.

This article discusses the dangers of nuclear plants; the then-existing "regulatory scheme"; licensing procedures then prevailing; adequacy of licensing procedures; and experience versus prediction in the licensing process. The article on the whole is a plea for protection of the public interest.

Handl, Gunther. **"Transboundary Nuclear Accidents: The Post-Chernobyl Multilateral Legislative Agenda."** *Ecology Law Quarterly* 15:2 (1988), 203–248.

The article treats the following subjects: internationally binding safety standards; monitoring compliance with safety standards; the expansion of international exchanges of nuclear safety information; means to mitigate the effects of nuclear accidents; the status of IAEA conventions; reparation of transboundary nuclear harm; and standards of source state liability and related matters.

Helm, Charles. **"Is Opposition to Nuclear Energy an Ideological Critique?"** *American Political Science Review* 82:3 (September 1988), 943–946.

"In the June 1987 issue of this *Review*, Stanley Rothman and S. Robert Lichter offered evidence to support their argument that 'the new environmental movement in the United States is partly a symbolic issue,' that elites in the news media and in public interest groups misrepresent the dangers of nuclear energy as a surrogate for more direct criticism of liberal capitalism in the United States. In this controversy, Charles J. Helm expresses skepticism about the Rothman-Lichter line of argument; and they respond" (p. 943). The Rothman-Lichter response is found on pp. 947–951.

Horn, Michael. **"Nuclear Energy Safety."** *Harvard International Law Journal* 28:2 (Spring 1987), 558–567.

A discussion of the Convention on Early Notification of a Nuclear Accident (opened for signature on September 26, 1986, and entered into force on October 27, 1986), and the Convention on Assistance in the Case of a Nuclear Accident or Radiological Emergency (opened for signature on September 26, 1986, and entered into force February 26, 1987).

Jacks, W. Thomas. **"The Public and the Peaceful Atom: Participation in AEC Regulatory Proceedings."** *Texas Law Review* 52:3 (March 1974), 466–525.

This article deals with the extent to which members of the public are allowed to participate in the nuclear regulatory process. It treats such topics as the dangers of the nuclear generating process (e.g., loss of coolant, earthquakes, sabotage, radiation release from routine operations, effects on aquatic life); licensing procedures; functional and dysfunctional activities of intervenors; and the proper role of intervenors. Also provides some recommendations.

Kaplan, Morton. **"The Nuclear Non-Proliferation Treaty: Its Rationale, Prospects and Possible Impact on International Law."** *Journal of Public Law* 18:1 (1969), 1–20.

This article focuses on the rationale, the prospects, and the impact on international law of the nuclear nonproliferation treaty. The major conclusion is that the treaty will probably fail because it is largely unenforceable: How will those nations currently possessing nuclear power prevent those not possessing it from acquiring it?

Key-Smith, Frances S. **"Atom Bomb and Monroe Doctrine."** *The Journal of the Bar Association of the District of Columbia* 13:10 (October 1946) 449–454.

An argument that maintaining atomic secrets will continue to protect the Western Hemisphere and, especially, the U.S. form of republican government.

Lass, Leslie. **"The Price-Anderson Act: If a 'Chernobyl' Occurs in the United States, Will the Victims Be Adequately Compensated?"** *Glendale Law Review* 7:2 (1987), 200–216.

The Price-Anderson Act ensured that claimants have an asset pool from which damages may be recovered. Without this act, the possibility is real that utility companies would be unable to pay claims arising out of major accidents. The article argues that Congress should implement a more relaxed standard for proving causation, should extend the statute of limitations to at least 40 years after a nuclear accident, and should state whether punitive damages would be allowed in the case of recklessness or indifference to the rights of others. Victims of nuclear accidents should not bear the burden of uncertainty during recovery from their injuries.

Lewis, Leonard J., and C. Keith Rooker. **"Domestic Uranium Procurement—History and Problems."** *Land and Water Law Review* 1:2 (1966), 449–471.

This article examines the exploration, development, and production of domestic uranium deposits; discusses the history of evaluation of the rigidly controlled program of the regulation of these factors; and considers stretchout contracts involving purchase obligations, computation of royalties, and related issues.

Magee, John. **"The Uranium Mill Tailings Radiation Control Act of 1978."** *Ecology Law Quarterly* 8:4 (1980), 801–809.

This article discusses the hazards of uranium mining, emphasizing that concern over these hazards has been only a recent development. It considers federal regulation and provides an analysis and assessment of the environmental effects of the act.

Miller, Byron S. **"A Law Is Passed—The Atomic Energy Act of 1946."** *University of Chicago Law Review* 15:4 (Summer 1948) 799–821.

An excellent and detailed account of the development of the Atomic Energy Act of 1946, from the May-Johnson Bill through various committees of the Senate, the McMahon Bill, final passage, and the primary issues. It also discusses the major alignments in the debate over the act.

"National Energy Forum 1978: Government Helping or Hurting?" A **Symposium.** *University of Tulsa Law Journal* 13:4 (1978), 659–801.

This symposium includes articles on coal production and conversion; oil and gas regulation; environmental restrictions on exploration and development of oil and gas; the Federal Energy Regulatory Commission (FERC) and natural gas regulation; and a good section on nuclear energy that includes plant regulation, proposed nuclear legislation, state regulation of nuclear power, and storage and disposal of radioactive wastes.

Neel, James N., Jr. **"Federal or State Jurisdiction over Atomic Products and Waste—A Dilemma."** *Kentucky Law Journal* 50 (1961–1962), 52–60.

This article discusses the role of the states in assuming authority over byproduct, source, and special nuclear materials. Although a major focus of the article is Kentucky, it has general applications and deals at length with the provisions of the Atomic Energy Act of 1954.

Newman, James R., and Byron S. Miller. **"Patents and Atomic Energy."** *Law and Contemporary Problems* 12:4 (Autumn 1947), 746–764.

This article discusses the juxtaposition of the need for security in atomic energy matters and the right to protect private property. Patent provisions proved to be one of the most controversial issues discussed during the debates on the Atomic Energy Act of 1946. The article discusses such matters as the devices used in the production of fissionable materials and military weapons; the devices used in research; reporting procedures; licensing and royalties; compensation; and related topics.

"Nuclear Waste Disposal: A Symposium." *Tennessee Law Review* 53:3 (Spring 1986), 475–678.

This symposium is composed of eight articles dealing with "nuclear waste, what good is it?"; the law of high-level nuclear waste; high-level waste repository siting; public participation in waste management programs; options for gathering information about waste shipments; the debate on mixing nuclear and chemical wastes; sites for low-level waste; and the role of the proposed host state for waste materials.

"Nuclear Weapons and Constitutional Law: A Symposium." *Nova Law Journal* 7:1 (Fall 1982), 1–178.

The 15 articles in this symposium focus on such matters as nuclear weapons and constitutional law; protecting posterity; nuclear war as the end of law itself; nuclear weapons policy; the frailties and the strengths of the Constitution to deal with nuclear weapons; international law as the law of the land; the wisdom required to deal with nuclear policy; the notion that law may not in fact resolve the nuclear debate; the question as to whether nuclear weapons may be unconstitutional; and related subjects.

Oppenheimer, J. Robert. **"Contemporary Problems of Atomic Energy."** *Oklahoma Bar Association Journal* 22:12 (March 31, 1951), 457–465.

In this article, Dr. Oppenheimer discusses a broad range of issues related to the early development of the atom, atomic energy, and especially its potential wartime uses. The article also touches upon policy, protection against the abuse of atomic energy, military and civilian options, and a range of related topics.

Rocchio, David M. **"The Price-Anderson Act: Allocation of the Extraordinary Risk of Nuclear Generated Electricity: A Model Punitive Damages Provision."** *Boston College Environmental Affairs Law Review* 14:3 (1987) 521–560.

This article discusses, among other things, the development and implementation of the Price-Anderson Act, its legislative history, its judicial interpretation, and suggested reforms. The article also presents a model statutory provision.

Rothman, Stanley, and S. Robert Lichter. **"The Nuclear Energy Debate: Scientists, the Media, and the Public."** *Public Opinion,* August/September 1982, 47–52.

This article reports the results of an opinion survey of the attitudes of Americans toward nuclear energy. It demonstrates, for example, that while scientists and nuclear experts are overwhelmingly in favor of accepting nuclear risks and having plants locate in their cities, and strongly possessed of the belief that we have sufficient knowledge to solve any nuclear problems, public support has tended to decline. The role of the media in this anomaly is discussed.

Ruebhausen, Oscar M. **"Toward a New Atomic Policy."** *The Record of the Association of the Bar of the City of New York* 8:5 (May 1953), 229–242.

This article discusses the "healthy concern" that Americans were entering into regarding the nuclear policy of the United States during these early years of atomic development. The article argues basically that the "solution for our present uncertain state of affairs lies in increased and informed public discussion" (p. 229).

Ruebhausen, Oscar M., and Robert B. von Mehren. **"The Atomic Energy Act and the Private Production of Atomic Power."** *Harvard Law Review* 66:8 (June 1953), 1450–1496.

This article discusses the development of atomic power, examining technical and economic facts; the industrial participation program; possible institutional patterns (such as government monopoly, partnership between government and industry, and regulated private enterprise); various legal problems (e.g., monopoly, secrecy, patents, antitrust); and, in general, attempts to show "where the nation now stands in the development of commercial power from atomic energy and how it got there" (p. 1495).

Schwan, Charles E., Jr., and Stuart Urbach. **"The Suggested State Radiation Control Act."** *Kentucky Law Journal* 50 (1961–1962), 13–28.

This article reviews the history of the State Radiation Control Act, including Public Law 86-373, from the time of the enactment of the Atomic Energy Act of 1954. It points out that there was a "lengthy, deliberate, and careful" drafting process of the act. The provisions of the act are discussed and the role of state participation in the regulation of nuclear materials is examined.

Seaborg, Glenn T. **"Nuclear Power—Status and Outlook."** *Atomic Energy Law Journal* 12:1 (Spring 1970), 36–58.

In this reprinted speech, Seaborg discusses the fact that nuclear power has become an important and rapidly growing element in the energy process; indeed, he anticipated that within 30 years nuclear power would be generating over half of the nation's electrical power. His remarks emphasize the importance of the breeder reactor and its usefulness, and suggest greater public participation in the siting of facilities. Future challenges are also discussed.

"A Symposium on Atomic Energy." *Texas Law Review* 34:6 (June 1956), 799–923.

A technical symposium dealing with such issues as the rules of practice of the Atomic Energy Commission, the licensing and regulating of private atomic activities, compliance with regulations, patents, international business aspects of the Atomic Energy Act of 1954, mining rights, and uranium tax problems.

"Symposium on Atomic Energy and the Law." *California Law Review* 46:1 (March 1958), 3–98.

Six articles focus on such topics as the law of torts and atomic energy; liability in nuclear accidents; legislative readjustments in federal/state regulatory powers; patent protection in the area of nuclear energy; federal licensing; and state regulation of atomic hazards.

"Symposium on Atomic Power Development." *Law and Contemporary Problems* 21:1 (Winter 1956), 1–210.

The nine articles of this symposium focus on atomic power development; the changing role of the Atomic Energy Commission; democratic control of the development of atomic energy; public investment; information control; patent aspects; the role of public electrical power; international aspects of atomic energy; and the role of the states in the development and control of nuclear energy.

"A Symposium on Nuclear Energy and the Law." *Vanderbilt Law Review* 12:1 (December 1958), 1–228.

This symposium focuses on lawyers' responsibilities in the nuclear age; international cooperation and the peaceful uses of atomic energy; atomic energy and world trade; the effects of radiation; tort liability; the law of reactor safety; workman's compensation; labor relations; antitrust provisions; federal support of power development; and some legal aspects of atomic development in the United Kingdom. A good bibliography of materials up to the date of publication is also included.

Walker, John S. **"Legal Control of Thermonuclear Energy: The Atomic Energy Act and the Hydrogen Program."** *Michigan Law Review* 52:8 (June 1954) 1099–1136.

A discussion set in the context of the development of the hydrogen bomb and the Atomic Energy Act of 1946, this article considers the McMahon Act and whether it can be relied upon to provide for control of thermonuclear energy. The article concludes with the argument that "thermonuclear energy must be accorded the perspective and the awful prestige which are its due.. . .[F]resh and searching legislative effort is a basic first step which is completely within our power and our duty to take" (p. 1136).

Walske, Carl. **"The Outlook for the U.S. Nuclear Industry."** *Nuclear Europe* 10 (October 1983), 21–24.

The article discusses the need for new nuclear plants, generation of electricity, and future production in a context of sustained energy growth. In general, the article is highly optimistic about the use of nuclear power in the future, stating that "the long-term outlook for the nuclear option remains excellent" (p. 21).

Wolf, Martin L. **"Some Legal Aspects of the Atomic Energy Act."** *The Georgetown Law Journal* 36 (1947–1948), 73–86.

This is an overview of the early development of the Atomic Energy Act from the date of the Einstein letter to Franklin D. Roosevelt in 1939. It provides a brief legislative history of the act; discusses the powers of the Atomic Energy Commission; examines congressional control of the commission; describes presidential powers under the act; discusses restrictions the act places on freedom of speech and press; describes patent controls and licensing; and refers to international controls and the practical difficulties encountered.

Bibliographies

Atomic Energy Commission Group, United Nations Department of Security Council Affairs. **An International Bibliography on Atomic Energy.** 2 vols., supplements. New York: United Nations, 1949–1952.

These volumes and their supplements contain thousands of references (in several languages) to books, documents, pamphlets, articles, audio-visual aids, and other materials that deal with political, economic, social, and scientific aspects of atomic energy. It is an extraordinarily comprehensive bibliography and a good basic research tool.

Boswell, Jane E. **A Bibliography of Current Materials Dealing with Atomic Power and Related Atomic Energy Subjects for Non-Specialists and Lay Persons.** Detroit: G. H. Craig Fund for Peaceful Atomic Development, Inc., 1955.

A bibliography for the general reader. It avoids highly technical matters and is aimed at overall enlightenment of the lay public.

Browne, M. L. **"Legal Aspects of Atomic Power Plant Development: A Selective Bibliography."** *Atomic Energy Law Journal* 13:1 (Spring 1971), 50–75.

Most of the citations in this bibliography are from the 1950s and some are from the 1960s. The material is arranged under four subjects: background, regulation and licensing, liability and safety, and insurance. It is a useful source for government documents of the period, but many of the entries are of comparatively less scholarly value.

Burns, Grant. **The Atomic Papers.** Metuchen, NJ, and London: Scarecrow Press, 1984. 323p. ISBN 0-8108-1692-X.

This bibliography is subtitled "A citizen's guide to selected books on the bomb, the arms race, nuclear power, the peace movement, and related issues." Its coverage is extensive, but its selections seem to indicate an antinuclear bias.

Controlled Fusion Atomic Data Center. **Atomic Collisions Bibliography Categorizations List.** Oak Ridge, TN: Oak Ridge National Laboratory, 1986. 1p.

This is a list of bibliography categories used by the Controlled Fusion Atomic Data Center. It also contains references to reviews, books, bibliographies, abbreviations, and a country code.

Energy Information Administration. **EIA Publications Directory 1987: A User's Guide.** Washington, DC: National Energy Information Center, U.S. Department of Energy, 1987. 125p.

This is one of the annual user's guides provided by the U.S. Department of Energy. Its many entries cover such topics as coal and coal products, natural gas, nuclear fuels, solar energy, electric power, nuclear power plants, and energy planning and policy. The annotations are excellent; it is one of the better sources with which the layperson can begin a literature review.

Goehlert, Robert. **Studies on Energy Policy: A Selected Bibliography.** Monticello, IL: Vance Bibliographies, December 1982. 14p. ISSN 0193-970X.

Although not focused on nuclear energy, this is an excellent, brief bibliography covering the late 1970s and early 1980s. It includes references to journal articles and major books.

Hazelton, Penny. **"The Literature Labyrinth of Nuclear Power: A Bibliography."** *Environmental Law* 6:3 (Spring 1976), 921–943.

A selected, general bibliography of bibliographies, government documents, "current awareness tools," books, and legal periodical articles from 1957 to about 1975. It is not as extensive as some bibliographies, but will provide the reader with a useful introduction to the middle years of atomic energy literature.

International Atomic Energy Agency. **List of Bibliographies on Nuclear Energy.** Vienna, Austria: International Atomic Energy Agency, 1970.

This list covers bibliographies related to nuclear energy in a wide range of subfields and in various countries working in the area of atomic energy development.

Los Angeles County Law Library staff. **"Atomic Energy Bibliography."** *Utah Law Review* 5 (1956), 136–140.

This bibliography consists of general articles and articles pertaining to mining law, public lands, and prospecting; atomic energy administration and control; atomic energy and private industry; insurance, patents, and taxes; medicine; and atomic warfare. It is interesting to note that the Murphy bibliography, published in 1958, contains most of the material cited here.

Losee, M. W. **"Blueprint for Atomic Energy Literature: Legislative and Legal."** *Law Library Journal* 53 (1960), 184–196.

Publications from the following sources are annotated by the author: (1) U.S. Atomic Energy Commission, (2) Joint Committee on Atomic Energy, (3) other federal government organizations, (4) private organizations, (5) material related to state and local governments, (6) international organizations. This is a very good overview of the literature in the fields indicated.

McCormack, J. A. **Bibliography on Uses of Radioactive and Stable Isotopes in Industry; A List of Selected References.** TID-3511. Washington, DC: U.S. Atomic Energy Commission, 1957. 27p. Available from Office of Technical Services, U.S. Department of Commerce, Washington, DC.

This bibliography is composed of 455 references to articles from the open literature of the time; it includes an author index and literature reference sources.

Murphy, Eileen. **"Atomic Energy and the Law: A Bibliography."** *Vanderbilt Law Review* 12:1 (December 1958), 229–270.

This is an excellent early bibliography, divided into seven sections: (1) legislation on atomic energy, 1946–1958; (2) Joint Committee on Atomic Energy publications, 1945/46–1958; (3) books (the bibliographer has annotated them); (4) U.S. and foreign periodicals (again annotated); (5) a selected list of law review articles, 1946–1948; (6) a selected list of nonlegal periodical articles, 1955–1958; (7) sources (such as the Office of Technical Services, Microcopy, AEC Depository Libraries).

Nuclear America: A Historical Bibliography. Santa Barbara, CA: ABC-CLIO Information Services, 1984. 184p. ISBN 0-87436-360-8.

This bibliography contains abstracts of 824 articles drawn from ABC-CLIO Information Services' database. All of the entries relate directly to the United States, and are organized around the following topics: "The Road to Hiroshima"; "The Development of Nuclear Energy"; "The Balance of Terror"; "Attempts at Nuclear Arms Control"; and "Nuclear Reactors and Public Reaction." This volume is an indispensable introduction to materials published on the topic between 1973 and 1982.

Rycroft, Robert W., Timothy Hall, Don E. Kash, and Irvin L. White. **Energy Policy-Making: A Selected Bibliography.** Norman: University of Oklahoma Press, 1977. 179p. ISBN 0-8061-1448-7.

Although not annotated, this bibliography provides a good introduction to energy literature through the mid-1970s. Nuclear energy is treated in the context of a broad approach described in the introductory essay as an attempt "to provide guidance in understanding contemporary substantive issues."

Sandia National Laboratories. **Bibliography of Published Radioactive Material Transportation Reports Produced by Sandia National Laboratories, 1979–July 1, 1988.** Albuquerque, NM: Sandia National Laboratories, 1988.

This is a bibliography containing hundreds of references to reports produced by Sandia on a wide-ranging series of subjects, e.g., radioactive waste management, measurements in high-intensity fires, materials issues in cask development, potential environmental impact of radioactive material transportation to the first repository site in the United States, and many other topics related to radioactive materials transportation. An extraordinarily comprehensive list.

Sinnott, J. P. **"A Bibliography of Early Radiation Damage Litigation in the United States."** *Atomic Energy Law Journal* 3 (1961), 23–31.

A narrow bibliography, but extremely useful to those interested in all the cases involving radiation damage case law in the United States up to 1961.

Technical Information Service Extension, U.S. Atomic Energy Commission. **Cumulated Numerical List of Available Unclassified U.S. Atomic Energy Commission Reports.** TID-4000-2d ed. Oak Ridge, TN: 1956. 244p. Available from Office of Technical Services, U.S. Department of Commerce, Washington, DC.

Section 1 of this document lists all AEC unclassified reports abstracted in *Nuclear Science Abstracts,* volumes 1–8, and its predecessor, *Abstracts of Declassified Documents,* volumes 1–2. Section 2 lists all non-AEC reports appearing in the same journals; sections 3 and 4 are the same as the Numerical Index of Reports in *Nuclear Science Abstracts.*

———. **What's Available in the Unclassified Atomic Energy Literature.** TID-4550-4th rev. Oak Ridge, TN: 1958. 60p.

This is a very useful guide to available literature sponsored by the Atomic Energy Commission and how to find and use it.

U.S. Nuclear Regulatory Commission. **Regulatory and Technical Reports (Abstract Index Journal).** Washington, DC: Regulatory Publications Branch, Division of Freedom of Information and Publications Services, Office of Administration and Resources Management, U.S. Nuclear Regulatory Commission, 1988. 47p.

This is an excellent bibliography for the specialist or more technically trained reader. It consists of bibliographic data and abstracts for the formal regulatory and technical reports of the Nuclear Regulatory Commission staff and its contractors. Single copies may be acquired from the National Technical Information Service, Springfield, Virginia 22161.

Voress, Hugh E. **Bibliographies of Interest to the Atomic Energy Program.** TID-3043-rev. ed. Washington, DC: U.S. Atomic Energy Commission, 1958. Available from Office of Technical Services, U.S. Department of Commerce, Washington, DC.

This is a collection of various bibliographies on a variety of subjects that relate to the overall development of the nuclear energy program in the United States, generally up to 1958.

Books and Monographs

Allardice, Corbin, and Edward R. Trapnell. **The Atomic Energy Commission.** New York: Praeger, 1974. 236p. ISBN 0-275-55460-1.

This is a comprehensive account of the Atomic Energy Commission. It traces the origins of the commission from Albert Einstein's letter of August 2, 1939, to Franklin D. Roosevelt to the creation of the Atomic Energy Act of 1946, which gave control of the commission to civilians. A separate chapter describes the organization of the old Atomic Energy Commission and the relationship of universities and industries engaged in atomic research to the Atomic Energy Commission.

Clarfield, Gerard H., and William M. Wiecek. **Nuclear America: Military and Civilian Nuclear Power in the United States, 1940–1980.** New York: Harper & Row, 1984. 518p. ISBN 0-06-015336-9.

This book is described as "the first complete, comprehensive history of United States nuclear policy from 1940 to 1980" (dust jacket). It covers events from the development of the atomic bomb through the policies of various administrations, ending with the Carter administration.

Clark, Ronald W. **The Greatest Power on Earth: The International Race for Nuclear Supremacy.** New York: Harper & Row, 1980. 342p. ISBN 0-060-14846-2.

This book traces the history of nuclear power from the 1930s through the invention of the bomb, tending to emphasize the military. The author writes from a British perspective, but the topic is treated in terms of its international implications. A very well written book that serves as a highly useful treatment of the subject.

Cohen, Bernard L. **Before It's Too Late. A Scientist's Case for Nuclear Energy.** New York: Plenum Press, 1983. 292p. ISBN 0-306-41425-2.

This book is a plea for the development of nuclear energy. It covers such topics as the difficulties the public has in understanding the problem of nuclear power, the question of the dangers of radiation, meltdown accidents, how to understand risk, the hazards of high-level radioactive waste, plutonium and the nuclear bomb, terrorist activity, the costs of nuclear power, the solar "dream," public opinion and the polls, "questions from the audience," and an unabashed appeal for help in solving the world's energy crisis. It is an excellent book and a good antidote for the doomsayers.

Colglazier, E. William, ed. **The Politics of Nuclear Waste.** New York: Pergamon Press, 1982. 264p. ISBN 0-08-026323-2.

Various experts address the issues of nuclear waste management, the problems resulting from congressional and executive branch factions, the conflict between federal and state levels, and public participation in decision making, among other topics.

Committee for the Compilation of Materials on Damage Caused by the Atomic Bombs in Hiroshima and Nagasaki. **Hiroshima and Nagasaki: The Physical, Medical, and Social Effects of the Atomic Bombings.** Eisei Ishikawa and David L. Swain, trans. New York: Basic Books, 1981. 706p. ISBN 0-465-02987-6.

This is probably the definitive study of the effects of the attacks on Hiroshima and Nagasaki. The work suggests that the consequences of the bombings were horrifying; the text is supported by graphic illustrations.

Evans, Nigel, and Chris Hope. **Nuclear Power: Futures, Costs, and Benefits.** Cambridge: Cambridge University Press, 1984. 171p. ISBN 0-521-261910.

Although this book has a British focus, it does present a very useful summary of the development of nuclear power in North America, Western Europe, the Pacific, and the developing world. There is a particularly good section on meltdown risks and informative discussions on the economics of nuclear energy and trade in nuclear electricity.

Goldschmidt, Bertrand. **The Atomic Complex: A Worldwide Political History of Nuclear Energy.** La Grange Park, IL: American Nuclear Society, 1982. 520p. ISBN 0-89448-550-4.

A review of the international development of nuclear energy. This book discusses the major decision makers and the primary political developments in the international arena of nuclear power development. International nuclear power organizations and the emerging science and technology of nuclear power are discussed in the context of the international political history of nuclear power.

Grotwohl, Manfred. **World Energy Supply: Resources, Technologies, Perspectives.** Berlin and New York: Walter de Gruyter, 1982. 450p. ISBN 3-11-008153-9.

This is a highly technical book dealing with the interdisciplinary and international ramifications of the future supply of world energy. It takes the position that "controlled nuclear fusion will eventually be possible" and that this will result in "a practically unlimited supply of energy" (p. 3).

Groves, Leslie R. **Now It Can Be Told: The Story of the Manhattan Project.** New York: Harper, 1962. 465p. ISBN 0-306-70738-1. Reprinted 1975, DaCapo.

This is a first-person account of the history of the Manhattan Project by the U.S. general who directed it—very interesting reading.

Gyorgy, Anna, and friends. **No Nukes: Everyone's Guide to Nuclear Power.** Boston: Southend Press, 1979. 478p. ISBN 0-89608-007-2.

An extremely interesting book that deals with such subjects as the history of nuclear energy, the economics of nuclear power, alternatives to nuclear power, the international ramifications of nuclear energy, and a national overview in terms of "educate, agitate, organize." The book clearly expresses an antinuclear point of view.

Hewlett, Richard G., and Oscar Anderson, Jr. **The New World, 1939–1946.** vol. 1. 766p. ISBN 0-87079-471-X.

Hewlett, Richard G., and Francis Duncan. **Atomic Shield, 1947–1952.** vol. 2. 718p. ISBN 0-87079-473-6.

Hewlett, Richard G., and Francis Duncan. **A History of the United States Atomic Energy Commission.** 718p. ISBN 0-271-00103-8.

University Park, PA: Pennsylvania State University Press, 1962, 1969.

These volumes are the definitive and exhaustive history of the U.S. Atomic Energy Commission. They are meticulously detailed; the casual reader might find them difficult. Nevertheless, they are worth consulting for the best treatment of the subject.

Holl, Jack M., Roger M. Andrews, and Alice M. Buck. **United States Civilian Nuclear Power Policy, 1954–1984: A Summary History.** Washington, DC: U.S. Department of Energy, 1986.

Available from the Technical Information Service, U.S. Department of Commerce, Washington, DC.

Hunt, S. E. **Fission, Fusion, and the Energy Crisis.** 2nd ed. Oxford: Pergamon Press, 1980. 166p. ISBN 0-08-024734-2.

This book deals with the atom and its nucleus, fission, the bomb, uranium reactors, enriched reactors, control and safety, long-term economics, short-term economics, national nuclear programs, nuclear power and the environment, renewable energy resources, and the concept of a fusion program. It is an excellent introduction to the concept of atomic energy.

Institute for Contemporary Studies. **Options for U.S. Energy Policy.** San Francisco: Institute for Contemporary Studies, 1977. 317p. ISBN 0-91761-620-0.

In this book, 12 economists and engineers who specialize in energy policy devote their attention to energy problems related to national security, the environment, safety, and the general role of government in the policy process. Nuclear power is treated particularly from the perspectives of proliferation and the problems of safety and the environment.

International Atomic Energy Agency. **Environmental Aspects of Nuclear Power Stations.** Proceedings of a symposium. New York. August 10–14, 1970. Vienna: International Atomic Energy Agency, 1971. 970p.

An excellent early introduction and survey of the problems related to siting of nuclear power stations and nuclear power as an energy source, standards for effluent control, monitoring, steam power, and site selection and benefit-risk assessment.

Jungk, Robert. **Brighter than a Thousand Suns: A Personal History of the Atomic Scientists.** James Cleugh, trans. New York: Harcourt, Brace, 1956, 1958, 1970. 369p. ISBN 0-15-614150-7.

This is an early history of the development of nuclear energy. It is particularly concerned with the personal relationships among the scientists who worked on the atomic bomb. Originally written in German, it presents an interesting central European view of events leading to the development of nuclear power.

Kash, Don E., and Robert W. Rycroft. **U.S. Energy Policy: Crisis and Complacency.** Norman: University of Oklahoma Press, 1984. 334p. ISBN 0-8061-1869-5.

This book argues, quite effectively, that the United States does not have an energy policy, and that the Reagan administration in particular has been responsible for "a radical departure from traditional U.S. policy-making processes." Although the development of nuclear energy is viewed by the authors as one element on "the path to stability," they are doubtful that the issues surrounding nuclear energy permit anything but pessimism about its future.

Katz, James Everett. **Congress and National Energy Policy.** New Brunswick, NJ: Transaction Books, 1984. 287p. ISBN 0-87855-486-6.

This book provides an excellent overview of the impact of Congress upon the attempts to develop a national energy policy for the United States. The author provides interesting insights into the dynamics of Congress and the policy-making process. Nuclear energy policy, per se, is not a major emphasis, but the book leads to an understanding of how Congress is involved in the energy policy process.

Kursunoglu, Behram, and Arnold Perlmutter, eds. **Directions in Energy Policy: A Comprehensive Approach to Energy Resource Decision-Making.** Cambridge, MA: Ballinger Publishing Company, 1979. 519p. ISBN 0-88410-089-8.

This volume presents statements on the major issues involving the production and use of various energy forms, by economists, physicists, engineers, legal scholars, political scientists, industrialists, and various government officials. The primary conclusion is that nuclear energy provides the only viable avenue of transition toward the quest of a practical energy policy for the future.

Lilienthal, David E. **Atomic Energy: A New Start.** New York: Harper & Row, 1980.

Lilienthal was the first chairman of the Atomic Energy Commission. In this book, he generally supports the development of nuclear energy, but suggests that safety may not have been given enough consideration. He also recommends that alternatives to the light-water reactor be energetically sought out.

Lilienthal, David E. **The Atomic Years: 1945–1950.** New York: Harper & Row, 1964. 666p.

This is the second volume of Lilienthal's diary entries. His comments provide a type of insider's view of the early years in the development of the Atomic Energy Commission and also portray the positions that required critical examination during these early years of the evolution of atomic energy in the United States.

Lipschulz, Ronnie D. **Radioactive Waste: Politics, Technology, and Risk.** Cambridge, MA: Ballinger Publishing Company, 1980. 247p. ISBN 0-88410-621-7.

This book deals with such subjects as the nature and hazards of radioactivity; the nuclear fuel cycle; management, storage, and disposal of waste; the history of waste management; and the requirements for a successful program of waste management. It includes several appendixes, a glossary, references, and a bibliography.

Lowinger, Thomas C. **Energy Policy in an Era of Limits.** New York: Praeger, 1983. 223p. ISBN 0-03060-423-0.

This book, in the author's words, "contains a detailed albeit selective evaluation of the formulation and implementation of United States energy policy in the post oil-embargo period. . . .[I]t seeks to gain a better understanding of the reasons and factors behind our all too obvious inability to forge an effective and consistent set of energy policies in the past decade" (pp. 5–6). Chapter 4 in particular discusses the "critical state" of the role of the nuclear industry in the formulation of contemporary energy policy in the United States, and takes the position that "the failure to realize the full potential of nuclear power could jeopardize efforts to reduce our oil dependence and to ensure an adequate provision of electricity" (p. 6).

Murphy, Arthur W., ed. **The Nuclear Power Controversy.** Englewood Cliffs, NJ: Prentice-Hall, 1976. 184p. ISBN 0-13-625582-5.

This is a brief and excellent treatment of the controversy over the development of nuclear energy. Each chapter is written by an expert on the respective subject; topics covered include safety aspects of nuclear energy, economics of electrical power generation, the likelihood of developing nuclear energy in the context of institutional and social

structures, the regulation of nuclear plants, exports and nonproliferation strategies, and related subjects. The study concludes with the
question, "Nuclear power: How much is too much?"

National Academy of Sciences. **U.S. Energy Supply Prospects to 2010.**
Washington, DC: National Academy of Sciences, 1979. 213p. ISBN
0-309-02936-8.

This book discusses such matters as the current energy picture, electricity, oil and gas, coal, and advanced energy resources. Chapter 5, in
particular, deals with nuclear energy: technology, the fuel cycle, issues
and constraints, growth scenarios, and related subjects.

Nesbit, William, ed. **World Energy: Will There Be Enough in 2020?**
Decisionmakers Bookshelf, vol. 6. Washington, DC: Edison Electric
Institute, 1979. 74p. ISBN 0-931032-06-7.

This publication provides a very useful discussion of the demand and
supply of energy including sections on oil, natural gas, coal, nuclear,
geothermal, hydraulic, solar, and hydrogen. The introduction summarizes the major issues involved in meeting energy needs to the year 2020.

Patterson, Walter C. **Nuclear Power.** 2nd ed. New York: Penguin
Books, 1983. 256p. ISBN 0-14-02-2499-8.

This is possibly the best one-volume introduction to the entire topic of
nuclear energy policy for the layperson. The author, a Canadian, writes
from a British point of view, treating both technical and historical events
in nuclear power and reactor development. He retains a rather skeptical
point of view about nuclear energy but, at the same time, attempts a cool
objectivity.

Penner, S. S., ed. **Energy: Volume III Nuclear Energy and Energy
Policies.** One of a three-volume set of lecture notes. Reading,
MA: Addison-Wesley Publishing Company, 1976. 713p. ISBN 0-201-
05564-3.

This volume consists of a series of highly technical lectures on nuclear
fission energy, breeder reactors, controlled thermonuclear fusion, environmental aspects of nuclear power applications, nuclear strategies, and
energy policies. Clearly too complex for the beginner, but for someone
who desires a broad overview in a more advanced stage, it is nothing
short of excellent.

Rose, David J. **Learning about Energy.** New York and London: Plenum
Press, 1986. 508p. ISBN 0-306-42124-0.

A highly technical but excellent introduction to the range of issues surrounding the entire energy topic, with emphasis on the technological aspects. It treats such subjects as how to think about energy, time perspectives and economics of energy policy, acid deposition and global carbon dioxide, the rational uses of energy, oil and gas reserves, coal and its derivatives, nuclear power, solar power, and energy storage and electric system integration. The book provides a holistic view of the energy problem.

Rosenbaum, Walter A. **Energy, Politics, and Public Policy.** 2nd ed. Washington, DC: CQ Press, 1987. 221p. ISBN 0-87187-412-1.

This book presents an excellent overview of the current apparent indifference in the United States with respect to the development of a viable energy policy. The book emphasizes the political nature of the development of energy policy and addresses the important issues of government institutions, political culture, and political history in development of policy. Chapter 5, "The Politics of Inertia: Nuclear Power," is a particularly good overview of the difficulties of developing a workable nuclear policy.

Seaborg, Glenn T., and William R. Corliss. **Man and Atom: Building a New World through Nuclear Technology.** New York: Dutton & Co., 1971. 411p. ISBN 0-52515-099-4.

The authors discuss a wide range of peaceful applications of nuclear energy as a means of solving modern society's most urgent energy problems. They approach the uses of nuclear energy with a set of facts and assess the future of fission and fusion power. This is an optimistic view of the potential of nuclear energy.

Simpson, John, ed. **Nuclear Non-Proliferation: An Agenda for the 1990s.** Cambridge: Cambridge University Press, 1987. 237p. ISBN 0-521-33308-3.

This book provides an excellent overview of nonproliferation efforts since the adoption of the nonproliferation treaty in 1968. Individual experts treat subjects including the international political system of the 1990s, the development of new technologies, the existence of nuclear arsenals, the options for strengthening nonproliferation in the 1990s, and the issues and prospects for the future. The book contains a copy of the nonproliferation treaty.

Sweet, William. **The Nuclear Age: Atomic Energy, Proliferation, and the Arms Race.** 2nd ed. Washington, DC: Congressional Quarterly, Inc., 1988. 340p. ISBN 0-87187-466-0.

An informative overview of the nuclear power situation during its "mid-life crisis." It treats the widening nuclear debate, nuclear energy from the perspective of how reactors work, nuclear economics, uncertain risks and unsolved problems, the issues of nuclear proliferation, and the arms race. It concludes with comments on a "post-nuclear age" and has a good list of suggested readings.

U.S. Congress. **Nuclear Power in an Age of Uncertainty.** Washington, DC: U.S. Congress, Office of Technology Assessment, February 1984. OTA-E-216.

An excellent overview of such subjects as the seven-sided nuclear debate, the uncertain financial and economic future of nuclear energy, various alternative reactor systems, the management of the nuclear enterprise, regulation of nuclear power, the likely survival of the nuclear energy industry in the United States and abroad, public attitudes, and policy options. There are appendixes dealing with acronyms and a glossary.

Weinberg, Alvin M., et al., Institute for Energy Analysis, Oak Ridge Associated Universities. **The Second Nuclear Era.** New York: Praeger, 1985. 460p.

A study concerned mainly with the decline of the nuclear era in the United States, it nevertheless argues that current nuclear reactors are much safer than those built in the past and suggests that the United States might be entering into a second nuclear era during which nuclear power might be restored as a leading energy provider.

Encyclopedias, Yearbooks, and Handbooks

Atoms for Peace Manual: A Compilation of Official Materials on International Cooperation for Peaceful Uses of Atomic Energy, December 1953–July 1955. Senate Document No. 55, 84th Congress, first session. Washington, DC: U.S. Government Printing Office, 1955. 615p.

A government document that assembles international materials on the peaceful uses of atomic energy and on international cooperation in this area.

Coffman, F. E., M. R. Murphy, K. W. Kearney, K. R. Schultz, and B. L. Scott. **Fusion Power by Magnetic Confinement: Questions and Answers.** Division of Magnetic Fusion Energy, May 1977. 41p. Available from National Technical Information Service, U.S. Department of Commerce, 5285 Port Royal Road, Springfield, Virginia 22161.

A very useful brief booklet, in question-and-answer format, that addresses such issues as perspectives on energy, the fusion process, the environmental impact and safety of the fusion process, magnetic fusion program goals, plasma physics, and reactor technology. It also contains a useful bibliography and a list of acronyms.

Dennis, Jack, and faculty members of the Massachusetts Institute of Technology. **The Nuclear Almanac: Confronting the Atom in War and Peace.** Reading, MA: Addison-Wesley Publishing Company, 1984. 546p. ISBN 0-201-05332-1.

This is an extremely useful overview of the entire gamut of nuclear energy as it has developed. It covers such topics as the Manhattan Project, the superbomb and Hiroshima and Nagasaki, the development of civilian authority over atomic affairs, nuclear weapons effects, nuclear war, biological and radiological effects, nuclear accidents, nuclear energy, international issues, and the future of responsible public policy. It is heavily illustrated with tables, diagrams, photographs, and charts.

Fusion in Our Future. N.p., n.d. 23p. For further information contact Fusion Power Associates, 2 Professional Drive, Suite 248, Gaithersburg, MD 20760.

This is an excellent brief overview of fusion energy and its many potential applications in electric power, medicine and health, food preservation, reactor fuel, defense, space propulsion, and other areas. It is beautifully illustrated and easily understood by the nonspecialist.

Glasstone, Samuel. **Sourcebook on Atomic Energy.** 2nd ed. Princeton: Van Nostrand, 1958. 641p. ISBN 0-88257-898-5.

This is an extensive handbook covering all aspects of the atomic energy field, with particular emphasis on the nuclear energy program of the federal government.

Goldblat, Jozef. **Arms Control Agreements: A Handbook.** New York: Stockholm International Peace Research Institute, Praeger, 1983.

This is an excellent overview, analysis, and assessment of arms control negotiations and agreements, free from government bias. It is intended as a handbook for students of arms control and disarmament as well as for politicians and laypersons. It contains the texts of and the parties to the major arms control agreements throughout history.

Kaku, Michio, and Jennifer Trainer. **Nuclear Power: Both Sides. The Best Arguments For and Against the Most Controversial Technology.** New York: W. W. Norton, 1982. 279p. ISBN 0-393-01631-5.

This is an attempt to clarify the nuclear controversy by presenting both sides of the issue. Twenty-one essays by authorities in physics, economics, industry, and other areas address opponents' views as well as laying out their own. This volume is intended as a sourcebook of information and is not aimed at winning the debate on either side.

Kinsman, Simon, et al., comps. and eds. **Radiological Health Handbook.** Cincinnati: Robert A. Taft Sanitary Engineering Center, 1957. 355p. Available from the Office of Technical Services, U.S. Department of Commerce, Washington, DC.

This is a useful reference book for training in radiological health. It contains a glossary, tables and charts of radiation data, and a table of isotopes.

League of Women Voters Education Fund. **The Nuclear Waste Primer: A Handbook for Citizens.** New York: Nick Lyons Books, 1985. 90p. ISBN 0-8052-6006-4.

This book attempts to present an unbiased view of the major facts about nuclear waste and how to deal with radioactive residues. The book is aimed at encouraging citizen involvement in the policy-making processes related to this issue. It contains lists of government agencies the citizen might contact, nongovernmental agencies involved in the issue, publications relevant to the topic, and a glossary. This is a brief but good introduction to the subject.

Lesko, Matthew. **Lesko's New Tech Sourcebook.** New York: Harper & Row, 1986. 726p. ISBN 0-06-181509-8.

A useful compendium of information dealing with all aspects of the new technology, including an excellent section on nuclear energy and where to find information on various aspects of the subject.

Makower, Joel, and Alan Green, eds. **Instant Information.** New York: Prentice-Hall, 1987. 768p. ISBN 0-13-467804-4.

A very useful book that provides information on a variety of subjects, including aspects of nuclear energy, especially organizations involved in disseminating information in connection with the subject.

Martocci, Barbara, and Greg Wilson. **A Basic Guide to Nuclear Power.** Washington, DC: Edison Electric Institute, 1987. 20p.

A booklet that explains how nuclear energy works and how it is used to make electricity. It offers a glossary of terms and discusses atoms, fission, heat production, electrical generation, radiation, the nuclear fuel cycle, nuclear waste, and nuclear power today. The pamphlet is written on the sixth-grade level.

National Bureau of Standards Handbooks. Washington, DC: U.S. Government Printing Office, 1949–1957.

These are recommended procedures for industrial and engineering practice and safety codes. Although somewhat dated, the handbooks reveal early concerns about standards of atomic safety. Those relevant to atomic energy are listed below.

Safe Handling of Radioactive Isotopes. 1949. 30p.

Control and Removal of Radioactive Contamination in Laboratories. 1951. 24p.

Recommendations for Waste Disposal of Phosphorus-32 and Iodine-131 for Medical Users. 1951. 11p.

Radiological Monitoring Methods and Instruments. 1952. 33p.

X-ray Protection Design. 1952. 36p.

Maximum Permissible Amounts of Radioisotopes in the Human Body and Maximum Permissible Concentrations in Air and Water. 1953. 45p.

Recommendations for the Disposal of Carbon-14 Wastes. 1953. 14p.

Safe Handling of Cadavers Containing Radioactive Isotopes. 1953. 15p.

Permissible Dose from External Sources of Ionizing Radiation. 1954. 79p.

Photographic Dosimetry of X- and Gamma Rays. 1954. 79p.

Protection against Betatron-Synchrotron Radiations up to 100 Million Electron Volts. 1954. 52p.

Protections against Radiations from Radium, Cobalt-60, and Cesium-137. 1954. 60p.

Radioactive Waste Disposal in the Ocean. 1954. 31p.

Regulation of Radiation Exposure by Legislative Means. 1955. 60p.

X-ray Protection. 1955. 41p.

International Coommission Radiological Units and Measurements. Report. 1956, 1957. 48p.

Design of Free-air Ionization Chambers. 1957. 16p.

Protection against Neutron Radiation up to 30 Million Electron Volts. 1957. 88p.

National Research Council Conference on Glossary of Terms in Nuclear Science and Technology. **A Glossary of Terms in Nuclear Science and Technology.** New York: American Society of Mechanical Engineers, 1957. 188p.

A list of some of the most important terms used in the development of nuclear science and nuclear technology.

Nuclear Proliferation Factbook. Washington, DC: U.S. Government Printing Office, 1985.

Prepared by the Environment and Natural Resources Policy Division, Congressional Research Service, Library of Congress for the Subcommittee on Arms Control, International Security, and Science and on International Economic Policy and Trade, Committee on Foreign Affairs, House of Representatives, and the Subcommittee on Energy, Nuclear Proliferation, and Federal Processes, Committee on Governmental Affairs, Senate.

Pearman, William A., and Phillip Starr. **The American Nuclear Power Industry: A Handbook.** New York: Garland Publishers, 1985. 112p. ISBN 0-8240-8968-5.

This book examines the scope, diversity, capacity, and control of nuclear power in the United States. Chapters focus on safety, environmental, and antitrust issues, as well as on case studies of selected nuclear power plants. An appendix containing federal government library resources on nuclear power is also included, and there is a selected bibliography.

Semler, H. Eric, James J. Benjamin, Jr., and Adam P. Gross. **The Language of Nuclear War: An Intelligent Citizen's Dictionary.** New York: Harper & Row, 1986. 256p. ISBN 0-06-096123-6.

This book is labeled as "[t]he first comprehensive, clearly written dictionary of nuclear terminology, history and strategy [that] provides a solid base for understanding what scientists, politicians, and experts are talking about concerning nuclear issues. It covers nuclear weaponry, strategies, treaties, reports, organizations, slang words, and history in its over 1200 entries."

Severud, Fred N., and Anthony F. Merrill. **The Bomb, Survival, and You: Protection for People, Buildings, Equipment.** New York: Reinhold, 1954. 264p. ISBN 0-686-34519-3. *Technical Supplement* by Kurt Bernhard and Fred N. Severud.

This handbook explains how existing and new structures can be strengthened to withstand atomic blasts of various magnitude. The *Technical Supplement* presents mathematical analyses of blast loadings.

United Nations Secretariat, Department of Conference Services. **Provisional Glossary on Atomic Energy.** Terminology Bulletin No. 115. New York: United Nations, 1955. 291p.

This book lists scientific and technical terms used in atomic energy, arranged in parallel columns, and gives the English, French, Spanish, and Russian equivalents.

U.S. Atomic Energy Commission. **Atomic Energy Facts: A Summary of Atomic Activities of Interest to Industry.** Nuclear Technology Series. Washington, DC: U.S. Government Printing Office, 1957. 216p.

The preface states: "This volume is intended primarily as a source book for industrial management. It is hoped, however, that teachers, writers, and others interested in atomic energy will find the book useful for their purposes."

U.S. Nuclear Regulatory Commission. **1988 Annual Report.** Washington, DC: U.S. Government Printing Office, 1989. 224p.

An excellent summary of the activities of the Nuclear Regulatory Commission covering such matters as nuclear reactor regulation, the cleanup at Three Mile Island, operational experience, nuclear materials regulation, safeguards, waste management, communicating with government and with the public, nuclear regulatory research, litigation, management and administrative services, and other subjects.

Journals and Periodicals

In a book this size, an attempt to include a comprehensive list of journals and periodicals that have included articles on nuclear energy policy is bound to end in frustration. Thousands of periodicals in the United States and around the world have contained articles dealing in one way or another with nuclear policy. Some of the best articles have appeared in law journals—a fact attested to by the number of articles drawn from them that have been included below. Even an attempt to list the law journals that have published articles on nuclear energy would itself require a small book. The authors have therefore excluded hundreds of periodicals that might have been mentioned in this section.

Annual Review of Nuclear and Particle Science. Annual Reviews, Inc., Palo Alto, CA. ISSN 0163-8998.

This annual review offers critical articles on nuclear science, nuclear physics, and particle science. It contains a selection of the year's leading research in the areas of nuclear and particle science.

Atomic Absorption Newsletter. The Perkin-Elmer Corporation, 761 Main Avenue, Norwalk, CT. Bimonthly. $14 per year.

This is a journal for technicians and scientists who work in the field of atomic absorption and chromatography. Each article includes an abstract of the findings.

Atomic Energy Law Journal. Management Reports, Inc., 89 Beach Street, Boston, MA 02111. Quarterly.

This journal discusses all aspects of atomic energy from a policy and legal perspective. Some examples of topics covered are standardization in nuclear power, the proper role of the public in nuclear decision making, licensing, national energy policy, and uranium enrichment.

Atomic Spectroscopy. The Perkin-Elmer Corporation, 761 Main Avenue, Norwalk, CT. 6/year. No charge. ISSN 0195-5373.

A journal containing articles on new applications and analytical data in atomic absorption spectrophotometry and its related disciplines of atomic fluorescence, atomic emission, and ICP-mass spectrometry. Most articles are written by professionals in the field of spectroscopy. This is an international journal that contains a current bibliography in the first and fourth issues of each year.

Bulletin of the Atomic Scientists. Educational Foundation for Nuclear Science, Inc., Kenwood, IL. Monthly. $24.50 per year; $2.50, individual copy. ISSN 0096-3402.

A popularly slanted journal that provides analyses of both civilian and military nuclear power, nuclear science, nuclear arms and weaponry, nuclear proliferation, and arms control. The journal is generally critical of the problems that have marked the evolution of the civilian development of nuclear energy and raises questions about nuclear power and nuclear weaponry.

Energy Abstracts for Policy Analysis. Office of Scientific and Technical Information, U.S. Department of Energy, P.O. Box 62, Oak Ridge, TN 37831. Monthly plus an index. Subscription available from the Superintendent of Documents, U.S. Government Printing Office, Washington, DC 20402.

This periodical is concerned with all aspects of the energy process, but is "limited primarily to nontechnological or quasitechnological articles or reports having significant reference value." It especially emphasizes "programmatic efforts; policy, legislative, and regulatory aspects; social, economic, and environmental impacts; regional and sectoral analyses, institutional factors, etc."

Energy Law Journal. Federal Energy Bar Association and the National Energy Law and Policy Institute, University of Tulsa College of Law. 2/year.

Functions of the periodical are "to promote the proper administration of the federal laws relating to production, development, conservation, transmission and economic regulation of energy."

Energy Policy. Butterworth Scientific, Ltd., P.O. Box 101, Sevenoaks, Kent TN15 8 PL, United Kingdom. Bimonthly.

International journal that includes articles on any aspect of energy policy and energy planning.

Energy Research Abstracts. Office of Scientific and Technical Information, U.S. Department of Energy, P.O. Box 62, Oak Ridge, TN 37831. Semimonthly. Subscription available from the Superintendent of Documents, U.S. Government Printing Office, Washington, DC 20402.

This journal "provides abstracting and indexing coverage of all scientific and technical reports, journal articles, conference papers and proceedings, books, patents, theses, and monographs originated by the U.S. Department of Energy, its laboratories, energy centers, and contractors."

Environment. Heldref Publications, 4000 Albemarle Street, NW, Washington, DC 20016. Monthly, combined issues in Jan./Feb. and July/Aug. $23 per year; $4.50, individual copy.

Publishes articles on all apsects of the energy situation.

Environmental Law. Lewis and Clark Law School students, Northwestern School of Law. 3/year.

This journal carries articles dealing with all aspects of energy, including nuclear power and its many nuances and ramifications.

Fusion Power Report. Business Publishers, Inc., 951 Pershing Drive, Silver Spring, MD 20910-4464. Monthly. $315 per year. ISSN 0276-2919.

This monthly newsletter aims at "complete coverage of worldwide fusion developments." It has included articles on such wide-ranging topics as the International Thermonuclear Engineering Reactor, efforts to declassify information related to the inertial confinement fusion program, personality profiles and appointments, work being undertaken in Japan, news briefs, and a calendar of events related to fusion activities.

International Journal of Applied Radiation and Isotopes. Pergamon Press, Elmsford, NY. $110 per year. ISSN 0020-708X.

A journal of nuclear medicine, it contains articles dealing with experiments and research in nuclear medicine and with the variety of procedures used in nuclear medicine and radionuclide preparation.

International Journal of Nuclear Medicine and Biology. Pergamon Press, Elmsford, NY. Quarterly. $135 per year. ISSN 0047-0740.

This journal publishes papers on various aspects of and research in nuclear medicine, radio immunoassay, and radionuclide assessment in medical practice and research. Quite specialized, but highly respected for its coverage and quality.

Journal of Energy and Development. International Research Center for Energy and Economic Development, University of Colorado. 2/year. $32 per year. ISSN 0361-4476.

Publishes articles on energy-related topics in conservation and environment, domestic and international issues, and others.

Nuclear Instruments and Methods in Physics Research. Physics Publishing, North Holland Publishing Company, Amsterdam, The Netherlands. Semimonthly. $260 per year. ISSN 0167-5087.

This journal provides a forum for discussion on research in all aspects of the interaction of energetic beams with atoms, molecules, and aggregate forms of matter. The journal publishes both theoretical and experimental papers based on original research.

Nuclear Law Bulletin. Organization for Economic Development and Cooperation. 2/year. $6.25 per copy. ISSN 0304-341X.

A journal established by the Nuclear Energy Agency of the Organization for Economic Cooperation and Development to promote the orderly development of the uses of nuclear energy for peaceful purposes. The journal seeks articles focusing on cooperative efforts between governments in developing nuclear energy. It also deals with regulatory policy, forecasts of uranium resources, production and demand, and cooperation in the field of nuclear energy information.

Nuclear Physics. North Holland Publishing Company, P.O. Box 211, Amsterdam, The Netherlands. Weekly. ISSN 0029-5582.

A journal devoted to the experimental and theoretical study of matter and their interactions. Most articles deal specifically with issues in nuclear physics and problems of the constituents of matter.

Nuclear Safety: A Technical Progress Overview. Office of Science and Technology Information, U.S. Department of Energy. Quarterly. $16 per year; $7.50, individual copy. Available from Superintendent of Documents, U.S. Government Printing Office, Washington, DC. ISSN 0029-5604.

A journal devoted to coverage of significant developments in the field of nuclear safety. It focuses on analysis and control of hazards associated with nuclear energy, operations involving fissionable materials, and products of nuclear fission and their effects on the environment. The journal is prepared for the U.S. Department of Energy and the U.S. Nuclear Regulatory Commission by the Nuclear Operations Analysis Center at the Oak Ridge National Laboratory.

Nuclear Science Abstracts. ERDA Technical Information Center, U.S. Department of Energy, Washington, DC. Semimonthly. 12 issues for $119; $7.40, individual copy.

Provides indexes to all literature of ERDA origin as well as nonnuclear information generated by foreign countries with which ERDA has cooperative agreements. This journal offers information on international nuclear literature.

Nuclear Science and Engineering. American Nuclear Society. Monthly. $125 per year; $34, individual copy. ISSN 0029-5639.

A technically oriented journal that publishes research in such areas as reactor performance, reactor kinetics, steam-explosion containment failure, and reactor theory.

OCRWM Bulletin. Office of Civilian Radioactive Waste Management, U.S. Department of Energy, Washington, DC 20585. Monthly.

A typical issue might include articles dealing with the status of cask design, limits for radiation doses, meetings of various agencies concerned with waste disposal and licensing, upcoming events, and a list of new publications and documents.

Physical Review: Nuclear Physics. American Physical Society. Monthly. $365 per year. ISSN 0556-2813.

This journal contains articles dealing with research and experiments on nuclear reactors, heavy ions, fission, intermediate energy, radioactivity, and nuclear structure.

Radiation Research. Academic Press, New York, NY. Monthly. $46 per year. ISSN 0033-7587.

This journal, a publication of the Radiation Research Society, publishes articles on physics, chemistry, biology, and medical research dealing with radiation effects and related subjects. Articles are accompanied by an abstract, references, and bibliography.

Scholarly Papers

Atomic Industrial Forum

The following professional papers are available from the Atomic Industrial Forum, Inc., 7101 Wisconsin Avenue, Bethesda, MD 20814-4891.

No. 231. *Fuel Cycle 1986.* Collected Papers. AIF Conference. Scottsdale, AZ. April 1–4, 1986. $187.50 (members); $375 (nonmembers).

No. 236. *Uranium 1986.* Collected Papers. AIF Conference. Moran, WY. September 14–17, 1986. $187.50 (members); $375 (nonmembers).

No. 238. *Reducing the Cost of Nuclear Power.* Collected Papers. AIF Conference. New Orleans, LA. May 18–21, 1986. $187.50 (members); $375 (nonmembers).

No. 239. *Management of Spent Fuel and Radioactive Wastes.* Collected Papers. AIF Conference. Washington, DC. September 16–19, 1979. $50 (members); $100 (nonmembers).

No. 240. *Waste Transportation and the Public: A Seminar for Public Information and Public Affairs Specialists.* Collected Papers. AIF Seminar. Albuquerque, NM. February 21–23, 1984. $125 (members); $250 (nonmembers).

No. 241. *Solutions to Nuclear Transportation Issues.* Collected Papers. AIF Conference. Monterey, CA. June 16–19, 1985. $50 (members); $100 (nonmembers).

No. 242. *The High Level Waste Business—Transportation, Storage & Disposal.* Collected Papers. AIF Conference. Charleston, SC. October 19–22, 1986. $187.50 (members); $375 (nonmembers).

No. 243. *Measurement of Radiation in and around Uranium Mills (PR3/9)*. Collected Papers. Cosponsored by Atomic Industrial Forum, Inc., U.S. Environmental Protection Agency, U.S. Energy Research and Development Administration, American Nuclear Society, and Health Physics Society. Albuquerque, NM. May 23–24, 1977. $20.

No. 244. *Radiation Issues for the Nuclear Industry*. Collected Papers. AIF Conference. New Orleans, LA. October 3–6, 1982. $50 (members); $100 (nonmembers).

No. 245. *Radiation Protection: Standards and Regulatory Issues*. Collected Papers. AIF Conference. Orlando, FL. October 7–10, 1984. $187.50 (members); $375 (nonmembers).

No. 247. *Licensing*. Collected Papers. AIF Conference. Dallas, TX. May 19–22, 1985. $50 (members); $100 (nonmembers).

No. 248. *Insurance Issues*. Collected Papers. AIF Conference. New Orleans, LA. January 21–25, 1985. $50 (members); $100 (nonmembers).

No. 249. *Legal Issues*. Collected Papers. AIF Conference. New Orleans, LA. January 21–25, 1985. $50 (members); $100 (nonmembers).

No. 250. *Nuclear Power Financing*. Collected Papers. AIF Conference. Las Vegas, NV. February 7–10, 1982. $50 (members); $100 (nonmembers).

No. 253. *Industry's Role in the Development of Fusion Power*. Collected Papers. AIF Conference. New York, NY. May 2–6, 1981. $50 (members); $100 (nonmembers).

No. 254. *Environmental Regulation: Looking Ahead*. Collected Papers. AIF Conference. Monterey, CA. June 11–14, 1978. $15 (members); $30 (nonmembers).

Bandrowski, Michael S. **"Regulation of Higher-Activity NARM Wastes by EPA."** Paper prepared for presentation at DOE's 10th Annual LLW Management Conference. Denver, CO. August 30–September 1, 1988.

The abstract of the paper reads, in part: "The U.S. Environmental Protection Agency . . . is currently developing standards for the disposal of low-level radioactive waste (LLW). As part of this Standard, EPA is including regulations for the disposal of naturally occurring and accelerator-produced radioactive material (NARM) wastes not covered under the Atomic Energy Act .. . . The regulations will cover only higher-activity NARM wastes, defined as NARM waste with specific activity exceeding two nanocuries per gram. The proposed regulations will specify that NARM wastes exceeding the above limits, except for specified exempted items, must be disposed of in regulated radioactive waste disposal facilities." Michael S. Bandrowski serves as a member of the U.S. Environmental Protection Agency, Office of Radiation Programs.

Clary, Bruce B., and Michael E. Kraft. **"Impact Assessment, Policy Failure and the Nuclear Waste Policy Act."** Paper prepared for presentation at the 1988 meeting of the Western Political Science Association. San Francisco. March 10–12, 1988.

The abstract states, in part: "The Nuclear Waste Policy Act established a process of environmental assessment which was to lead to the choice of a site for the nation's first nuclear waste repository. Due to the highly toxic nature of radioactive waste and the length of its potentially harmful effects, which can run into the tens of thousands of years, the central question which the assessments had to address was the extent to which a repository could isolate the waste from the environment. The purpose of this paper is to understand the policy impact of the assessments." Bruce B. Clary is in the Public Policy and Management Program of the University of Southern Maine, and Michael E. Kraft is in the Robert M. LaFollette Institute of Public Affairs, University of Wisconsin–Madison.

Finger, Harold B. **"The Environmental and Other Imperatives of Nuclear Power."** Paper prepared for the American Nuclear Society Topical Conference on Radiological Effects on the Environment Due to Electricity Generation. July 19, 1988.

This paper is a discussion, in part, of the environmental impact of manmade radiation. A major thesis of the paper is, "Our nuclear energy is safe; we do know how to handle the waste and have been doing so from the start; and nuclear energy is and always has been cost-competitive" (p. 1). The paper emphasizes the drive for excellence in the industry, the broad public acceptance of nuclear energy, some evidence of growing support in Washington to develop the industry, the need to invest in the future, and the necessity of nuclear energy to supply the country's future electrical needs. Harold B. Finger is president and chief executive officer of the U.S. Council for Energy Awareness.

Galpin, Floyd L., James M. Gruhlke, and William F. Holcomb. **"EPA's Low-Level and NARM Waste Standards: An Update."** Paper prepared for presentation at the Annual Meeting of the Conference of Radiation Control Program Directors, Inc. Nashville, TN. May 13–19, 1988.

The abstract reads in part as follows: "The Environmental Protection Agency . . . program to develop proposed generally applicable environmental standards for land disposal of low-level radioactive waste and certain naturally occurring and accelerator-produced radioactive wastes has been completed. The elements of the proposed standards include the following: (1) exposure limits for pre-disposal management and storage operations; (2) criteria for other regulatory agencies to follow in specifying wastes that are Below Regulatory Concern (BRC); (3) post-disposal exposure limits; (4) ground water protection requirements; and (5) qualitative implementation requirements." The authors are members of the U.S. Environmental Protection Agency, Office of Radiation Programs, Washington, DC.

Galpin, F. L., W. F. Holcomb, J. L. Russell, R. L. Clark, and R. S. Dyer. **"EPA's Regulatory Activities in Radioactive Waste Disposal."** Paper prepared for presentation at the Spectrum '88 International Topical Meeting on Nuclear and Hazardous Waste Management. Pasco, WA. September 11–15, 1988.

The abstract of the paper reads: "The USEPA has issued and is developing generally applicable environmental standards for the disposal of radioactive wastes. Standards have been issued for the disposal of spent nuclear fuel, high-level and transuranic wastes, and for uranium mill tailings. Standards are being developed for the land disposal of low-level radioactive wastes and for wastes considered 'Below Regulatory Concern.' Regulations for ocean disposal of low-level radioactive wastes are also under consideration." The authors are members of the U.S. Environmental Protection Agency, Office of Radiation Programs, Washington, DC.

7

Nonprint Materials
and Resources

PRINTED GUIDES AND OTHER RESOURCES dealing with nonprint
materials are listed in the Sources of Information section beginning on page 202. Addresses for industry associations and government departments and agencies that distribute nonprint
materials are given in the Sources of Materials section beginning
on page 203. Other distributors' addresses are included in the
entries for individual nonprint items.

Computer Software

Computer software packages prepared by DOE, the Nuclear
Regulatory Commission (NRC), and their contractors, as well as
the Nuclear Energy Agency in Saclay, France, are collected,
analyzed, announced, sample–problem tested (where appropriate), archived, and disseminated by the National Energy Software
Center, which is operated by the Office of Scientific and Technical
Information, Argonne National Laboratory. Over 1,700 computer programs are currently available. Among topics available
are nuclear physics and technology, power plant economics,
particle accelerators, magnetic fusion, radiological safety and
accident analysis, and others. Copies of the programs are available
from National Technical Information Service, 5285 Port Royal
Road, Springfield, VA 22161.

Databases

EIC/Intelligence
Energy Information System
245 West 17th Street
New York, NY 10011
(212) 337-6989

A division of the R. R. Bowker Company, the Energy Information System consists of print, microform, and computer-readable material covering the entire field of energy. Included is the Energyline database, which contains abstracts and indexes of literature from throughout the world. The system produces publications from the database and also offers a microfiche service for the text of articles found in Energyline. Containing some 80,000 records, Energyline is updated monthly. Energyline is accessible through Orbit Search Service, Dialog Information Services, Inc., and ESA/IRS. Magnetic tape copies of Energyline may be obtained from EIC/Intelligence. Publications include *Energy Information Abstracts* and *Energy Index and Abstracts Annual,* both available by subscription.

Electric Power Database (EPD)
Electric Power Research Institute (EPRI)
Technical Information Division
3412 Hillview Avenue
P.O. Box 10412
Palo Alto, CA 94303
(415) 855-2411

The EPD contains summaries of ongoing or completed research by the Electric Power Research Institute and by utilities in the United States, Canada, Japan, and Mexico. The database covers all aspects of energy, including nuclear power. The Electric Power Database can be searched online through Dialog Information Services, Inc. It is also searchable online through CAN/OLE to government agencies. EPRI publications include *EPRI Research and Development Projects* (annual) and *EPRI Guide* (three times a year; contains descriptions of reports, software, patents, videotapes, brochures, and other materials available from EPRI).

Energy and Economic Data Bank
International Atomic Energy Agency (IAEA)
P.O. Box 100
Wagramerstrasse 5
A-1400 Vienna
Austria
Tel. 0222 2360

This agency provides data to aid in long-term energy planning by the IAEA and its member states. The computer-readable data bank is composed of six files: information on energy production, consumption, and plant capacities; energy resources; nuclear reactors; population; national accounts; and forecasts. The agency publishes a Reference Data Series; No. 1 in this series is *Energy, Electricity, and Nuclear Power Estimates for the Period up to 2000.* Services are restricted to IAEA internal use.

Energy Information Administration (EIA) Electronic Publication System
National Technical Information Service (NTIS)
U.S. Department of Commerce
Springfield, VA 22161

Selected energy statistics are available electronically on the Energy Information Administration computer facility. Gain public access by dialing (202) 586-8658 for 300-baud or 1200-baud line speeds. Communications are asynchronous and require a standard ASCII-type terminal. There is no charge and no password is required but you must use your telephone number as a user identifier. The service is available seven days a week. Monthly statistics from the *Electric Power Monthly* are available on or about the first working day of each month. The EIA *Catalog of Data Files* describes data files currently available from NTIS:

> EIA's energy information is disseminated through a comprehensive publications program that includes statistical and data reports, reports containing analyses and projections, and directories.
>
> In addition, EIA makes available for public use a series of machine-readable data files and computer software models. The models are EIA software products used to assemble projections for certain EIA publications.
>
> The data files/models are made available for public use on computer readable magnetic tape. . . . In addition, the EIA data files are now available on 5¼″ floppy diskette for IBM-PC compatible microcomputers. . . .

Nuclear Science Abstracts (NSA)
Dialog Information Services, Inc.
3460 Hillview Avenue
Palo Alto, CA 94304
(800) 3-DIALOG

The NSA database contains international nuclear science and technology research results from the beginning of the nuclear era (early 1940s) through July 1976 (nuclear information collected since that time is in the Energy Database). NSA is available on DIALOG.

U.S. Department of Energy Databases

Controlled Fusion Atomic Data Center
Oak Ridge National Laboratory
P.O. Box X, Building 6003
Oak Ridge, TN 37831
(615) 574-4707

This office collects and evaluates all data in the field of interest to the controlled fusion research program. The center maintains computer-readable data files and a bibliography from 1978 to the present. Materials prior to that date are in printed form. Bibliographic data are searchable online. Its publications include books, reviews, bibliographic data, and compilations.

Coordination and Information Center (CIC)
Nevada Operations Office
P.O. Box 98521
Las Vegas, NV 89193
(702) 295-0731

This office deals with the collection and preservation of all records and data dealing with offsite radioactive fallout from all U.S. testing of nuclear devices. Public access is permitted; documents are unclassified. Its publications include a printed index to the document collection. Microfiche indexes to all documents are available. The CIC will conduct online searches upon request.

Energy Library
MA-232
Washington, DC 20585
(202) 586-5955

The library provides traditional and computer-based services on energy-related topics. Its holdings include materials on all forms of energy, including nuclear, and consist of 160,000 bound volumes, one million technical reports on microfiche, and 1,600 periodicals. Publications include *Databases Available at the Energy Library, Energy Library: Journals Available,* and *Energy Library: Guide to Services.* It maintains the following computer-based files: MARC-based catalog, searchable online through ORBIT as the POWER file; Users' Online Catalog; LIBUREP, a technical reports holdings list. DIALOG, BRS Information Technologies, Interactive Data Corporation, NEXIS, and other systems are also available.

Integrated Technical Information System (ITIS)
Office of Scientific and Technical Information
P.O. Box 62
Oak Ridge, TN 37831
(615) 576-1222

The Office of Scientific and Technical Information collects, evaluates, analyzes, stores, and disseminates energy information. It maintains the DOE Energy Database, the largest computer-readable, bibliographic file on technical aspects of energy in the world. It collects information on all aspects of energy, including fission and fusion. Over three million literature references are available and nearly 200,000 are added each year. It publishes over 20 periodicals dealing with various aspects of energy. The Energy Database is available for online searching through Dialog Information Services, Inc., STN International, and INKADATA (Informationssystem Karlsruhe) as well as through the Integrated Technical Information System (ITIS). It is also available by subscription on biweekly magnetic tapes. Other energy files are maintained. Services are mainly to the U.S. Department of Energy and its contractors, but may be available also to other agencies under special arrangements. The ITIS provides online access to: Energy Database; Management Information File; Report Holdings File; Research in Progress; Minority Economic Impact; and Limited File. ITIS also includes other features. Users generally include DOE and contractor library specialists, information managers, and researchers. It publishes the *ITIS User's Guide* and the *ITIS User's Directory*.

National Energy Information Center (NEIC)
Energy Information Administration
1F-048 Forrestal Building
1000 Independence Avenue, SW
Washington, DC 20585
(202) 586-1174

The NEIC is the central clearinghouse for those seeking information and assistance on energy topics. Its publications include the *Energy Information Directory*; *EIA Publications Directory: A User's Guide*; and *EIA Publications: New Releases*. Its services are available without restriction.

National Energy Software Center (NESC)
Argonne National Laboratory
9700 South Cass Avenue
Argonne, IL 60439
(312) 972-7250

The NESC maintains software in all subject-area programs of the Department of Energy and the Nuclear Regulatory Commission. Its publications include *Compilation of Program Abstracts*; *Computer Software Summaries*; *NESC Bulletin*; and *NESC Notes*. The main objective of the National Energy Software Center is to collect and distribute packages of machine-readable programs and related printed documentation. It also maintains ACCESS, an automated system providing storage, retrieval, modification, and report facilities for information resources that can be accessed through seven interrelated databases.

National Nuclear Data Center (NNDC)
Brookhaven National Laboratory
Building 197D
Upton, NY 11973
(516) 282-2902

The NNDC acquires, stores, processes, and disseminates nuclear data through publications of bibliographies and computer-based services from its machine-readable holdings. Its publications include the *NNDC Newsletter*, *Neutron Cross Sections*, and *Nuclear Data Sheets*. Its data can be accessed by the Cross Section Information Storage and Retrieval System, Evaluated Nuclear Data File, Computer Index of Neutron Data, Computerized Index to Integral Charged Particle Reaction Data, Evaluated Nuclear Structure Data, and Nuclear Structure References. Services are available without restriction in the United States and Canada.

Nuclear Data Project
Oak Ridge National Laboratory
P.O. Box X, Building 6000
Oak Ridge, TN 37831
(615) 574-4699

This agency is an evaluation center that maintains a complete computer-indexed library on published and unpublished references in experimental nuclear physics, and coordinates all of this material nationally and internationally. It edits the monthly journal *Nuclear Data Sheets*. The project maintains the following computer-based files: Evaluated Nuclear Structure Data File and Nuclear Structure References File. Services are provided to the relevant research communities.

Nuclear Facility Decommissioning and Site Remedial Actions
Oak Ridge National Laboratory
Information Research and Analysis Section
Remedial Action Program Information Center
P.O. Box X, Building 2001
Oak Ridge, TN 37831-6050
(615) 576-0568

The Nuclear Facility Decommissioning and Site Remedial Actions is a computer-readable bibliographic database covering contaminated sites and remedial actions taken. The database contains more than 5,500 records of information from 1948 to the present, and is updated on a daily basis. Its publications include *Nuclear Facility Decommissioning and Site Remedial Action, A Selected Bibliography.*

Nuclear Operations Analysis Center (NOAC)
Oak Ridge National Laboratory
P.O. Box Y
Oak Ridge, TN 37831
(615) 574-0391

This office analyzes and gathers information on nuclear power reactor operations and their safety. It maintains the computer-readable database of the National Safety Information Center and publishes a technical progress review called *Nuclear Safety* (a quarterly). It also publishes reports, indexed bibliographies, and summaries of activities. Services are provided without charge to NOAC sponsors and their contractors, and are available to others on a cost-recovery basis.

Reactor Safety Data Bank
Nuclear Regulatory Commission/Division of Reactor and Plant Systems (NRC/DRPS)
Idaho National Engineering Laboratory
P.O. Box 1625
Idaho Falls, ID 83415
(208) 526-9507

The NRC/DRPS was created to collect and disseminate the huge quantities of experimental data from domestic and foreign water-reactor safety programs and to store such data in a single data bank. The NRC/DRPS Reactor Safety Data Bank may be searched online or in batch mode. Printed copies of the database are available upon request.

General Online Databases Dealing with Government

CIS (1970–present)

This is the machine-readable format of the *Index to Publications of the United States Congress* put out by the Congressional Information Service. It provides excellent access to the vast array of reports and documents published each year by the hundreds of House and Senate joint committees and subcommittees of the U.S. Congress.

Comprehensive Dissertation Index (1861–present)

The definitive source of virtually every doctoral dissertation accepted by accredited U.S. universities since 1861. It is arranged by subject, title, and author. Useful in getting at some of the less available material on nuclear energy and energy policy.

Federal Index (October 1976–present)

Covers such topics as proposed federal rules and regulations, introductions of bills, speeches, roll call votes, hearings, court decisions, presidential vetoes, and executive orders. Federal documents such as the *Congressional Record, Federal Register,* presidential documents, and the publications on government agencies are indexed. An index to the *Washington Post* is also included.

Federal Register Abstracts (March 1977–present)

Covers in a comprehensive way actions of federal regulatory agencies as printed in the *Federal Register,* which is the official federal government publication dealing with proposed rules, legal notices, and government regulations.

Government Printing Office Monthly Catalog (July 1976–present)

Contains lists of publications issued by all agencies of the federal government. Reports, studies, fact sheets, handbooks, conference proceedings, maps, records of the hearings on private and public bills, and laws of the House and Senate are included.

Legal Resource Index (1980–present)

Indexes nearly 700 legal periodicals, law newspapers, and legal monographs. Useful in locating legal articles dealing with nuclear energy and nuclear law and current issues dealing with topics related to nuclear energy.

Pais International (1976–present)

This is the online version of the *Public Affairs Information Service* (PAIS). It provides references to all fields of the social sciences including articles in political science, public administration, international relations, economics, law, and public policy as these relate to nuclear affairs.

Social SciSearch (1972–present)

An excellent multidisciplinary database that indexes every important item from 1,000 of the most significant scientific journals worldwide. It also includes articles in the social sciences from some 2,200 other journals in the natural, physical, and biomedical sciences.

United States Political Science Documents (1975–present)

Includes references from all areas of political science, e.g., foreign affairs, international relations, public administration, economics, law, behavioral science, contemporary problems, world politics, and political theory and methodology.

Films, Videotapes, and Films Made for Television

Addresses for industry associations and government departments and agencies that distribute films, videotapes, and films made for television are included in the Sources of Materials section beginning on page 203. This section also provides additional information, such as the availability of catalogs or listings.

About Fallout

Type:	Color; 16mm film; ¾", Beta 2, VHS video
Length:	24 min.
Cost:	Rental $40, purchase $225 (film); purchase $110 (video)
Date:	1963
Source:	National Audiovisual Center
Title nos.:	112300/PY (film), A08956/PY (¾" video), A08958/PY (Beta 2 video), A08957/PY (VHS video)

This film uses both animation and live action to illustrate the basic nature of fallout radiation, its effects on the cells of the body, what radiation after a nuclear attack would do to food and water, and the simple common-sense steps that can be taken to guard against the dangers of radiation fallout.

The Atom: A Closer Look

Type:	16mm color film
Length:	30 min.
Date:	1980
Cost:	Write for information
Source:	American Nuclear Society
	555 North Kensington Avenue
	La Grange Park, IL 60525

This is a Walt Disney Educational Media creation produced in cooperation with the American Nuclear Society. The film examines such topics as nuclear power, atomic structure and radiation, and nuclear waste. It is especially good for students in grades 6 through 12. It is available from local chapters of the American Nuclear Society.

The Atom and the Environment

Type:	Color or black/white ¾" video
Length:	22 min.
Date:	1971
Source:	Handel Film Corporation
	8730 Sunset Boulevard
	West Hollywood, CA 90069

Examines the ecological effects of nuclear power.

The Atom Strikes

Type: Black/white; 16mm film; ¾″, Beta 2, VHS video
Length: 31 min.
Date: 1950
Producer: U.S. War Department
Sponsor: U.S. Army
Source: National Audiovisual Center
Title nos.:   00434/PY (film), A09490/PY (¾″ video), A13253/PY (Beta 2 video), A12254/PY (VHS video)

Gives an account of the first experimental atomic bomb blast in New Mexico. Also provides aerial views of Hiroshima and Nagasaki bombings with close-up shots of devastated areas. Produced by U.S. War Department, 1946. Released by U.S. Office of Education, 1950. This film is considered of historical value and does not necessarily reflect current policy or plans of the sponsoring agency.

The Bitter and the Sweet

Type: Color; 16mm film; ¾″, Beta 2, VHS video
Length: 30 min.
Cost: Rental $40, purchase $320 (film); purchase $110 (video)
Producer: U.S. Atomic Energy Commission
Source: National Audiovisual Center
Title nos.:   007053/PY (film), A03966/PYm (¾″ video), A03968/PY (Beta 2 video), A03967/PY (VHS video)

This film discusses the application of nuclear technology to the desalting of water, and gives a capsule report on the status of commercial desalting in the western hemisphere. It has won several awards.

Changes: The Human Reaction to Three Mile Island

Type: Color ¾″ video
Length: 28 min.
Cost: Rental or purchase; inquire
Date: 1979
Source: Pennsylvania State University
    Audio Visual Services
    University Park, PA 16802

In this presentation, seven people who live within 15 miles of the damaged nuclear power plant talk about the 1977 accident there and the impact it has had on their lives.

Coping with Crisis: Accident at Ginna

Type: ¾″, ½″ video
Length: 20 min.

Cost: Purchase $65, $35 AIF members
Date: 1982
Source: Atomic Industrial Forum (AIF)

This videotape involves the communications and public information activities that were undertaken during the January 25, 1982, Ginna nuclear power plant accident. The tape portrays an excellent example of response under pressure.

Danger: Radioactive Waste
Type: Color or black/white ¾″ video
Length: 50 min.
Cost: Purchase; inquire
Date: 1977
Producer: NBC
Source: Films, Inc.
    5547 North Ravenswood Avenue
    Chicago, IL 60640-1199

A look at the dangers of radioactive waste and at the efforts of the nuclear energy industry to deal with the problem.

The Day after Trinity: J. Robert Oppenheimer and the Atomic Bomb
Length: 60 min.
Source: Pyramid Films
    2801 Colorado Avenue
    Santa Monica, CA 90404

A documentary that explores Oppenheimer's role in the creation of the first atomic bomb and surveys the dramatic events that led up to its first test explosion on July 16, 1945.

Day One
Type: Television film
Length: 180 min.
Cost: For information, write CBS
Date: 1989
Source: CBS Video Library
    1211 Avenue of the Americas
    New York, New York 10036

A television dramatization of the book *Day One: Before Hiroshima and After* by Peter Wyden, this was a three-hour CBS movie presented on March 5, 1989. It emphasizes the roles of Albert Einstein, Leo Szilard, and especially J. Robert Oppenheimer and General Leslie Groves. These characters are played, respectively, by Peter Boretski, Michael Tucker, David Strathairn, and Brian Dennehy. The roles of presidents Franklin

Roosevelt (David Ogden Stiers) and Harry Truman (Richard Dysart) in the development of the atomic bomb, and hence the birth of the nuclear age, are also portrayed. The movie suggests that General Groves was highly instrumental in quashing arguments against the use of the bomb, and that scientific achievements ultimately took precedence over humane considerations.

The Day Tomorrow Began
Type: Color; 16mm film; ¾″, Beta 2, VHS video
Length: 30 min.
Cost: Rental $40, purchase $320 (film); purchase $110 (video)
Date: 1967
Title nos.: 001546/PY (film), A04253/PY (¾″ video), AO4255/PY (Beta 2 video), AO4254/PY (VHS video)
Source: National Audiovisual Center

This film describes and traces the history and development of the first atomic pile, along with the work of the scientific team that achieved the first sustained chain reaction on December 2, 1942.

Decision To Drop the Bomb
Type: Black/white film
Length: 82 min.
Source: Films Incorporated
             1144 Wilmette Avenue
             Wilmette, IL 60091

This film is largely a summary of the political, military, moral, and ethical issues involved in the decision by President Harry Truman to drop the first atomic bomb in order to bring the war against Japan to a rapid conclusion.

Electricity—The Way It Works
Type: 16mm color film
Length: 16 min.
Date: 1976
Source: King Features Entertainment
             235 East 45th Street
             New York, NY 10017

This film explains generation and transmission of electricity and discusses alternative fuels such as coal, hydropower, nuclear energy, and others.

Endless Energy: The Promise of Fusion
Type: Beta, VHS video
Length: 7 min.

Cost: $25
Source: Fusion Power Associates

This video produced by Fusion Power Associates introduces lay audiences to fusion. Easily understandable, it is great as an introduction for speakers or as an educational aid by itself.

Energy and Nuclear Power

Type: Color or black/white ¾" video
Length: 14 min.
Producer: Guidance Associates, Motion Media
Date: 1977
Source: The Center for Humanities
              Communications Park
              Box 1000
              Mount Kisco, NY 10549

This program examines nuclear power and speculates on whether or not it is capable of solving the energy crisis in the United States.

Eniwetok—A Radiological Cleanup

Type: Color; 16mm film; ¾", Beta 2, VHS video
Length: 12 min.
Cost: Purchase $125 (film), $95 (video)
Date: 1975, released 1981
Producer: U.S. Defense Nuclear Agency
Source: National Audiovisual Center
Title nos.: A07505/PY (film), A07506/PY (¾" video), A0750/PY (Beta 2 video), A07505/PY (VHS video)

This film covers the use of Eniwetok Atoll as a nuclear test site from 1948 to 1958. It describes the five years of planning for the actual cleanup project, the radiation safety and monitoring program, and the resettlement program. Shows how debris and soil were monitored before disposal to Runit Island and the new homes and crops of the people who returned to Eniwetok in April 1980.

The First Twenty-five Years

Type: Color; 16mm film; ¾", Beta 2, VHS video
Length: 29 min.
Date: 1973
Producer: U.S. Atomic Energy Commission
Sponsor: U.S. Department of Energy Planning
Source: National Audiovisual Center
Title nos.: 005391/PY (film), AO3987/PY (¾" video), AO3989/PY (Beta 2 video), A03988/PY (VHS video)

Concentrates on the development of the first atomic bomb and the first hydrogen bomb. Gives a historical perspective on the role played by the Los Alamos Scientific Laboratory in the development and advancement of the nuclear age. Deals with the remarkable group of scientists gathered at Los Alamos by Dr. Robert Oppenheimer.

Fitting the Pieces ... Managing Nuclear Waste
Type: 16mm film; ¾", ½" video
Length: 25 min.
Cost: Purchase $350 AIF members, nonmember prices on request
Source: Atomic Industrial Forum (AIF)

This film deals with the questions of defining high-level radioactive waste and how to manage and control it. Answers to these questions and to others involved in this controversial issue are fully and simply discussed in this comprehensive documentary. An animated sequence traces spent nuclear fuel's route to a geologic repository deep underground. It is appropriate for junior high school students and those older. Produced for the Atomic Industrial Forum and the U.S. Committee for Energy Awareness; related printed materials are provided.

Fusion: Energy's Space Program
Type: 16mm film; Beta, VHS video
Length: 30 min.
Cost: Rental $20 (film), purchase $25 (video)
Source: Fusion Power Associates

Narrated by former astronaut Neil Armstrong, this film compares the challenge of the fusion energy program to that of the space program in the early 1960s. Appropriate for technical and nontechnical audiences.

Fusion: The Energy Promise
Type: Color or black/white ¾" video
Length: 56 min.
Cost: Rental or purchase, inquire
Date: 1976
Producer: WGBH Boston, BBC
Source: Time-Life Video
             1271 Avenue of the Americas
             New York, NY 10020

This program—an episode from the television series "Nova"— recounts events in the international race to produce a successful fusion reaction.

Hiroshima: A Document of the Atomic Bombing
Type: Black/white film, some color scenes
Length: 28 min.

Source: American Friends Service Committee
15 Rutherford Place
New York, NY 10003.

Wilmington College Peace Resource Center
Pyle Center, Box 1183
Wilmington, OH 45177.

A documentary of the bombing of Hiroshima, with shots taken during the weeks immediately following the attack. The film is interspersed with footage illustrating medical and psychological consequences of the bombing.

Hiroshima/Nagasaki: August 1945
Type: Black/white film
Length: 16 min.
Source: Museum of Modern Art
Circulating Film Program
11 West 53rd Street
New York, NY 10019.

American Friends Service Committee
15 Rutherford Place
New York, NY 10003.

Wilmington College Peace Resource Center
Pyle Center, Box 1183
Wilmington, OH 45177.

This film depicts the devastation and agony resulting from nuclear war. It includes footage of the Hiroshima and Nagasaki bomb bursts.

In Our Own Backyards: Uranium Mining in the United States
Type: Color or black/white ¾″ video
Length: 29 min.
Cost: Purchase or duplicating license; inquire
Date: 1982
Producer: Eleventh Hour Films
Source: Bullfrog Films
Oley, PA 19547

Examines various aspects of uranium mining in the United States.

Into the Atom: The Electric Connection
Type: 16mm film; 1″, ¾″, ½″ video (PAL standard)
Length: 9 min., 40 sec.
Cost: Purchase $150, $120 AIF members
Date: 1984
Source: Atomic Industrial Forum (AIF)

Through animation and special effects photography, the viewer is taken into the fundamentals of the atom. Produced in cooperation with the U.S. Committee for Energy Awareness, it is excellent for junior high school audiences and those older. Also provided is a film user's guide and related printed material.

Is Nuclear Power Safe? (Parts A and B)
Type: Color ¾" video
Length: 60 min.
Cost: Rental or purchase; inquire
Source: American Enterprise Institute for Public Policy Research
1150 Seventeenth Street, NW
Washington, DC 20036

Melvin B. Laird moderates a panel discussion on the title question; panel members include consumer advocate Ralph Nader.

The New R.C.R.A.
Type: Color; ¾", Beta 2, VHS video
Length: 180 min.
Cost: Purchase $140 (¾"), $450 (Beta 2, VHS)
Producer: U.S. Office of Solid Waste Management
Source: National Audiovisual Center
Title nos.: A12255/PZ (¾"), A12256/PZ (Beta 2), A12257/PZ (VHS)

This videocassette describes a teleconference that explains the major provisions of the New Resources Conservation and Recovery Act, which became effective November 8, 1984. The videocassette is particularly useful for those who handle hazardous waste. It has won the Gold Award at the Information Film Producers of America Festival.

The New Superfund—What It Is, How It Does—A Series
Type: Color; 6 videocassettes; ¾", Beta 2, VHS
Length: See individual titles, below
Cost: Purchase $775 (¾"), $585 (Beta 2, VHS)
Date: 1987
Producer: U.S. Office of Solid Waste Management
Source: National Audiovisual Center
Title nos.: A16464/PZ (¾"), A16466/PZ (Beta 2), A16465/PZ (VHS)

On March 5, 1987, the U.S. Environmental Protection Agency presented a national teleconference on the new superfund hazardous waste cleanup law. This legislation, entitled Superfund Amendments and Reauthorization Act of 1986 (SARA), was signed by the president on October 17, 1986. The program is designed to provide an overview of the changes and new provisions in superfund. Panels of EPA and other agency managers discuss changes in the cleanup process (including cleanup standards, state involvement, and new requirements for federal facilities). The presentation is appropriate for the general public, industry, environmental groups, trade associations, and universities. An 11-page handout sheet is included. Titles of the individual tapes are as follows:

"Changes in the Remedial Process: Cleanup Standards and State Involvement Requirements," 62 min.

"Changes in the Removal Process: Removal and Additional Program Requirements," 48 min.

"Enforcement and Federal Facilities," 52 min.

"Emergency Preparedness and Community Right-to-Know," 48 min.

"Underground Storage Tank Trust Fund and Response Program," 21 min.

"Research and Development/Closing Remarks," 33 min.

Now that the Dinosaurs Are Gone
Type: 16mm film; ¾", ½" video
Length: 26 min.
Cost: Purchase $350, $250 AIF members
Source: Atomic Industrial Forum (AIF)

This is an explanation of nuclear power and its role in our evolutionary energy growth. It covers the advantages of nuclear power and answers many of the questions often posed by the public. It features Drs. Dixy Lee Ray, Norman Rasmussen, and Ralph Lapp. It is an excellent reference resource.

Nuclear Countdown
Type: Color film
Length: 28 min.
Source: Journal Films, Inc.
             930 Pitner Avenue
             Evanston, IL 60202

This is a documentary on the arms race, especially the danger involved in the worldwide proliferation of nuclear weapons. The film emphasizes the successes, the failures, and the inadequacies of arms control negotiations and agreements up to the time it was made.

Nuclear Electricity and You
Type: 13-part video series; ¾",½"
Length: 28 min. each
Cost: $650 for series, $60 each for AIF members; nonmember prices on request

Date: 1983
Source: Atomic Industrial Forum (AIF)

This series covering various issues of nuclear power is designed for cable television broadcast. It includes film inserts, interviews with key nuclear figures, and lively panel discussions.

Nuclear Energy
Type: Color video
Length: 30 min.
Cost: Rental or purchase; inquire
Producer: Nebraska ETV Council for Higher Education (NETCHE)
Source: NETCHE
Box 83111
Lincoln, NE 68501

Describes in technical terms how nuclear fission produces energy and how this energy is converted into electricity.

Nuclear Energy: A Perspective
Type: Color or black/white ¾" video
Length: 29 min.
Date: 1981
Producer: Exxon Corporation
Source: New York State Education Department
Center for Learning Technologies
Media Distribution Network
Room C-7, Concourse Level
Cultural Education Center
Albany, NY 12230

A view of nuclear power from a positive perspective.

Nuclear Energy: The Question before Us
Type: Color ¾" video
Length: 23 min.
Date: 1981
Source: National Geographic Society
Seventeenth and M Streets, NW
Washington, DC 20036

This program takes viewers inside a nuclear power facility to describe how it produces electricity. Advantages and drawbacks of nuclear energy are examined.

Nuclear Power: An Introduction
Type: 16mm film; ¾", ½" video
Length: 20 min.

Cost: Purchase $200, $150 AIF members (film); purchase $150, $100 AIF members (video)
Date: 1976
Source: Atomic Industrial Forum (AIF)

This is a basic explanation of the atom, the fission process, and how a nuclear power plant actually works. Various reactor designs are described and compared. Dr. E. Linn Draper, formerly of the University of Texas, is featured. A transcript is provided.

Nuclear Power: Pro and Con
Type: Color or black/white ¾″ video
Length: 50 min.
Date: 1977
Source: CRM/McGraw Hill Films
          674 Via de la Valle
          P.O. Box 641
          Del Mar, CA 92014

This program features nuclear energy proponents and opponents debating the issue of whether nuclear power production should continue in the face of its inherent risks. Available in a single- or two-part version.

On the Move
Type: Color; 16mm film; ¾″, Beta 2, VHS video
Length: 28 min.
Cost: Purchase $295 (film), $110 (video)
Producer: U.S. Atomic Energy Commission
Source: National Audiovisual Center
Title nos.:   007282/PY (film), A09539/PY (¾″ video), A13707/PY (Beta 2 video), A09580/PY (VHS video)

This film explains many aspects of packaging and shipping radioactive materials, including the extreme concern and caution taken for safety in normal and accidental environments.

Operation Crossroad
Type: Black/white; 16mm film; ¾″, Beta 2, VHS video
Length: 27 min.
Cost: Purchase $165 (film), $110 (video)
Date: 1949
Source: National Audiovisual Center
Title nos.:   002542/PY (film), A13710/PY (¾″ video), A13711/PY (Beta 2 video), A13712/PY (VHS video)

This is a film record of the Able and Baker atomic bomb tests at Bikini.

Operation Greenhouse

Type:	Color; 16mm film; ¾", Beta 2, VHS video
Length:	25 min.
Cost:	Rental $40, purchase $265 (film); purchase $110 (video)
Date:	1952
Producer:	U.S. Atomic Energy Commission
Sponsor:	U.S. Energy Resources Development Administration
Source:	National Audiovisual Center
Title nos.:	002643/PY (film), A13716/PY (¾" video), A13717/PY (Beta 2 video), A13718/PY (VHS video)

Describes the scientific and technical operations of the Atomic Energy Commission during the nuclear weapons test at Eniwetok in the spring of 1951. It depicts the blast and thermal effects of the explosions on different types of structures. This film is considered of historical value and does not necessarily reflect current policy or plans of the sponsoring agency.

Operation Smash Hit

Type:	16mm film; ¾", ½" video
Length:	10 min.
Cost:	$35 AIF members, nonmember prices on request
Date:	1984
Source:	Atomic Industrial Forum (AIF)

In 1984 the British Central Electricity Generating Board (CEGB) ran an unmanned diesel train, traveling at 100 miles an hour, into a nuclear fuel cask prototype. The film chronicles the event, showing the diesel being destroyed while the cask, designed to transport spent fuel rods, emerges unscathed. This televised demonstration, witnessed by millions, showed the CEGB's confidence in the cask's strength and ability to provide safe containment. Sir Walter Marshall, CEGB chairman, is interviewed.

Properties of Matter

Type:	Black/white; 16mm film; ¾", Beta 2, VHS video
Length:	15 min.
Cost:	Rental $40, purchase $90 (film); purchase $90 (video)
Date:	1974
Producer:	U.S. Air Force
Source:	National Audiovisual Center
Title nos.:	A08886/PY (film), AO8887/PY (¾" video), AO8888/PY (Beta 2 video), AO8889/PY (VHS video)

This film defines matter and gives examples of matter in various states. It illustrates the makeup of an atom and discusses the atomic construction of conductors, semiconductors, and insulators. It uses demonstrations to show how to determine whether a material is a conductor or an insulator and how materials exhibit different characteristics when they are subjected to extreme voltages or impurities are added.

Radiation in Medicine and Industry
Type: ¾", ½" video
Length: 20 min.
Cost: Purchase $75, $50 AIF members
Date: 1980
Producer: Consumers Power Company
Source: Atomic Industrial Forum (AIF)

A Hershey, Pennsylvania, physician discusses his experiences with the public during and following the Three Mile Island accident. Dr. Arnold Muller describes the misinformation being spread at that time and offers basic radiation information. Produced by Consumers Power Company.

Radiation . . . Naturally
Type: 1", ¾", ½" video
Length: 28 min.
Cost: Purchase $375, $275 AIF members
Date: 1981
Source: Atomic Industrial Forum (AIF)

With low-level radiation existing naturally all around us, this film explores radiation's sources, benefits, and risks. The viewer is taken from high in the Rockies to Saint Peter's Square in Rome on this educational journey. The film helps dispel the mysteries and myths surrounding radiation. Geared for all general audiences; related printed materials are provided.

The Science of Managing Nuclear Waste
Type: 16mm film; ¾", ½" video
Length: 18 min.
Cost: Purchase $195
Date: 1986
Source: Atomic Industrial Forum (AIF)

This program, produced for the U.S. Committee for Energy Awareness and the Atomic Industrial Forum, discusses high-level radioactive waste, specifically spent (used) fuel rods from commercial nuclear power plants. The film contains excellent explanations of waste shipping and repository site characterization. Good for general public use.

The Sea We Cannot See
Type: Color; 35mm film; ¾", Beta 2, VHS video
Length: 28 min.

Cost: Rental $40, purchase $295 (film); purchase $110 (video)
Date: 1973
Producer: U.S. Atomic Energy Commission
Sponsor: U.S. Office of Energy Planning
Source: National Audiovisual Center
Title nos.:   005064/PY (film), A00945/PY (¾" video), A139843/PY (Beta 2 video), A12147/PY (VHS video)

Indicates where background radiation comes from and discusses low-level radiation as it is used in medicine and dentistry as well as the effects of X-rays, TV sets, and nuclear power installations. Also explains the federal radiation protection standards policy that was set as far back as 1929.

Selected Atomic Industrial Forum (AIF) Stock Footage

Type: 16mm film; 1", ¾", ½" video
Cost: Prices on request
Date: 1985
Source: Atomic Industrial Forum (AIF)

Some of the best pieces of footage from AIF-produced films and videotapes.

SL-1 Accident, Phases 1 and 2

Type: Color; 16mm film; ¾", Beta 2, VHS video
Length: 43 min.
Cost: Purchase $455 (film), $1,400 (video)
Date: 1962
Producer: U.S. Atomic Energy Commission
Sponsor: U.S. Energy Resources Development Administration
Source: National Audiovisual Center
Title nos.:   003484/PY (film), AO8737/PY (¾" video), A13885/PY (Beta 2 video), A13886/PY (VHS video)

Uses actual and reenacted scenes to present an account of what happened in phases 1 and 2 following the accidental nuclear explosion of January 3, 1961.

SL-1 Accident, Phase 3

Type: Color; 16mm film; ¾", Beta 2, VHS video
Length: 57 min.
Cost: Rental $40, purchase $605 (film); purchase $155 (video)
Date: 1962
Producer: U.S. Atomic Energy Commission
Sponsor: U.S. Energy Resources Development Administration
Source: National Audiovisual Center
Title nos.:   003483/PY (film), A08736/PY (¾" video), A13887/PY (Beta 2 video), A13888/PY (VHS video)

This film documents what was done with the SL-1 reactor and building following the accidental nuclear explosion that occurred January 3, 1961, and provides a reenactment of the accident using animation. It also presents a postulation of the cause.

Target Nevada

Type:	Color; 16mm film; ¾″, Beta 2, VHS video
Length:	14 min.
Cost:	Purchase $150 (film), $95 (video)
Date:	1962
Producer:	U.S. Defense Nuclear Agency
Source:	National Audiovisual Center
Title nos.:	A08197/PY (film), A08198/PY (¾″ video), A08199/PY (Beta 2 video), A08200/PY (VHS video)

This film recounts the story of the U.S. Air Force support to the Atomic Energy Commission on continual atomic tests. It covers the delivery of the atomic bomb and shows aerial views of nuclear explosions plus the monitoring of blast areas. It explains the preparation for atomic strikes, including the use of the air weather service for atomic cloud sampling. It shows an observer viewing an atomic explosion and the effect of atomic bursts on the eyes, which is referred to as flash blindness. The film was produced by the Defense Nuclear Agency in 1962 and released by the Department of Defense in 1980.

War and Peace in the Nuclear Age

Type:	13-part series; ¾″, ½″ video
Length:	60 min. each
Cost:	Purchase $45 each, $500 series (¾″); purchase $29.95 each, $350 series (½″); off-air taping and duplication licenses also available
Date:	1989
Producer:	WGBH Boston and Central Independent Television, England, with NHK, Japan
Source:	The Annenberg/CPB Project c/o Intellimation P.O. Box 1922 Santa Barbara, CA 93116-1922

Originally presented on public television, the series of tapes consists of the following programs:

"Dawn" describes the development of the first atomic bomb

"The Weapon of Choice" explores the origins of the cold war from 1947 to 1953

"A Bigger Bang for the Buck" has to do with military planning during the Eisenhower administration

"Europe Goes Nuclear" addresses the strategic developments with respect to the role of nuclear weapons in the defense of Europe

"At the Brink" deals with the Cuban missile crisis of October 1962

"The Education of Robert McNamara" examines the succession of nuclear strategies implemented under McNamara's leadership as secretary of defense

"One Step Forward . . ." is an analysis of the Nixon-Kissinger era of detente with the Soviet Union

"Haves and Have-Nots" explores the relationship between nuclear power and nuclear weapons proliferation

"Carter's New World" analyzes the U.S. domestic political atmosphere and international events such as the Iran hostage crisis and the Soviet invasion of Afghanistan

"Zero Hour" examines the role of nuclear weapons in Europe during the 1970s and 1980s

"Missile Experimental" focuses on the perceived vulnerability of the U.S. intercontinental ballistic missile force to Soviet attack

"Reagan's Shield" deals with the Strategic Defense Initiative (so-called star wars program)

"Visions of War and Peace" examines the future of the nuclear age in light of past performance

A textbook (The *Nuclear Age Reader*) and study guide to accompany the series when presented as a course are also available.

The War Game
Type: Film
Length: 49 min.
Source: Films Incorporated
            1144 Wilmette Avenue
            Wilmette, IL 60091

A quite realistic depiction of an atomic attack on England sometime in the future after diplomatic efforts have failed and nations have been placed in essentially uncompromisable positions.

War without Winners
Type: Color film
Length: 28 min.

Source: Films Incorporated
1144 Wilmette Avenue
Wilmette, IL 60091

American Friends Services Committee
15 Rutherford Place
New York, NY 10003.

Physicians for Social Responsibility
P.O. Box 144
Watertown, MA 02172

Interviews are conducted with Paul Warnke, former chief negotiator for SALT, Dr. George Kistiakowsky, former scientific advisor to President Eisenhower, and a number of other experts, workers, and students on their hopes and fears about nuclear warfare.

Web of Life—Endless Chain
Type: Color; 16mm film; ¾", Beta 2, VHS video
Length: 28 min.
Cost: Rental $40, purchase $295 (film); purchase $110 (video)
Date: 1972
Producer: U.S. Atomic Energy Commission
Sponsor: U.S. Office of Energy Planning
Source: National Audiovisual Center
Title nos.: 02225/PY (film), A01299/PY (¾" video), A14163/PY (Beta 2 video), A10056/PY (VHS video)

A special no-narration version of the motion picture *Endless Chain*. It uses poetry, music, and nature photography to depict the work being done by the Atomic Energy Commission at its ecological study sanctuary in the state of Washington.

Nonprint Media Materials and Productions

Displays

Atoms for Peace . . . A Spark for Life

This table-top display graphically addresses the atom's place in industrial, medical, and everyday applications. The exhibit fits on a six-foot table and consists of four panels, each measuring 25 inches by 44 inches. Packed in its own shipping case, it weighs 40 pounds.

Nuclear Energy for America

Three changeable graphic panels depict major nuclear energy issues— such as the need for electricity, nuclear reliability, safety, and waste disposal. The exhibit includes a literature cabinet and an interactive computer complete with color graphics and a videotape player. It requires a 10- by 10-foot space with a clearance of eight feet and uses a standard 110v outlet. When in storage or transit, the exhibit fits in four crates with a total weight of 1,500 pounds.

Electronic News Releases

Decommissioning a Nuclear Power Plant
Type: ¾" video
Cost: $40 AIF members, nonmember prices on request
Date: 1985
Source: Atomic Industrial Forum (AIF)

Covers nuclear plant retirement and decommissioning, demonstrating feasibility and technology. It is excellent for local media to adapt for their own use and encourages accurate information dissemination.

Nuclear Expedition
Type: ¾" video
Cost: $16 AIF members, nonmember prices on request
Date: 1985
Source: Atomic Industrial Forum (AIF)

This 90-second feature invites the public to visit any of the more than 80 energy information centers across the United States and Canada. It is designed for use in news broadcasts as well as in information centers.

Slides and Slide Programs

Electricity and the Environment
Type: 16mm color film
Length: 23 min.
Date: 1984
Source: Magic Lantern
925 Penn Avenue
Pittsburgh, PA 15222

The film focuses attention on the commitment of the utility industry to the protection of our environment. It is especially useful for showing how environmental control systems work in coal and nuclear plants. The film is good for students in high school and beyond.

Endless Energy: The Promise of Fusion
70 slides in binder; script included.
Cost: $50
Source: Fusion Power Associates

A compilation of 70 slides in a loose-leaf binder with narrative text to be used for introductory presentations on the development of fusion energy.

Hazardous Wastes—The Gross National By-Product
44 color slides, 2″ x 2″; 1 audiocassette, 2-track, MONO, with audible and inaudible advance signals; script included.

Cost:	$40
Date:	1976
Producer:	U.S. Office of Solid Waste Management
Source:	National Audiovisual Center
Title no.:	007918/PY

This series of slides explains what hazardous wastes are and how they are produced. It discusses how they are treated, transported, and disposed of. It summarizes the problem and suggests ways for citizens and public interest groups to take constructive action to cope with hazardous waste materials.

Nuclear Energy Issues and Information
78 slides; audiocassette; script included.

Date:	1980
Source:	National Society of Professional Engineers
	2029 K Street NW
	Washington, DC 20006

This series of slides describes the operation of nuclear plants, radiation, and the accident at Three Mile Island. It also treats conservation, oil supplies, and nuclear waste repositories. Good for students in junior high and beyond.

Nuclear Power Inside and Out
20-slide package; explanatory text included; periodic updates available.

Cost:	$100, AIF members $60
Source:	Atomic Industrial Forum (AIF)

The basics of a nuclear power plant and its operation are described with precise detail in this 20-slide resources package. Text accompanies maps, photos, and schematics to thoroughly illustrate and explain the nuclear power processes to all audience levels. An excellent basic resource.

Uranium: The Facts
Slide program; script included.

Cost:	$125, $75 AIF members
Date:	1981
Source:	Atomic Industrial Forum (AIF)

Uranium mining and milling activities are explained in this complete industry wrap-up. Prepared for those working in the field, this scripted slide program also serves well as an educational tool for all audiences.

Uranium: The Facts of Mill Tailings
78 slides.
Cost: $125, $75 AIF members
Date: 1984
Source: Atomic Industrial Forum (AIF)

This program addresses questions raised by the public about this form of radioactive waste—what tailings are, how they were created, and how they are managed. Adaptable to the public as well as to uranium industry workers.

Why Nuclear Energy? A Slide Talk with a Moral
Slide program.
Cost: $100, $75 AIF members
Date: 1977
Source: Atomic Industrial Forum (AIF)

Excellent for nontechnical audiences, this program gives straightforward information on why our economy needs energy and how nuclear technology helps to meet that need. It also makes an effective employee orientation. Over 130 slides, including original cartoon drawings.

Sources of Information

Educators Guide to Free Films. Educators Progress Service, Inc., 214 Center Street, Randolph, WI 53956. Annual, 1941– . $27. ISSN 0070-9395.

Educators Guide to Free Filmstrips and Slides. Educators Progress Service, Inc., 214 Center Street, Randolph, WI 53956. Annual, 1949– . $20.

Free and Inexpensive Materials: A Selected List of Guides to Sources. Reference Guides, General Reading Rooms Division, Library of Congress, Washington, DC 20540. ISSN 0163-1357.

Index to Free Educational Material—Multimedia. Los Angeles: National Information Center for Educational Media, University of Southern California, 1978. 238p.

Sources: A Guide to Print and Nonprint Materials Available from Organizations, Industry, Government Agencies, and Specialized Publishers. Gaylord Professional Publications, P.O. Box 61, Syracuse, NY 13201. 3/year, Vol. 1– (Winter 1977–). $60 per year.

Published in association with Neal-Schuman Publishers. Includes "Index to Free and Inexpensive Materials."

Video Rating Guide for Libraries. Santa Barbara, CA: ABC-CLIO, Inc. 1990– . $89.50 per year.

Published quarterly, the guide reviews and rates VHS-format videos, including topics on nuclear energy and waste management (see the Social Sciences–Political Science and Pure Sciences–Environment & Ecology sections). Subject, title, and audience indexes in each issue, cumulated annually in the October issue.

The Video Source Book. Detroit: Gale Research Inc., 1989. $199.

Compiled from distributor and producer information, this reference covers videos in all formats. Entries are presented in alphabetical order by title, and include brief annotations. Indexed by subject and main category.

The Workbook. Southwest Research and Information Center, P.O. Box 4524, Albuquerque, NM 87106. 8/year, November 1974– . $7 per year for students and senior citizens, $10 for individuals, $20 for institutions.

A "catalog of sources of information about environmental, social and consumer problems," much of which is free and inexpensive. Covers such subjects as agriculture, consumer affairs, energy, health care, pollution, etc.

Sources of Materials

Atomic Industrial Forum, Inc.
7101 Wisconsin Avenue
Bethesda, MD 20814-4891.

Fusion Power Associates
2 Professional Drive
Gaithersburg, MD 20879
(301) 258-0545.

National Audiovisual Center
8700 Edgeworth Drive
Capitol Heights, MD 20743-3701
(301) 763-1896

This office distributes audiovisual programs produced by the federal government. The center also provides captioned films for the deaf. Audiovisual materials may be rented, previewed, or purchased at low cost. A subject catalog of audiovisual holdings and film loan referrals are available.

National Energy Information Center
Energy Information Administration
U.S. Department of Energy
Forrestal Building, EI-231, Room 1F048
1000 Independence Avenue, SW
Washington, DC 20585
(202) 586-1170

Among other things, the center operates the Energy Information Administration microfilm document control center, providing access to data collection surveys and historical documents available to the public.

Office of Scientific and Technical Research
U.S. Department of Energy
P.O. Box 62
Oak Ridge, TN 37831
(615) 576-1155

This office manages the technical information program of the Department of Energy. Among other things, it maintains the DOE Energy Database, which holds approximately two million citations to technical energy literature. It also maintains the central DOE Research in Progress database; provides online retrieval through DOE; and offers microfiche publication services for technical reports to DOE and its contractors.

Policy Development and Information Systems Division
Research and Special Programs Administration
U.S. Department of Transportation
400 7th Street, SW, Room 8112
Washington, DC 20590
(202) 366-4555

This office serves as a central, computer-maintained, management information system supporting the multimodal transportation of hazardous materials. The Hazardous Materials Information System provides direct retrieval, through six major subsystems, of the available information on incident data, inspection/enforcement results, indexes of regulations, interpretation of regulations, status of approvals, and status of exemptions. Requests for information will be honored, and limited direct access can be arranged.

Remedial Action Program Information Center
Oak Ridge National Laboratory
P.O. Box X, Building 2001
Oak Ridge, TN 37831-6050

This center operates the Nuclear Facility Decommissioning and Site Remedial Actions database. This database serves as a comprehensive source of technical information pertinent to the Department of Energy's Remedial Action Program. The database is managed by the staff of the Remedial Action Program Information Center (RAPIC). Computerized literature searches of RAPIC databases are available upon request at no charge.

U.S. Department of Energy
Forrestal Building, CP-24, Room 8G048
1000 Independence Avenue, SW
Washington, DC 20585
(202) 896-4670

This division is responsible for establishing policy and providing oversight of the Department of Energy's public affairs activities. Among other things, the division manages and reviews all audiovisuals and exhibits produced through the Department of Energy. Write or call the Office of Audiovisuals and Exhibits at the above address. Also see the listings for the National Energy Information Center and the Office of Scientific and Technical Research in this section.

Glossary

activation products   Atomic fragments that have been absorbed by the steel of the reactor or by minerals in the cooling water. These fragments give off radiation for many years.

agreement state   A state of the United States that has entered into an agreement with the Nuclear Regulatory Commission to assume regulatory responsibility for radioactive materials within its borders, in compliance with Section 274 of the Atomic Energy Act of 1954, as amended.

alpha particle   A positively charged particle made up of two neutrons and two protons. An alpha particle cannot penetrate clothing or the outer layer of the skin. An alpha particle is emitted during decay of some radioactive nuclei, but is heavy and slow-moving and has little biological impact unless inhaled or ingested.

aquifers   Rock, sand, or gravel (water-bearing formations), through which water moves much more rapidly than in other formations, which have lower permeability.

atom   The basic component of all matter. An atom is made up of protons and neutrons.

atomic energy   A term that relates to the production of energy by nuclear fission.

atomic mass   The number of protons and neutrons in an atom.

backfill   The materials used to fill in around casks after they have been placed in a repository or a shallow land burial trench.

background radiation   Radiation originating from radioactive materials that occur naturally in the environment, e.g., solar and cosmic radiation, other radioactive substances in the atmosphere, the earth, building and construction materials, and even the human body itself.

base load   The normal, more or less constant demand for energy from a given system.

base loaded   Maintaining a power station at its maximum load because it is one of the lowest-cost power producers in the system.

baseline information   Information collected concerning social, physical, and biological data at or near a site before the development of an energy facility.

beta particle   A negatively charged particle that has mass and charge equal to that of an electron, relatively short range, and low ability to penetrate other materials.

biomass   Organic material that can supply heat.

boiling-water reactor   A nuclear reactor cooled by water that is boiling as it passes through the core. This coolant directly produces the steam that generates electricity. The steam is radioactive and the turbine must be shielded if the steam is to be used directly.

breeder reactor   A nuclear reactor that creates more fissionable material than it consumes. Thus, the reactor is said to "breed."

British thermal unit   The amount of heat required to raise the temperature of one pound of water by one degree Fahrenheit. It is abbreviated BTU.

canister   The outermost container, composed of stainless steel or an innert alloy, in which glassified high-level waste or spent fuel rods are placed.

capital costs   The amount of money needed to build, or the amount of money invested in, such a building as a power plant.

carrier   An individual who transports passengers or property by land or water as a common, contract, or private carrier or by a civil aircraft.

cask   A container that shields canisters or radioactive materials during transportation.

catalyst   A substance that promotes a chemical reaction without actually changing itself.

cesium   Element 55. Cesium-137 is a radioactive fission product having a half-life of 30 years.

chain reaction   A series of nuclear fissions that take place in a reactor core; a reaction that causes its own repetition. The neutrons produced in one fission collide with other nuclei, which in turn give off neutrons that collide with still other nuclei. The action thus repeats itself.

chemical contamination A process of introducing hazardous materials into a critical system such as ground water or a river system.

chemical reaction A process during which one or more chemical materials change into one or more chemically different materials.

cladding Any material that is used to enclose nuclear fuel. It is a protective alloy shielding, made of stainless steel or of some alloy, in which fissionable fuel is inserted.

cogeneration Producing heat and electricity from a common source.

commercial wastes Low- and high-level radioactive wastes produced by commercial nuclear power plants, industry, and other institutions such as hospitals and universities.

commissioning The lengthy process by which a nuclear plant is made operational. The process involves construction and demonstration of conformity to specific acceptance tests and performance criteria.

condenser The apparatus that cools steam and transforms it back into water.

containment building A structure, made of thick, steel-reinforced concrete, that surrounds the pressure vessel and other components of the nuclear reactor. It is constructed and designed to prevent radioactive materials from being released into the atmosphere in the remote possibility that they might escape from the pressure vessel.

containment system Those elements that make up the packaging intended to retain radioactive materials during their transportation.

contamination The process of causing materials to become impure or foul by the introduction of undesirable substances.

control rods Long, thin rods, made of material that absorbs neutrons, that slow down a chain reaction by capturing neutrons that would otherwise create more fissions. They are positioned among fuel rods so that they regulate the chain reaction. They are some of the major components of light water reactors.

control room The room in a nuclear power plant in which operators and technicians monitor and control the activities of the plant. The equipment contained in the control room enables the technicians to observe what is occurring in the reactor and in other locations of the installation.

conversion The transition of one energy form to another energy form.

coolant   Fluid that is circulated through the core of a reactor to remove heat generated as a result of the fission process. It may be any gas or liquid, and may be referred to as a reactor coolant or a primary coolant.

cooling pond   Most often a manmade body of water used by electrical generating systems to dissipate heat, largely through evaporation.

cooling system   The system that carries the coolant through the nuclear power plant.

cooling tower   A tall, chimney-like structure used to remove heat from cooling water in the condenser. The cooling tower prevents thermal pollution of lakes and rivers.

core   The central part of a nuclear reactor where the nuclear chain reaction is started, maintained, and controlled. It contains the fuel rods, the moderator, and the control rods. A coolant is continuously circulated through the core to absorb the heat produced by fission.

critical   The condition of a nuclear reactor when it is capable of sustaining a chain reaction. A subcritical reactor is no longer able to sustain a reaction, while a supercritical reactor is more than capable of just sustaining a reaction.

critical mass   The minimum mass of fissionable material, having a specific geometric arrangement and composition, that will sustain a fission chain reaction.

curie   A unit of measurement used to describe the intensity of radio-activity contained in materials. It is based on the radioactivity of one gram of radium and is equivalent to 37 billion disintegrations per second.

daughter   This is a nuclide resulting from the radioactive decay of another nuclide, which is called the parent.

decay   The disintegration of the nucleus of an unstable nuclide because of the emission of charged particles and/or of photons.

decommission   Removing a nuclear power plant from service and safely disposing of its nuclear reactor when its service life has been completed.

decontamination   The removal of radioactive material from the surface or insides of another material.

defense wastes   Radioactive wastes created by defense research projects, naval reactors, production of weapons and weapons materials, the decommissioning of nuclear-powered ships, and reprocessing spent fuel.

disposal The permanent removal of radioactive wastes from the human environment.

dose The quantity of radiation or energy absorbed by an object. It is measured in RADS.

electric energy The flow of charged particles.

electron The smallest particle with a negative electrical charge. The electron is one of three basic particles that make up the atom. The electron determines the chemical behavior of elements, and their flow through a conductor is known as electricity. An electron can be stopped by only a few millimeters of plastic, for example, but it is of special danger if taken into or onto the body's surface.

element Any of the known substances that cannot be chemically broken down and of which all known matter is composed.

emergency core cooling system A safety system intended to prevent fuel from melting if, in a nuclear reactor, there is a sudden loss of coolant. It consists of pipes, valves, and water supplies that will flood the reactor in case of an emergency.

emission standards A law or ordinance that places limitations on the amount of pollutants that a given source may release.

energy Simply, the capacity to do work. Energy may be mechanical, chemical, electrical, nuclear, heat, or light.

energy policy The set of public policies adopted by a nation that deal specifically with the establishment of an energy development program, production and assessment of energy needs, and rules and regulations to maintain energy security.

energy security The situation in which a nation maintains and protects crucial reserves of oil, gas, electricity, etc., for the purpose of providing emergency long-term services to meet potential energy needs during a time of national emergency.

enrichment The process by which the isotope of a given element is increased. It is the process of increasing the number of fissionable atoms in nuclear fuel.

entombment The decommissioning of a nuclear facility by sealing it in concrete.

environment The ecological context of all organisms: The physical, chemical, and biotic variables that act upon organisms and determine their form and survival.

environmental effect   The impact that human beings and their inventions and products have on the environment.

environmental impact statement   A report presenting results of a systematic analysis of the short- and long-term effects of a proposed development on the surrounding environment.

exposure   The ionization produced by X-rays or gamma rays. Exposure may be either acute (high-level of short duration), or chronic (low-level of long duration).

fast breeder reactor   A reactor cooled by liquid sodium rather than water. The conversion of uranium to plutonium is so efficient in a fast breeder reactor that it creates more fuel than it consumes.

fertile material   Material made of atoms that readily absorb neutrons to produce fissionable materials. Fertile material alone cannot sustain a chain reaction.

fissile (or fissionable) material   Atomic materials that readily fission when struck by a neutron. Some of the best examples of fissile materials are uranium-235 and plutonium-239.

fission   The splitting of a heavy nucleus into two more or less equal parts (nuclei of lighter elements) that is accompanied by release of large amounts of energy and one or more neutrons. Although fission can occur spontaneously, it is generally caused by nuclear absorption of gamma rays, neutrons, or other particles.

fission products   The atoms formed when uranium is split in a nuclear reactor. These produces are generally radioactive.

fuel   Fissile and fertile materials, which are basically chain-reacting.

fuel cell   A cell that converts chemical energy to electrical energy.

fuel cycle   The entire series of procedures involved in supplying fuel for nuclear reactors. The fuel cycle begins with mining of ore, and then includes refining, fabrication of fuel elements, using these fuel elements in a reactor, and dealing with spent fuel and radioactive waste products. A fuel cycle starts with uranium and creates plutonium as a byproduct. Fuel cycles may be closed (in which case reprocessing of spent fuel is included) or open (in which case the cycle does not include the reprocessing stage). Future fuel cycles may use thorium and produce the fissile isotope uranium-233.

fuel pellets   Cylindrical units of uranium oxide about ¼-inch thick and ½-inch long that are used as fuel in a nuclear power plant.

fuel rods The rods that contain fuel pellets. They are 12 to 14 feet long.

fuel storage pond a pond made of concrete and lined with steel that contains water in which irradiated fuel is kept after it has been removed from the nuclear reactor. Fuel is stored in this container until its activity has decayed to the desired level and it can be removed from the site. The water is a coolant and a shield against radiation.

fusion The process by which certain light atomic nuclei are combined to form heavier nuclei, resulting in the release of great energy.

gamma ray A form of radiation characterized by high energy and short wavelength. A gamma ray can be stopped by lead. A gamma ray is similar to an X-ray and generally is highly penetrating.

gas-cooled reactor A nuclear reactor in which a gas, such as carbon dioxide, is used as the coolant.

geiger counter An electronic device used to detect and measure radiation.

generator A device that converts mechanical energy into electrical energy.

half-life The number of years required for a radioactive material to lose 50 percent of its activity by decay. This may be a very long time. For example, in the case of the radioisotope plutonium-239, it takes 24,000 years for one pound to be reduced to one-half pound.

heat energy Energy that causes a rise in temperature and an increase in the speed of the molecules in matter.

heat rate A measure used to determine the amount of fuel used in the production of electricity and/or of thermal energy.

heavy metals Metals having an atomic weight generally above 40.

heavy water Water that consists of molecules in which the chemical hydrogen is in the form of deuterium. Heavy water is used as a moderator in some nuclear reactors.

high-level waste Highly radioactive material that contains fission products, uranium traces, and other elements, resulting from the chemical reprocessing of spent fuel. High-level waste must be solidified before it can be disposed of.

high-temperature gas-cooled reactor A nuclear reactor that is cooled by helium.

hot A term meaning highly radioactive.

integrated waste-management system A waste management system in which all of the components are coordinated to work together, usually including a monitored retrievable storage system.

interest groups A collection of individuals formed to pursue common aims or interests. Interest groups normally align themselves around narrow issues over which they hope to use their advocacy and influence to bring about change or a solution, from their point of view, of public policy issue.

interim storage The temporary holding of nuclear wastes on or away from the generator site when disposal space is not readily available.

intermediate-level waste Solid wastes that exceed the boundaries considered for low-level wastes but that do not need produce the heat of radioactive decay.

intermediate load The demand from an energy system that falls between the base load and the peak load.

ion This is an atom or a molecule that has lost or acquired one or more electrons.

ionization The process by which negatively charged electrons break away from the atom, leaving an ion, or positively charged particle.

isotopes Atoms that have the same number of protons but a different number of neutrons. Isotopes may have varying nuclear properties, e.g., one isotope may not fission at all while another isotope of the same atom may fission easily.

kilowatt 1,000 watts. A measurement of the rate of generation or consumption of electricity.

kilowatt-hour The amount of energy that will be spent by using 1,000 watts of electricity for one hour.

kinetic energy Energy associated with matter in motion.

krypton This is element 36. It does not interact chemically with any other element. Krypton-85 is a radioactive fission product found in spent reactor fuel that is released during reprocessing.

latent period The period of apparent inactivity between the time of exposure to radiation and the onset of the final stage of radiation sickness.

leaching The dissolving of substances through permeable materials, such as the dissolving of chemicals by percolation through soil or ground water.

light-water reactor A common term that describes all nuclear reactors that use ordinary water as their coolant. Pressurized-water reactors and boiling-water reactors, which are the most frequently used reactors in the United States, are included under the category of light-water reactors.

liquid metal fast breeder reactor A nuclear breeder reactor that is cooled by the circulation of a liquid metal such as sodium.

liquid waste This is a liquid radioactive waste produced by one of the waste streams of the nuclear cycle. It may be dilute or highly concentrated with radioactivity.

load The actual demand for electric or thermal energy at a specific time.

load cycle pattern The changes in demand from an energy system over a specified time period.

loss-of-coolant accident An accident at a nuclear reactor during the course of which the primary system loses coolant.

low-level waste Radioactive waste that contains only small amounts of radioactivity. It poses relatively few health hazards and is usually disposed of by land burial.

mill tailings The fine, gray sand left over after the refining of uranium ore to extract uranium oxides. Mill tailings have 700 trillionths of a curie per gram of radioactivity.

millirem A dosage of radiation equal to one-thousandth of a rem. According to national government guidelines, the average person may receive up to 500 millirem per year; the average American may actually receive 150–200 millirem per year from all radiation sources.

moderator A unit of a light-water reactor used during the fission process to slow the speed of neutrons emitted so they can be more readily absorbed by other nuclei. Water and graphite are typical moderator materials.

molten salt breeder reactor A nuclear reactor that uses a molten salt mixture that contains uranium and thorium as both fuel and coolant and produces more uranium than it consumes.

monitored retrievable storage The temporary storage of waste or spent fuel under conditions where it would be continuously monitored and in such a way that it could be retrieved for shipment to a permanent repository. Especially involved are such matters as spent fuel consolidation, packaging, and other waste-handling activities.

neutron   An atomic particle that has no electrical charge. Neutrons, together with protons, make up the portion of the atom called the nucleus. Electrons, which are negatively charged, orbit the nucleus.

neutron poison   Any materials that will absorb neutrons. These materials can interfere with the fissioning process or may be used to control it.

nuclear energy   The energy released when the nucleus of an atom splits or when two nuclei fuse; the energy created by fission and fusion.

nuclear fission   Splitting of the nucleus of a heavy atom into parts. When the nucleus of the uranium atom is split, this fission is accompanied by the release of tremendous energy.

nuclear fusion   The combining of the nuclei of two atoms. When the nuclei are combined, tremendous energy is released.

nuclear island   The entire nuclear reactor apparatus: buildings, equipment, and auxiliary and emergency systems.

nuclear pile   A device for controlling a nuclear chain reaction during the creation of atomic energy. A pile is made up of uranium and some moderating material such as graphite.

nuclear power   The power—electricity—generated by the process of nuclear fission.

nuclear reactor   A device in which a controlled nuclear reaction is maintained, usually for the purpose of generating electrical power.

nuclear steam supply system   A nuclear reactor and its associated equipment required to make the steam that drives the turbines to produce electricity.

nuclide   A type of atom having specific mass, atomic number, and nuclear energy state, which determine its other properties, including radioactivity.

once-through fuel cycle   A fuel cycle in which nuclear materials are placed into a reactor only once and are not recycled.

operating costs   The cost of keeping a power plant running once it has been built.

operating license A legal document that permits the operation of a nuclear power plant.

peak load The level of greatest demand for energy from a system, measured daily, seasonally, or annually.

plutonium An element produced from uranium in the core of a reactor. It fissions easily and may be used as nuclear fuel.

policy agenda The demands registered by the public or by groups upon which legitimate government bodies choose to act.

policy evaluation The assessment, estimation, and/or appraisal of the success, failure, or impact of specific public policies.

policy formulation The process of developing alternative solutions to deal with public problems.

policy implementation The activity of putting a public policy into effect. This process involves the application of solutions to specific public problems.

policy process The entire system of developing policies as solutions to public problems. The process involves deliberate courses of action designed by legitimate government officials to remedy a problem or a matter of concern to the body politic in general.

pollution To make physically unclean or impure. The term is widely used to describe the process by which the human environment is damaged by intentional and unintentional defiling of the earth and its atmosphere.

potential energy Energy that is capable of being produced. Nuclear energy is potential energy; when fission occurs, heat and light are given off.

power plant A nuclear plant and its attendant apparatus that produces electricity.

pressure-tube reactor A nuclear power reactor in which fuel is placed inside hundreds of tubes able to withstand circulation of the high-pressure coolant.

pressure vessel The steel enclosure surrounding a reactor core. Able to withstand high pressures and high temperatures, its function is to prevent the escape of radioactive material.

pressurized-water reactor A nuclear reactor that is cooled by water maintained at a high pressure to prevent it from boiling. The primary coolant passes through the reactor core and transfers its heat to a secondary cooling system from which steam is produced.

primary coolant The liquid or gas used to cool the fuel elements.

proliferation The spread of nuclear weapons to those nations not currently possessing them.

proton A tiny particle that carries one positive charge of electricity. It is one of the three particles that make up an atom.

public policy Both a plan and a set of actions undertaken by a public agency to carry out objectives of government. Public policy affects all people on the local, state, and national levels.

qualifying facility A cogenerator or a small power producer that meets the provisions of the Public Utilities Regulatory Policies Act of 1978, the requirements of the Federal Energy Regulatory Commission, and is owned by someone not mainly concerned with the generation or sale of electric power.

rad (radiation absorbed dose) The amount of ionizing radiation absorbed by any material, such as human tissue.

radiant energy The energy transmitted by waves or particles.

radiation The particles and electromagnetic waves emitted from the center of an atom during radioactive disintegration. Prolonged exposure to these particles and rays may be harmful.

radioactive waste Waste materials produced by a nuclear facility. They may be sold, liquid, or gas.

radioactivity The spontaneous emitting of alpha or beta particles or gamma rays on the part of some elements such as uranium.

radioisotope An unstable isotope of an element that will eventually undergo radioactive decay.

radon A radioactive gas is produced by the decay of one of the daughters of radium. If inhaled in relatively unvented areas for a long period of time, it may induce lung cancer.

reactor Any facility that contains a controlled nuclear fission chain reaction. Among its functions may be generating electricity, carrying on nuclear research, or producing plutonium for nuclear bombs. Included in a reactor are fissile material (such as uranium or plutonium), the moderator, a control system, and a provision for the removal of heat by a coolant.

reactor vessel The container of the nuclear core. It may be a steel pressure vessel, a prestressed concrete vessel, or a low-pressure vessel.

reactor year   The operating of one nuclear reactor for one year.

recycling   The reusing of fissionable material in irradiated fuel.

refueling   The removal of spent fuel from and the introduction of new fuel into a nuclear reactor.

regulatory policy   Specific public policy designed to control, restrict, or structure specific types of activities. Regulatory policy is specified in regulations, rules, and procedures, most of which govern certain kinds of conduct and activities.

rem   An acronym for roentgen equivalent man; a unit of ionizing radiation.

repository   A permanent disposal facility for high-level or transuranic wastes and spent fuel.

reprocessing   The chemical treatment of spent nuclear reactor fuel that separates the plutonium and uranium from the fission products.

roentgen   The unit of exposure to gamma rays or X-rays, named after William Roentgen, who discovered X-rays in Munich in 1895.

safeguards   Procedures, regulations, and instrumentation aimed at detecting and preventing the diversion of nuclear materials to unauthorized persons or institutions.

safety system   Any combination of electrical, mechanical, or instrumentation systems aimed at maintaining the safety of both the reactor and the public in general.

scram   A rapid shutdown of the chain reaction by introduction of neutron absorbers.

secondary system   The nonnuclear part of a power plant that actually generates the steam and produces the electricity.

shielding   Materials—usually concrete, water, and lead—placed around radioactive materials to protect personnel and the environment against the dangers of radiation exposure.

shutdown   The cessation of nuclear plant operation for any reason.

spent fuel   Fuel that has been "burned" in a nuclear power plant's reactor to the point where it no longer contributes efficiently to the nuclear chain reaction. Spent fuel is thermally hot and highly radioactive, and is removed from the reactor.

spent fuel pool   A deep pool of water close to a nuclear reactor in which spent fuel from a power plant is stored temporarily.

steam generator   A machine that uses heat in a pressurized-water or gas-cooled reactor power plant to produce the steam to run turbines.

storage   The isolation and recovery of radioactive materials. Storage facilities require constant human monitoring and maintenance as well as protection from human intrusion for specific periods of time.

tailings   The residue left during preparation of an ore.

technology   The methods and means by which the practical purposes of sustaining human life and comfort are achieved.

thermal pollution   Pollution by heat, as by the discharge of warm water into rivers. This has the effect of raising the temperature of the water to unnatural levels, thus adversely affecting the system.

thermal reactor   A nuclear reactor in which the chain reaction is sustained mainly by fission stimulated by thermal neutrons.

thorium-232   A natural, fertile isotope from which the fissile isotope uranium-233 can be bred.

tokamak   A doughnut-shaped nuclear fusion device.

transuranic wastes   Waste materials contaminated with uranium-233 and its daughter products, certain isotopes of plutonium, and nuclides with atomic numbers greater than 92 (uranium). Such wastes are produced primarily from reprocessing spent fuel and from use of plutonium in fabrication of nuclear weapons.

turbine   A rotary engine made up of blades attached to a shaft. A turbine converts the kinetic energy of a fluid to mechanical energy.

turbine generator   The turbine that is linked to a generator that produces electric power.

uranium   An element commonly used as fuel in a nuclear reactor. It is a hard, shiny, metallic element that is radioactive.

uranium milling   The process by which uranium is removed from uranium ore.

uranium-233   A fissile isotope similar in weapons quality to plutonium-239.

uranium-235   The uranium isotope that accounts for less than one percent of all natural uranium.

uranium-238   The uranium isotope that accounts for more than 99 percent of all natural uranium.

vitrification   Radioactive wastes in the form of glass.

voltage   Potential electrical energy.

waste disposal system   The entire collectivity of facilities, apparatus, personnel, and sites to be established by the U.S. Department of Energy for the permanent disposal of spent fuel and high-level waste.

watt   The measure of the rate of generation or consumption of electrical energy.

watt-hour   The amount of energy that will be expended by use of one watt of electricity for one hour.

yellowcake   A yellow powder, mostly uranium, produced by pouring crushed uranium ore into an acid that dissolves the uranium. This acid, when drained from the crushed ore and dried, leaves a yellow powder called yellowcake.

zircalloy   An alloy of zirconium and tin used to make fuel rods used in a nuclear power plant.

zirconium   A metallic element with a high melting point that is very resistant to corrosion.

Acronyms and Abbreviations

AC	alternating current
ACRS	Advisory Committee on Reactor Safeguards
AEC	Atomic Energy Commission (United States)
AGR	advanced gas reactor
AIF	Atomic Industrial Forum
ANL	Argonne National Laboratories
ANS	American Nuclear Society
BTU	British thermal unit
BWR	boiling-water reactor
CAA	Clean Air Act
CEQ	Council on Environmental Quality
CONAES	Committee on Nuclear and Alternative Energy Systems
CWA	Clean Water Act
DC	direct current
DHLW	defense high-level radioactive waste
DOE	Department of Energy (United States)
DOI	Department of the Interior (United States)
DOT	Department of Transportation (United States)
EEI	Edison Electric Institute
EIA	Energy Information Administration
EIS	environmental impact statement
ENO	extraordinary nuclear occurrence
EPA	Environmental Protection Agency (United States)
ERDA	Energy Research and Development Administration
FBR	fast breeder reactor
FEA	Federal Energy Administration (United States)

FEMA	Federal Emergency Management Agency
FEO	Federal Energy Office
FERC	Federal Energy Regulatory Commission
FPC	Federal Power Commission (United States)
FR	Federal Register

| GCR | gas-cooled reactor |

HEDL	Hanford Engineering Development Laboratory
HEU	highly enriched uranium
HLW	high-level radioactive waste
HMI	hazardous material incident
HNTA	Hazardous Materials Transportation Act
HTGR	high-temperature gas-cooled reactor
HWR	heavy water reactor

| IAEA | International Atomic Energy Agency |
| IEA | International Energy Agency |

| JCAE | Joint Committee on Atomic Energy (U.S. Congress) |

| kW | kilowatt(s) |
| kWh | kilowatt-hour |

LASL	Los Alamos Scientific Laboratory
LBL	Lawrence Berkeley Laboratory
LLL	Lawrence Livermore Laboratory
LLW	low-level radioactive waste
LMFBR	liquid metal fast breeder reactor
LWR	light water reactor

MED	Manhattan Engineering District, the official code name for the World War II effort to build an atomic bomb
Mound	Mound Laboratory
mW	megawatt(s)

NAS	National Academy of Sciences
NCRP	National Commission on Radiological Protection
NEPA	National Environmental Policy Act
NPT	Non-Proliferation Treaty
NRC	Nuclear Regulatory Commission (United States)
NSF	National Science Foundation

OPEC	Organization of Petroleum Exporting Countries
ORNL	Oak Ridge National Laboratory
OTA	Office of Technology Assessment (U.S. Congress)
PHWR	pressurized heavy water reactor
PNL	Batelle Pacific Northwest Laboratories
PPPL	Princeton Plasma Physics Laboratory
Pu-239	plutonium-239
PURPA	Public Utility Regulatory Policies Act
PWR	pressurized-water reactor
R&D	research and development
RAM	radioactive materials
RAM/AIDB	RAM Accident/Incident database
RAMPAC	radioactive materials packaging
RL	radiation level
Sandia	Sandia National Laboratories
SIPI	Scientists' Institute for Public Information
SIPRI	Stockholm International Peace Research Institute
Sr-90	strontium-90, a radioactive isotope
TMI	Three Mile Island
TRU	transuranic
U-235	uranium-235
U-238	uranium-238
W	watts(s)

Index

McFeely Library

George School

Newtown, PA   18940